ROOT AND BRANCH

Charles Hamilton Houston, Thurgood Marshall,
and the Struggle to End Segregation

RAWN JAMES, JR.

BLOOMSBURY PRESS

New York   Berlin   London

Published by Bloomsbury Press, New York

ISBN 978-1-59691-606-7

Typeset by Westchester Book Group
Printed in the United States of America

Book Club Edition

For my parents, Rawn Sr. and Sara James

CONTENTS

ROOT AND BRANCH

1

SOUTHERN JUSTICE ON TRIAL

THE FOXHUNTING SET OF Loudoun County, Virginia, had been on edge for weeks even before the two women were found murdered. With alarming ease, burglars had been stealing china, jewels and even furniture from the Georgian homes scattered atop the rolling hills that lay about forty miles northwest of Washington, D.C. No suspects had been taken into custody, and homeowners in towns like Leesburg were oiling their rifles for more than mere sport during the first weeks of 1932.

On one mild January night, furniture designer Paul Boeing retired to "the big house" of his family's estate, where he slept warily prepared to defend the property against any would-be intruders. Boeing awoke the next morning after an uneventful sleep, donned an overcoat atop his pajamas, slid on an old pair of shoes and welcomed the crisp morning with a stroll across the lawn to the cottage where his sister and her maid had spent the night.[1]

His knocking went unanswered. Boeing opened the door, stepped into the cottage and jumped back outside as if thrown by a man twice his size. His sister, Agnes Boeing Ilsley, lay beaten to death on the cottage floor; Mina Buckner, Agnes's maid, lay dead in the next room with her skull crushed and one hand stiffly clutching her set of false teeth. Investigators later found the scratched bits of a black person's hair and skin caked in blood beneath Agnes's fingernails.

Before the sun struck noon that day, a band of white men had swarmed through several towns in Loudoun County searching for the man they were convinced had murdered the socially prominent Mrs. Ilsley and her maid.[2] Despite the fact that several of the men were well-to-do members of the county's gentry, their group comprised a lynch mob. They planned to find the murderer, torture him, castrate him and kill him.

But by nightfall it had become clear to them that they were not going to find the killer. It would be more than a year before they learned that the man they sought, George Crawford, was arrested in Boston. It would be another year before the Loudoun County courthouse resonated for the first time with the voice of an African American lawyer rising in defense of Crawford, by then formally accused of murdering the two women. And it would be a few months after that when a writer for the *Washington Post* declared, "If there ever was a lucky Negro, he is George Crawford."[3]

In 1932, the chief executive of the National Association for the Advancement of Colored People had straight blond hair and blue eyes, a thick mustache and a thin man's tendency to disappear inside double-breasted suits. By all accounts Walter White looked Caucasian. "My skin is white," he wrote on the first page of his autobiography, "my eyes are blue, my hair is blond. The traits of my race are nowhere visible upon me."[4] The mailman's son could have passed out of the colored world and lived his life as a white man. If he and his father had not been attacked by a white mob during the Atlanta race riots of 1906, perhaps he would have "crossed over" like thousands of African Americans did each year. But Walter was thirteen years old on that searing September night when Atlanta burned anew, when he and his father defended their home against a mob of white men wielding fire and yelling, "That's where that nigger mail carrier lives! Let's burn it down!"[5] Gunshots scattered the horde, and the shaken blond boy decided that he forever would be black.

Ten years later White joined the NAACP after graduating from the Atlanta University. Field Secretary James Weldon Johnson, impressed with White's volunteer efforts in the Atlanta branch, hired him as an assistant field secretary. The young staffer's transracial appearance quickly proved an invaluable asset: From 1918 to 1929, White repeatedly went undercover to mingle with Klansmen and murderers and bloodthirsty lots. Posing as a white man, he investigated forty-one lynchings and eight race riots. He publicized their stories and plans through the NAACP. For life White was haunted by what he saw and heard during those eleven years.

The fight against lynching became Walter White's crusade. He wrote several critically acclaimed books on the subject, and, after working his way up to become the NAACP's chief executive, he vowed to use every means at his disposal to stop the brutal killings. In his New York City office in January 1933, White read in the newspapers that a black man was arrested in Boston and had confessed to murdering two white women in rural Virginia the year before. Eight days after confessing, however, the suspect claimed that he had not killed the women and in fact had been in Boston when the crime occurred. Several witnesses substantiated his alibi. Nonetheless, authorities in Massachusetts began making arrangements to extradite the suspect, George Crawford, to Virginia.

The entire affair looked to Walter White like a legally sanctioned lynching. While it could not patrol the swamps and thickets where white mobs slaughtered black men, the NAACP could stand guard against America's courtrooms' becoming the sites of slaughter. George Crawford's life could be saved if the association could keep him from being extradited to Virginia.

LOUDOUN COUNTY PROSECUTOR John Galleher had rushed to Massachusetts upon word of Crawford's arrest, pausing only for his own wedding in Washington. The morning after the wedding night, Galleher left for Boston with his bride in tow, on what the Associated Press called "an extradition honeymoon."[6]

After his arrest, Crawford's NAACP lawyers, led by Bostonian Butler Wilson, fought extradition on the grounds that black citizens were excluded from Virginia's juries in violation of the Fourteenth Amendment's guarantee of equal protection of the laws. The lawyers persuaded federal judge James A. Lowell and he ordered Crawford released. "Why send this man back to Virginia when I know and everyone knows the Supreme Court will say his trial is illegal?" the judge demanded. "The lawyers are the only ones who will get anything out of it. The whole thing is absolutely wrong."[7]

Virginia appealed, with its attorney general exclaiming, "Why, under [Lowell's] ruling, it would be illegal to try any colored person before a Virginia jury for any offense!"[8] Likewise infuriated by his professed reliance on "Yankee common sense," Congress impeached Judge Lowell, who suddenly fell sick. Ten days later the sixty-four-year-old judge died in Newton, Massachusetts.

The circuit court of appeals overturned Lowell's ruling. It held that because Virginia did not by statute exclude African Americans from jury service, its juries were constitutionally sound; whether or not black people ever actually served on Virginia's juries was irrelevant. Crawford's attorneys appealed to the Supreme Court, but the justices declined to hear the case. The thirty-two-year-old black man was returned to Loudoun County to stand trial for capital murder.

Before returning to Virginia with his bride, Galleher spoke of the defendant to the press. "We want to give him plenty of time to get counsel and otherwise prepare his defense. But court is in session now and I see no reason for delay." Galleher pointedly added, "I will recommend that Crawford be placed in the Alexandria jail in lieu of being brought to Leesburg in advance of trial."[9] Alexandria was two counties east of Leesburg; Loudoun County's prosecutor was afraid that Crawford, like so many black defendants held in southern jails, would be kidnapped and lynched if he spent a night in the Leesburg jail.

WITH GEORGE CRAWFORD DESTINED for trial and the nation now interested in his fate, Walter White was more determined than ever to save Crawford's life. As perhaps the most well-connected black man in the nation, White had his pick of America's most accomplished progressive attorneys to represent the suddenly famous defendant. The man at the top of his list was the dean of the Howard University School of Law and a graduate of Amherst College and Harvard Law School. His tireless work and controversial decisions had elevated the school from one that accepted high school graduates to one fully accredited by the American Bar Association. But Charles Hamilton Houston promptly replied with his regrets. "This case is far too big to be sloppily prepared. I would not be equal to the task," Houston explained, "because it would mean that I would have to give up all work here at the University. It would be impossible to do both jobs at the same time."[10] The school year had already begun by October 1933 and it was too late for the dean to apply for a leave of absence. Before signing off, however, Houston conceded that "if Crawford could be tried by all Negro counsel, it would be a turning point in the legal history of the Negro in this country."[11]

Walter White was nothing if not perceptive. He knew that Charlie Houston did not write incidentally; if White could guarantee him an all-black legal team, Houston might reconsider. As a law student ten years earlier, Houston had become the first African American to serve on the *Harvard Law Review.* A tall, sandy-toned man, Houston wore meticulously tailored suits that betrayed his unwavering attention to detail. His gray-eyed gaze smoldered. He was brilliant and disciplined perhaps to a fault.

For his part, Houston believed Crawford's case could mature to legal significance: The road to saving the innocent man's life almost certainly led to the Supreme Court of the United States, where Crawford's lawyers would argue that a state's excluding black citizens from juries as a matter of practice was as unconstitutional as excluding them as a matter of law. Success would be monumental, but if they lost, Walter White feared, "all the gains in jury service may be wiped out and Negroes be set back thirty years."

White assured Houston command of an all-black legal team. Less than one week later, the dean agreed to serve as lead counsel on his first murder case. Fellow Washingtonians Edward P. Lovett, James G. Tyson and Leon A. Ransom would assist him, and all would work for free. Except for Ransom, who was a professor at Howard, Crawford's lawyers were Houston's former students. They would be assisted by one of Houston's favorite students in the third-year class at Howard Law, a lanky Baltimore native named Thurgood Marshall.

They immediately filed a motion to quash Crawford's indictment on the grounds that African Americans were, as a matter of long-standing practice, excluded from Loudoun County's grand juries. Although this argument had failed in Massachusetts, if Houston lost the motion during this, the trial stage, and his client was convicted, then he could base an appeal on the issue. A hearing was scheduled for November 6, 1933.

VIRGINIA GOVERNOR JOHN GARLAND POLLARD personally appointed Judge James L. McLemore to try the case. With his full head of silver hair parted sharply down the middle, McLemore was a judge partial to brass collar-clips and a courtroom of the utmost order. He understood the case's national import, however, and granted the lawyers latitude at the hearing. Crawford's defense team called no fewer than forty-six witnesses, including forty-one African American residents of Loudoun County, the county's clerk of court and the sheriff. Five of the prosecution's twelve witnesses were members of the county's board of supervisors.

Houston asked the court if he could call to the stand Judge J. R. Alexander, who had drawn the jury list. When Judge McLemore balked at the idea of a fellow jurist facing cross-examination, Houston replied that Judge Alexander could face criminal prosecution under an 1875 federal statute that made it illegal to exclude anyone from a jury based on a "previous condition of servitude"—that is, former slaves. Houston argued that although he had no intention of seeking Judge Alexander's prosecution, he deserved the chance to question the judge under oath, particularly in light of the federal statute expressly addressing the issue at hand.[12]

Judge McLemore relented and ordered his fellow Virginia judge to take the stand. Silence froze the courtroom as the clerk swore a judge onto the witness stand.

Judge Alexander was, as Houston later described, "a slow and reluctant witness." After establishing that Alexander had been a judge since May 1929 and that he did in fact draft the list from which the Crawford jury was drawn, Houston asked, "Did you or did you not consider the Negro population?"

"I considered the population as a whole. I didn't know whether they were white or colored."

Were *any* Negroes on the list of prospective jurors?

No, but the men on the list were well qualified, with individual reputations for honesty, intelligence and reliability. The men on the list were *a little above the average.*

Wasn't it the custom in Loudoun County to choose only white citizens for jury duty?

Well, yes, but there were only two Negroes in the county qualified to serve on a jury and they were not selected for the Crawford case.

Because they were Negroes?

No. The entire population was considered. Most people were not selected.[13]

Houston did not expect Judge Alexander to admit to deliberately excluding African Americans from the jury. By questioning him, the jury commissioners and several black residents of Loudoun County, he was constructing a record of operative facts: There were black people in Loudoun County qualified to serve on juries, but no black person had ever been selected to serve on a jury, and this was because black people were, as a matter of long-standing practice, excluded from jury service.

After all the witnesses had been heard, Judge McLemore announced that he was ready to hear closing arguments on the defendant's motion to disband the jury.

"All the testimony here today," Houston commenced in his clipped diction, "shows there have been no Negroes on grand juries or trial juries in Virginia, so their deliberate exclusion must be admitted by the Commonwealth. Public policy in Virginia is that Negroes are not to serve on juries." He motioned to Judge Alexander, who had returned to his seat in the gallery. "Judge Alexander has been revolving around a closed circle—a wheel excluding all Negroes. In other words, a caste system is prevalent in Virginia and the South." The caste system resulted in the systematic exclusion of black Virginians from juries. Even if they were "considered," they were never chosen for grand jury duty because of their race, and that violated the federal Constitution.

Loudoun County prosecutor John Galleher, in his rebuttal, denied that black people were excluded from the grand jury that indicted George Crawford. "The sole issue," he said, "is whether Judge Alexander excluded Negroes solely on account of their race. The Commonwealth denies Negroes were excluded, denies there are Negroes in Loudoun County qualified for grand jury service and denies that the constitutional rights of Negroes were invaded. Judge Alexander selected an intelligent class of people he thought would measure up to the requirements of law."[14]

As the lawyers finished making their arguments at the long day's end, perhaps no one was more relieved than the defendant, who wore a gray suit and whose forehead, according to the *Washington Post*, was "wrinkled by frowns."[15] Crawford had appeared bored throughout the day, as if the high-stakes legal wrangling holding hundreds spellbound was but a distant annoyance.

After hearing all the witnesses testify, Judge McLemore ruled for the commonwealth. Because Virginia law did not preclude African Americans from serving on grand juries, the fact that no black person had ever done so was irrelevant. The judge removed his gold-rimmed glasses before explaining his decision from the bench in a dripping gentleman's drawl: "The judge is charged with a serious responsibility in selecting grand juries. He must choose intelligent men. Intelligence usually means a high order of reasoning power, a higher thinking power as distinguished from the senses of memory. An intellectual person is one who is elevated a little above what we would term a plain citizen. A good citizen, just as good a citizen as exists anywhere, might prove not to have the intellectual qualities which would make him the best material for grand jury service. The judge has to decide that question when he selects the grand jury list, and if he decides it honestly and conscientiously and includes no colored people among the 48 men selected, the list is still a perfectly good list." Judge McLemore concluded that the judge who selected the grand jury "did not exclude anyone because of race or color."

Charles Houston rose and, with his fingertips glanced atop counsel's table, said to the judge, "I respectfully request a ruling on testimony that Judge Alexander picked the grand jury from his personal acquaintances. Your honor should say something about the caste system existing in Virginia. Inside the circle are white people. Outside are black people. Black people cannot get inside."[16] Spectators in the crowded courtroom whispered at the lawyer's measured audacity.

Judge McLemore's gavel remained idle as he restored order by raising his tone just enough to convey irritation. "If I have any doubts," he assured defense counsel, "I always lean toward the colored man. I carry no feelings myself. We're perfectly conscious that the social caste is well marked in Virginia. I have nothing to add to my decision."[17]

Although delivered by a grand jury from which black citizens were effectively excluded, George Crawford's indictment would stand. On the courthouse's steps Houston was surrounded by scribbling reporters who asked if he would seek to move the trial. He pounced on the question: "Loudoun County and Virginia justice [are] as much on trial as Crawford."[18] Because the crime was committed in Loudoun and Crawford was indicted in Loudoun, the rural county was where he should be tried. If Houston seemed uncharacteristically charged during the impromptu press conference, it was with good reason: McLemore's ruling had given him the very issue he wanted to appeal if his client was convicted.

THE TRIAL WAS SCHEDULED to begin on December 12, 1933. The NAACP immediately sought to raise funds for Crawford's defense. "It will take money to fight this case properly," Walter White explained at a fund-raiser at the Nineteenth Street Baptist Church in Washington, D.C. "There is a tremendous amount of investigation to be done and many services have to be paid before we even go to trial." He hastened to add, "Mr. Houston and his associates are glad to give their services without fee, because of the importance of this case to colored people everywhere. The NAACP needs, then, a fund for expenses in the case, not a real defense fund. Even so, the amount needed is large."[19] He noted that, including the hearings in Boston, the organization already had spent $1,503.44 on Crawford's case.

While White worked the telephones and cables both to raise money and to keep the case in national news reports, Houston and his team began constructing their defense. No hotels in or around Leesburg accepted African American customers, so the NAACP implored local black residents to lodge the lawyers. It was expensive and time-consuming for them to travel the eighty-mile round-trip from Washington to Leesburg each day of trial preparation, but Loudoun County's black residents uniformly declined to let the trial team into their homes. Along with their suits and typewriters, the lawyers carried the danger of violence; any family known to lodge the Washingtonians would make its home a target for attack. Loudoun County's white residents were vocal in their desire to be rid of Crawford's defense team.[20]

Howard Law School provided the lawyers' base of operations. Thurgood Marshall had spent hours researching the case's complex issues. The opportunity to practice the tenets of social engineering exhilarated him: Not only was the defense team trying to save a man's life, but it was determined to change a legal system that every one of Houston's students and cocounsel had come to believe was unconstitutional.

Marshall was not content to provide just research assistance to George Crawford's defense. His outsized personality and legal acumen enabled the third-year law student to interject himself into strategy debates with Professor Ransom and Dean Houston. Walter White, who attended some of the late-night sessions at Howard, could scarcely believe the temerity of the young man who one day would lead the NAACP to its greatest victories. In the library Marshall challenged his professors as ardently as they challenged him in the classroom.

Throughout their investigation and during what promised to be a difficult trial, Charles Houston and his team spent two hours in a car each day, traveling to and from a county where no hotel, motel or house would shelter them for the night. It was an unforeseen practical burden but, even so, was a minor inconvenience compared with the facts uncovered by their investigation.

CRAWFORD'S GIRLFRIEND, Bertie DeNeal, had verified his alibi. Both she and George Crawford, she had said, were in Boston the night the two white women were murdered. Houston was outlining cross-examinations based on this alibi when he learned that DeNeal had turned state's witness; she would testify that Crawford was in Loudoun County on the night of the murders and that his alibi was untrue.

Houston sped to the Alexandria jail to confront his client. Was DeNeal telling the truth? Had Crawford been lying to him, the courts, the NAACP?

Yes, Crawford confessed from his cell. He was present when the women were killed, but he did not kill them. He had only wanted to steal from the cottage. His accomplice in the burglary, Charley Johnson, had attacked the women while a horrified Crawford hid in the next room.

Houston considered his wiry client through the iron bars. George Crawford had been born in Richmond, Virginia, where he had lived for most of his life. In 1921, he was convicted of receiving and concealing stolen goods and was sentenced to three years in the state penitentiary. He escaped from prison within a year and lived on the lam for months. He might have remained a free man had he not gotten arrested on a charge of grand larceny. This time Crawford was sentenced to five years. In 1925, he escaped from prison for the second time but was recaptured the next day. The next time Crawford saw freedom was the day before Thanksgiving 1930, when the Commonwealth of Virginia released him into the morning sun. With his checkered past and discredited alibi, Houston could not put Crawford on the witness stand.

Charles Houston returned to Washington beneath a pall. Most if not all of what Crawford had confessed in Boston was true: He was a lookout in a burglary when his accomplice committed two murders. The law unequivocally held him as culpable as if he had wielded the weapon himself. From these facts, Houston had to construct a defense that would save his client from the electric chair.

ON THE MORNING OF DECEMBER 12, 1933, George Crawford arrived at the Loudoun County courthouse in a four-car convoy. Twenty-five state and county police officers, armed with shotguns, clubs, tear gas and revolvers, surrounded the diminutive defendant as he shuffled the short distance from the police car to the courthouse's doors. An integrated crowd of six hundred spectators jostled in the street while three hundred more, including Governor Pollard, filled every courthouse seat. Wearing metal police helmets, officers stood guard at each exit and waded through the throngs to maintain order.[21] There would be no disturbances during this first day of trial, however, as the townspeople were more interested in finding seats than registering protest. Their composure was rewarded as soon as the jury filed into place: Loudoun County's jury commissioners had selected two bankers, a businessman and nine farmers to serve as jurors—all of them were white men. (Virginia's General Assembly did not allow women to serve on juries until 1950.)[22] Houston immediately moved to disband the jury on the grounds that black residents had been excluded from the jury pool.

Judge McLemore spent the day hearing arguments on the matter and before announcing his decision from the bench. It was the same decision he had reached when the defense sought to quash Crawford's indictment. The only difference was his conceding that Houston's argument—excluding black citizens from juries as a matter of practice violated the same constitutional principle as excluding them by law—presented a question that was "not free from difficulty."[23]

The judge then adjourned court for the day. Tomorrow the trial would begin in earnest and the defendant would live or die on the jury's verdict.

BOTH PROSECUTION AND DEFENSE counsel realized that the crux of the trial was the confession George Crawford had given in Boston. If Judge McLemore refused to allow the confession to be read in court and entered into evidence, then, as the *Washington Post* observed, the prosecution's case would "collapse." The commonwealth's lawyers waited until the end of their case to offer the confession into evidence.[24]

Houston objected, arguing that the state had obtained the confession through coercion and "undue inducement." Because he felt coerced into making the confession, Crawford had refused to sign the document the morning after he had confessed.

"I cannot say that this man was forced," McLemore ruled. "I am going to let the confession in for two reasons: first, because I think it is admissible, and second, because if I am wrong, there are courts which can reverse me." It was a cavalier note to a momentous decision.

Crawford's confession was damningly specific. He admitted to waiting in the kitchen while his accomplice, a rail-thin black man named Charley Johnson, stole some items. When Johnson encountered the two women, he killed them—to Crawford's shock and dismay. Upon seeing Agnes Ilsley's bloodied body lying in her bedroom, Crawford yelled at Johnson, "Man, you didn't have to do that!"[25] Their robbery job had become a double murder and they had to escape Virginia before sunrise. The men stole Mrs. Ilsley's car and drove to South Washington, Virginia, where they hopped aboard a freight train bound for Pittsburgh.

Immediately after the jury listened to a reading of Crawford's confession, the prosecution rested its case.

The prosecution had offered no evidence that Crawford had killed the two women. To the contrary, the state's entire case was predicated on a confession in which the defendant strenuously maintained that he neither killed the women nor wanted his accomplice to kill them. The state also failed to present any evidence to show that the murders were premeditated. So the defense called to the stand only three witnesses, all of them African American former army officers. Houston called them to rebut the testimony of a prosecution witness who testified that Crawford bragged in Boston that he had "killed two white women in Virginia." Houston rested his case after the third witness.[26]

In a closing argument immediately lauded for its measured appeal to the distinction between justice and retribution, Charles Houston reasoned that his client's life should be spared because he was not the murderer. His argument correctly presumed that the jury had accepted Crawford's confession as true. Arguing against the confession would ensure Crawford's execution. Houston instead opened with a concession. "I have no words to palliate this offense. Every white woman and every black woman is entitled to safety in her bed. But I ask you to consider the fact that you haven't got Charley Johnson, who, if you accept the confession—and you must accept it unless the Commonwealth's case is to collapse completely—Johnson actually committed the murders while Crawford waited outside.

"You've got George Crawford, and I put it to you that Crawford is not the killer type." Houston gestured toward the little defendant slouched behind him. "You have seen him here in the courtroom, how respectful he is, how he bobs up with a smiling greeting to acquaintances, including the slain woman's brother, who came to testify against him. He is a thief, yes—but not the killer type."[27]

Reminding jurors that the prosecution failed to present evidence that Crawford did anything but wait in another room while the women were murdered, Houston continued: "There is nothing in the record to show that Crawford would have harmed a hair of Mrs. Ilsley's head. There is a grave distinction between Crawford and the actual killer.

"Now gentlemen, if you are going to find the defendant guilty, I ask you to consider two things: I ask you to consider the prisoner's background. He went away from Middleburg with Bertie DeNeal, who later left him to return to her family. A homeless, hungry dog, he wandered in circles, drawn back to Virginia with no idea of the fate awaiting him, then thrust into this awful tragedy by a will stronger than his own.

"I ask you to consider this: If you ever hope to catch Charley Johnson and put him in the chair for this dastardly crime, there is only one man who can help you do it." Houston reached the fulcrum of his argument; his eyes locked with the jurors'. "If you ever hope to catch the man who really is guilty, don't wipe out George Crawford. If you do wipe him out, Charley Johnson is gone forever. Although there are two honest women lying in their graves, the law does not say that you must take an eye for an eye and a tooth for a tooth, regardless of the degree of guilt of the accused. But I submit to you, gentlemen, that if you find George Crawford guilty, this is not a case for the supreme penalty."[28]

The case went to the jury on December 16, 1933, at nine thirty in the morning. Not once during the trial was the race of either the victims or the defendant mentioned by either side. After the jury had retired from the courtroom to deliberate, Judge McLemore expressed his admiration for the manner in which the lawyers for both sides conducted themselves. "I came expecting to find instances of race prejudice," he admitted from the bench. "But it never has been my privilege to try a contested case of this sort where the temper in the courtroom has been as splendid as it has been here. The people have been dignified and reserved. This case has been an oasis in the desert. I have caught a new vision of what can be and what ought to be in the conduct of a criminal trial."[29]

AFTER FOUR SECRET-BALLOT VOTES in just ninety-five minutes, the jurors found George Crawford guilty of first-degree murder. This surprised no one. The jury then recommended that Crawford be sentenced to life imprisonment. Judge McLemore promptly agreed and announced the sentence to a stunned courtroom.

The defendant appeared elated to have escaped the electric chair, smiling broadly as he assured the judge that he had "nothing to say." Before he was taken into custody, Crawford, still smiling, turned to shake Houston's hand. A short while afterward, Crawford would plead guilty to the charge of murder in the case of Mina Buckner, Agnes Ilsley's maid; it was unlikely that a second Virginian jury would spare his life. George Crawford spent his remaining days in the Richmond State Penitentiary.

THE DAY AFTER THE VERDICT, the *Washington Post* reported that "it had been a foregone conclusion among the neighbors and acquaintances of the slain society woman that the verdict would be death. But if there was any dissatisfaction, it was not voiced by the citizens, who struggled to the exits to see the prisoner whisked away to jail at Alexandria and thence to Richmond."[30] Although they had sought the death penalty, the prosecution team announced that they were "satisfied" with the life sentence. John Galleher assured citizens that the authorities' search for Charley Johnson would continue in earnest; in fact, police in Richmond had a lead on Johnson's whereabouts.

The jurors later told reporters that they spared George Crawford because they were persuaded by Houston's argument that if Crawford were executed, the authorities would have a much more difficult time bringing

Charley Johnson to justice. Because the jurors believed Crawford's confession, they believed that it was Johnson and not Crawford who had killed the women. Crawford's guilt was indirect and legal, but Johnson's was direct and moral, and the jurors wanted him to pay with his life.

State police officers guarded Charles Houston, his associates and their wives until they were safely out of Leesburg. Walter White issued a statement extolling the case as "an outstanding example of successful legal defense." In the aftermath of the case, counties in Virginia began to include African Americans in their jury pools, and the press reported effusively about the dean of Howard Law School, who, "without ever yielding a point of law, had set a high standard of gentleness and courtesy for his opponents at the bar."

For his part, the Crawford case left Houston physically and emotionally exhausted. In the ensuing months, some African American newspapers would question his trial decisions, contending that he had "agreeably compromised" with the prosecution by failing to argue his client's innocence.[31] The accusations stung, and prompted Houston and Leon Ransom to write a lengthy rebuttal widely printed in the African American press. "In their disposition of the Crawford case," the two lawyers wrote, referring to themselves in the third person, "counsel were not trying to establish any universals. They were dealing with a concrete case in a concrete way."[32] Houston had defended his client as best as facts allowed, and now George Crawford was sitting in prison instead of on death row. It was, admittedly, wearying solace for the man who was suddenly the most famous black lawyer in American history.

2

AMBITIOUS, SUCCESSFUL, HOPEFUL DREAMS

Had his life been a little more fair or comfortable, Thurgood Marshall would not have met Charles Hamilton Houston until years later, perhaps when Houston served as the NAACP's special counsel and Marshall volunteered legal advice to its Baltimore chapter. Howard Law School was for Marshall, as it was for most of its students in 1930, the campus of last resort. The University of Maryland Law School was near his parents' home but did not accept black applicants; his mother dissuaded him from submitting a futile application. He could not afford any of the northern law schools that admitted a few African Americans each year. Howard Law School was all that remained. This was the first time segregation had determined his course, and it wounded him deeply.

He was born in Baltimore in 1908, but Thurgood's family moved to Harlem when he was two years old and still named Thoroughgood. His was a family given to imposing first names. Although born to parents named Willie and Norma, he had relatives named Fearless, Ravine and Olive Branch. Uncle Fearless, called Uncle Fee, was his favorite. Young Thoroughgood was so pretty "he should have been a girl," and everyone called him Goody.[1] When the Marshalls moved back to Baltimore to care for Norma's mother, the six-year-old announced that his name was now Thurgood, a contraction to which he clung so strongly that his mother agreed to change his birth certificate. Thoroughgood and Goody no more,

Thurgood ecstatically learned that his family would be moving in with Uncle Fee, whose given name, aptly, was Fearless Mentor.[2]

Uncle Fee lived in an integrated neighborhood, which distinguished Thurgood's childhood from that of nearly every other African American of the time, including Charles Hamilton Houston. Uncle Fee's mostly black neighborhood in Old West Baltimore included families recently arrived from Russia, Italy and Germany. Thurgood's dad was often away working as a porter on the trains and Fearless had no children of his own. Thurgood and his older brother, William Aubrey, treasured the hours together when Uncle Fee arrived home each day from his job as the B & O Railroad president's personal attendant.[3]

By the time he turned seven, Thurgood had a job of his own, earning ten cents a day helping in the Jewish-owned grocery store next door to Uncle Fee's house. He enjoyed playing with the owners' son Sammy, but the two boys attended different schools; Thurgood attended the local elementary school for black children. His summer vacation was a month longer than Sammy's.

Thurgood attended high school in a hometown hardening into a southern mold. Baltimore had managed to avoid the racial violence that burned through Washington after World War I, but white politicians nonetheless invoked the specter of that unrest in the face of the Great Migration that was bringing thousands of African Americans from the Deep South to border and northern states. Most who reached Baltimore were bound for New York, but enough decided to cast their lots in Charm City that Baltimore's white residents, formerly divided into religious, ethnic and linguistic factions, united in racial solidarity. The NAACP's Baltimore chapter swelled in response.

Such a political environment made inevitable the black high school's descent into disrepair. A few years after his family moved out of Uncle Fee's and into a home of their own, Marshall enrolled in "Colored High." The school had no library, gym or cafeteria. The books were old discards from white schools. Half a lifetime later when he argued that separate could never be equal, Colored High was still with him.

He graduated from high school one semester early so that he could go to work full-time. His brother was a junior at Lincoln University in

Pennsylvania, where Thurgood planned to enroll, and the family would struggle to send both sons to college. Every bit helped.

CHARLES HOUSTON'S EARLY CHILDHOOD, like Thurgood's, bubbled over with family and neighborhood friends. But where the Baltimore boy knew work as well as play, the sheltered Washingtonian, born thirteen years earlier, in 1895, blossomed in a cocoon of play and study. He and his parents lived in a row house at 1705 Tenth Street NW, on the outskirts of a part of Washington called Strivers' Section, where many African American professionals owned houses and raised families. Two months after Charlie's ninth birthday, a group of neighborhood parents whom the *Washington Post* called "Negro Aristocracy" brought a case before the D.C. commissioners in which they sought to shut down a "poolroom" run by a man named Charles Cutch. The citizens declared that theirs was "the best colored section in the city" and noted that pictures of their houses were shown at the recent Paris Exposition. A poolroom had no place among "the rising colored generation."[4]

Indeed, Charlie's playmates were, like him, scions of Washington's black society. Parents in Strivers' Section worked to protect their children from the lash of segregation that afflicted their downtown workdays; they shielded the children from the disease and crime-ridden alleys in which so many Washingtonians lived and died. Their row house roofs boasted tiled designs as ornate as the matriarchs' Sunday church hats. Children like Charlie learned to speak in the proper manner that, to this day, still manages to separate some black children from others. As carefree as it likely seemed to the young boy, his was a purposeful upbringing. Days spent dashing back and forth in childhood fervor and evenings spent practicing the piano comprised a hard-earned utopia beyond the bounds of which lay the sort of horror with which no child could have been expected to deal well.

Charlie's father, William, spent his days working for the federal government and his nights pursuing a law degree. He served as chairman of the board of the Pen and Pencil Club, and on the eighty-sixth anniversary of Frederick Douglass's birth William opened a celebratory meeting at Gray's Hall on Sixteenth and M streets NW. The club's logo was printed in gold on the back of the program. The menu was decorated with a tiny quill pen and pencil; pink baby ribbon and little red hearts reminded members that it was Valentine's Day. The evening's entertainment included the on-stage presentation of Cupid and Puck, the latter character played by seven-year-old Charlie Houston.[5]

A few years earlier, Charlie's parents had enrolled him in Washington's segregated school system. In 1901, the young boy stepped into the wide hallways of Garrison Elementary, just a few blocks from home, where he became a good but not exceptional student. He attended summer school and read voraciously, his books and the family's piano swiftly becoming his favored companions. By the time he graduated from Garrison and applied to the prestigious M Street School, Charlie had developed the trait that would define his academic and professional life: a zealous work ethic whose cause and effect were a yearning impatience.

INITIALLY FOUNDED in a church basement in 1870 as the Preparatory High School for Negro Youth, the M Street School was the only high school available for African American students in Washington, D.C. The school stood just beyond the shadow of the Capitol dome and enjoyed a stellar reputation nationwide. In 1898, the all-black student body at M Street scored higher on the city's standardized tests than their white counterparts at Eastern High. Parents moved hundreds of miles to Washington just to send their children to the scrubbed-clean school. Even though it lacked such basic amenities as lockers and grass on its front lawn, the school boasted a faculty worthy of a small college: Many teachers held Ph.D.s; because so few colleges would hire black professors, the instructors migrated to the only black high school in the country that consistently graduated college-bound students.

Young Charlie Houston did well at M Street. Like all M Street students, he carried a course load that included English, French, Latin, history and math. He continued to attend summer school and graduated first in his class on June 11, 1911, at the age of fifteen.

His parents were doing well financially by then. His father had left the federal government in order to practice law full-time in his office at 1314 V Street NW, one block north of U Street, which was fast rising to become one of the cultural and commercial centers of black America. During the evenings, William Houston taught at his alma mater, Howard Law School.

Charlie's mother, Mary, had a hairstyling business that was booming with
the times; she regularly worked in the homes of senators and diplomats, always insisting on being let in through the front door and being addressed
by her white clients as "Mrs. Houston." The Houstons were ensconcing
themselves firmly in the District of Columbia's middle class and viewed
their son's college education as the most reliable way to ensure that he
would be able to stand on their shoulders.

During his senior year of high school, Houston was accepted into
Amherst College in Massachusetts. So comfortable had his life been to
this point that, once he had been accepted, there hardly was a doubt that
he would enroll in the exclusive institution. "Charlie was a rather spoiled
and self-centered child," his cousin William H. Hastie explained, "living a
rather comfortable and secluded life and not very acutely or painfully disturbed by American racism. If he was not pleased with the status of the
Negro, he was not greatly moved by it and had no passionate concern to
change it. All of that was changed by World War I."[6] But war was years and
a lifetime away as Charlie exulted in his Amherst acceptance letter.

His parents marshaled the last of their resources to enter him into
Amherst's class of 1915. He would be the only African American student
in his class, an uncomfortable position not unfamiliar to graduates of the
M Street School. As his train left Washington in the second week of September 1911, the energetic and bookish teenager felt the same anxiety as
any freshman bound for a seemingly faraway college. Charlie's apprehen-
sion certainly was heightened by the sequestered striver's life he had come
to know in black Washington. Indeed, there was no black Amherst; this
would be the only child's first foray into the America from which he long
had been shielded.

AFTER THE CRAWFORD TRIAL, Charles Houston did not return triumphantly
to Howard Law School; neither his client's guilty verdict nor Houston's
disposition allowed him to celebrate. He did, however, resume with renewed
confidence his duties as the law school's dean. That George Crawford's
all-black defense team had performed so admirably during the sensational
trial impressed not only the national media but also the citizens, both black
and white, of segregated Loudoun County, Virginia. In a county where black
men did not so much as make uninvited eye contact with whites, Houston

and his fellow attorneys had cross-examined the sheriff and challenged a judge in open court.

Their impeccable courtroom presentation, according to the influential *Richmond News Leader*, "itself gave to the trial a certain educational value."[7] White political leaders called themselves "impressed." These reactions validated the revolution Dean Houston had orchestrated at Howard Law School over the past four years. Even before the Crawford trial thrust him to national prominence, Houston was fundamentally changing what it meant for a black person to be a lawyer in the United States. He enacted sweeping reforms that transformed Howard Law School from what the city's wealthiest black residents called "a dummy's retreat" into an institution whose uncompromising rigor and singularity of purpose drew comparisons to the military academy at West Point.

Howard Law alumni in the 1930s were drastically different from their immediate predecessors. Through the 1920s, most black lawyers scratched out a living performing uncomplicated legal tasks for modest clients. Some of them had never attended law school, and most who had were alumni of Howard's unaccredited part-time law school. Earnest though they were, these attorneys could not be expected to mold gossamer points of constitutional law into the arguments Houston knew would be necessary in the coming years.

IN 1929, Justice Louis Brandeis, the first Jewish man appointed to the U.S. Supreme Court and an advocate for those abused under and by the law, ruefully told the president of Howard University, "I can tell most of the time when I'm reading a brief by a Negro attorney. You've got to get yourself a real faculty out there or you're always going to have a fifth rate law school. And it's got to be a full time and a day school."[8] Justice Brandeis was merely giving voice to what university president Mordecai Johnson had already decided to do.

Born in 1890 to former slaves in Paris, Tennessee, Johnson had earned degrees from Morehouse College and Harvard University by the time he became Howard's first black president in 1926. He was a formidable man with a light complexion, heavy eyebrows, a heavier preacher's voice and straight hair that all but abandoned him during his thirty-four-year tenure as Howard's president. His parents named him Mordecai because they believed him destined to deliver his people like the biblical hero in the Book of Esther who refused to bow to an unjust ruler. During his presidency, he delivered Howard University from the backwaters of higher education. Johnson increased Howard's annual congressional appropriation from a little over $200,000 to $7 million; he replaced lackluster professors with such luminaries as Ralph Bunche, John Hope Franklin and Charles Drew and considerably raised admission and academic standards.

Although armed with a doctorate in divinity, Johnson was an unabashedly pragmatic man. His force was fearless. When asked in 1922 to give the commencement address at Harvard University, the thirty-two-year-old embraced the opportunity to tell a nearly all-white audience that after having fought in the Great War, black people could no longer act like most white folks thought they should act. America's black citizens could no longer "talk like a Negro should talk, study like a Negro should study." Twelve million African Americans would "no longer feed on the bread of repression and violence. They ask for the bread of liberty, of public equality and public responsibility." Johnson believed that if it was to have any relevance to the lives of those whom it purported to serve, the nation's only university for black students had to be reborn as an accredited institution worthy of respect. The preacher-president assigned himself as midwife; labor pains would begin, he decided, in the law school.

MORDECAI JOHNSON BEGAN to search for someone to replace the vice dean of the law school's day program. He sought a scholarly lawyer who believed, as he did, that black folks should no longer depend on white attorneys to wage their legal battles. Their legal war would be won by black attorneys with a blood-stake in their cases' outcomes. Johnson soon settled on a thirty-four-year-old professor in Howard Law School's evening program who, along with his father, owned a small but prosperous downtown law firm.

At that moment, Charles Hamilton Houston was almost certainly the most academically accomplished African American attorney in history. As the only black student in Amherst's class of 1915, Charlie may have been stunted socially, but his racial isolation had failed to stunt his unwavering drive; he was inducted into Phi Beta Kappa and graduated with highest honors. A few years later, at Harvard Law School, he became the first

African American member of the law review. Mentored by future Supreme Court justice Felix Frankfurter, Houston again graduated with the highest honors offered by his school. Not content with a lawyer's Juris Doctor, he remained at Harvard to earn a Doctor of Juridical Science, a rarely earned degree equivalent to a Ph.D. in the law. Professor Frankfurter was by now so impressed with Houston that he recommended him for a prestigious traveling fellowship, which Houston won handily. As a Frederick Sheldon Fellow, Houston studied law at the University of Madrid and traveled through countries in Europe and Africa, before returning to a hometown poorer and more segregated than he had left it.

In Charlie Houston, Mordecai Johnson had found his man. He offered him the job at a salary that, although modest, would allow him to suspend his private practice and dedicate his full professional vigor to revolutionizing the day program at Howard Law School.

Despite Houston's being the evening program's most enthusiastic professor, Johnson could not be certain he would accept the position. William Houston's long-held dream of owning a successful law firm with his son had become a reality. Houston & Houston was a thriving concern, and over the past five years, Charlie had developed a stellar reputation and a diverse practice. Commercial litigation, trusts and estates, torts and family law comprised a book of business that hardly left him enough time to teach his night classes. Whereas Felix Frankfurter had taught him the value of social science evidence in arguing points of law, his father educated him in the practical mechanics of presenting a winning case for a paying client. Houston & Houston knew no shortage of such clients; Charlie's plain white business card bore in capital block letters a Northwest Washington office address that would remain unchanged for decades to come.

Houston had more than just his own financial security to consider upon receiving Johnson's offer. After returning to Washington from his traveling fellowship, he had married Margaret "Mag" Moran, a demure young woman of whom his family was quite fond and with whom he had pursued a long and complicated courtship. Their relationship tended to be more formal than warm even by the strict standards of Washington's early-twentieth-century African American elite. By now, however, the couple was trying to conceive, and the hope of incurring a father's expenses weighed in Houston's consideration of the $4,500 he would earn annually as the dean of Howard Law School's day program. In private practice, his income was sure to grow more rapidly than an academic salary world.

In the end, Houston felt compelled by conviction to accept Mordecai Johnson's offer. Professor Frankfurter had instilled in him the notion that every person "should know what they think and why they think it." As a law student, Charles Houston had come to think that "there must be Negro lawyers in every community."[9] Of the 12 million black people in America, only 1,100 of them were lawyers. Although "separate but equal" was the law in the South, separate and *unequal* was the reality—indeed, it was the very fabric on which American southern life was embroidered. Eventually it would take the Supreme Court, a president and the loaded rifles of the U.S. Army to tear up this stitching. But first there would be lawyers. If a new generation of African American lawyers was to litigate successfully against unconstitutional inequality, its members would have to be better educated and better trained than many of their white colleagues.

On the need for more and better-trained black lawyers, Houston and Johnson were in agreement. Each man saw his resolve mirrored in the other. Houston accepted the position of resident vice dean of the day program. Because the dean of the law school was an older white man whose work as a full-time judge occupied most of his time, Houston effectively would be running the day program. Mordecai Johnson excitedly informed the board of trustees and influential alumni that the best-educated black lawyer ever to practice in America was moving his files into 420 Fifth Street NW, the row house where Howard's part-time law students attended class between and after working full shifts beneath the Jim Crow caul that had lain itself across Washington, D.C., by the summer of 1929.

LIKE HOUSTON'S SIMMERING RESOLUTION, Washington's racial tensions were sparked in the ashes of America's victory in the Great War. In the blocks and miles surrounding the law school, the city's residents stewed in a kettle of racial hatred. The District, as Washingtonians still call their hometown, had erupted in 1919 with what newspapers deemed a "race riot," but what can more accurately be described as a four-day war. Ten years later, the District remained a city scarred. Its countless alleys brimmed with desperate and diseased shadows.

Until they were outlawed in 1850, the chatter-call of slave auctioneers had streamed through the open windows of the White House from across the street in Lafayette Square. Clusters of chained men, women and children clinked down Pennsylvania Avenue NW, bound for sale. Despite slavery's persistence in the capital, there thrived in the District black people free and strong; free blacks outnumbered slaves four to one. Civil War–era black Washingtonians flourished in the rocky, potted soil of segregation. Theirs was a world apart and within the Federal City, and it teemed with doctors, barbers, tailors, lawyers, teachers and all vocations in between.

As residents of the constitutionally created seat of the federal government, Washingtonians have little say in the management of their city. Congress and the president control the District, despite the fact that D.C. residents have no representatives or senators in Congress and could not vote in presidential elections until 1965. The city is locally governed by federal fiat. A president from Illinois or a senator from Alabama has more control over D.C.'s local affairs than do the city's locally elected council members.

Thus, slave-owning Washingtonians had no means by which to register an official political protest when, in the spring of 1862, President Abraham Lincoln abolished slavery in the nation's capital. The federal government compensated slaveowners for their lost property. As news of the emancipation spread down the coast, escaped slaves from the rebellious states poured into the District. Known as contrabands, these huddled masses swelled the city's African American population.

The next few years witnessed an unprecedented integration of black and white people in an American city. African Americans served in the District's police force and fire department. They exercised their numerical clout at the ballot box and began working for the federal government as laborers, cooks and clerks in integrated federal buildings. Not even a decade removed from the Civil War, some African American clerks supervised white employees. City residents sat in integrated trolley cars and sports venues. In deference to what District activists one hundred years later would call "home rule," Congress and the president permitted Washingtonians, three quarters of whom were white, to determine the path of their own affairs.

This modest progressivism ended when southerner Woodrow Wilson moved into the White House. After actively courting African Americans' votes during the 1912 election, Wilson segregated federal buildings. Restrooms, cafeterias and even office areas suddenly bore signs reading WHITES ONLY and COLORED. His administration demanded photographs from all federal job applicants. The government fired black employees for dubious reasons and refused to hire black applicants for reasons ungiven, casting many of D.C.'s African American families into poverty. When asked why he imposed segregation on federal workers, the president replied that "segregation was caused by friction between the colored and white clerks, and not done to injure or humiliate the colored clerks, but to avoid friction." Lest he be misunderstood, Wilson added, "It is as far as possible from being a movement against the Negroes. I sincerely believe it to be in their interest."[10] When the United States entered the "war to end all wars" during his second term, it did so with a segregated military commanded by leaders in a newly segregated government.

Nonetheless, African Americans by and large supported their country's involvement in the war. Charles Hamilton Houston was but one of thousands of black men to join the military, inspired by the belief that, by fighting abroad "to make the world safe for democracy," they might return to a homeland more inclined to grant them the rights promised to them at birth. As the army itself later would report in an official chronology, "The deeply entrenched negative racial attitudes prevalent among much of the white American population, including many of the nation's top military and civilian leaders, made it very difficult for blacks to serve in the military establishment of this period." Even before they returned home to segregated cities like Washington, "African American servicemen suffered numerous indignities and received little respect from white troops and civilians alike."[11] Lieutenant Houston would become but one of countless black soldiers to learn in horror that the soldiers most likely to maim or kill him wore American uniforms.

AFTER THE GREAT WAR WAS WON, veterans returned home to cities and counties whose alleys and woods rustled with murder. During 1919's first half, seven black veterans were tortured and lynched in America; each still wore his army uniform as his swollen body swung.

Steady jobs were hard to find for returning veterans of any race. President Wilson was replacing most remaining African American government employees with white applicants; there were not enough private or public sector jobs to put the crowded city to work. In the humidity of Washington's summer, white sailors panhandled downtown in their uniforms. Black soldiers who had fought in France listened incredulously as parents and wives explained that jobs available to them had all but disappeared.[12]

In Washington, a saloon-born rumor sparked fire. One muggy Saturday night in July 1919, white sailors, soldiers and marines were drinking in the bars clustered downtown when a canard crackled in the banter. The District's Metropolitan Police Department had arrested, questioned and released a black man suspected of sexually assaulting a white woman—and not just any white woman, either, but the wife of a fellow military man; a navy man in fact. The story snaked through the packed saloons and pool halls. Justice the horde demanded, and vengeance they would have.

They poured out of the bars, through the woods of the National Mall and down into an impoverished black neighborhood on the lowlands of Southwest D.C. They carried the pipes and lumber they'd found along their drunken march.

Charles Linton Ralls was enjoying an evening stroll with his wife, Mary, when the mob fell upon him. He was the first black man they saw and, for that, he was beaten to a bloody rag. About a block away, fifty-five-year-old George Montgomery was returning home with groceries in his arms. His purchases soon lay scattered near the dark corner of Ninth and D streets SW, waste for rats even before the mob cracked his skull with a brick.

The two broken but still breathing bodies lying in Southwest D.C. announced, in their awful heaps, that the nation's "Red Summer" had scorched its way into the District of Columbia. Race riots had burned through cities across the country and finally had reached the nation's capital. Local media abetted the conflagration; the *Washington Post* punctuated its Fourth of July week coverage with the headline NEGRO AGAIN ATTACKS, prompting the NAACP to urge the paper and its competition to stop "sowing the seeds of a race riot."[13] It was too late. The Red Summer's storm reached a capital city suddenly teeming with unemployed members of a racist military.

The violence rolled unabated from Saturday night into Sunday's dusk, by which time the mobs discerned that the District's seven-hundred-member police department was uninterested in intervening. Thousands of white veterans in uniform snatched black people from streetcars and sidewalks, and beat them without reason or mercy. Black women cried in the streets for God to save them. "Before I became unconscious," recalled Francis Thomas, a seventeen-year-old victim of the mobs' attacks, "I could hear [two black women] pleading with the Lord to keep them from being killed." A twenty-two-year-old black man, Randall Neale, was walking near Fourth and N streets NW when a white marine shot and killed him from a passing trolley car.[14]

By Sunday night black Washington had had enough. Veteran sharp-shooters cleaned their rifles before scaling walls to the roof of Howard Theatre. U Street NW was their Rubicon and they defended it against white invasion. The *Washington Post* reported, "In the negro district along U Street from Seventh to Fourteenth streets, the negroes began early in the evening to take vengeance for the assaults on their race in the down-town district the night before." After securing their neighborhoods, some black men went on the offensive, pulling unsuspecting white riders from streetcars and beating them to pleading ruins. Ten white and five black residents would die that night. An African American teenage girl shot and killed a police officer. Black and white men fired at each other from moving cars. The nation's capital was at war with itself.[15]

On the fourth day of bloodshed, after the streets, alleys and trolley cars were stained red, President Woodrow Wilson decided that he should act. He ordered nearly two thousand military servicemen into Washington to crush the violence and restore order. The troops justifiably expected to meet fierce resistance from the warring residents. Hundreds of guns had been bought and sold during the past three days alone. Saloons and taverns closed; local officials pleaded for calm. It seemed the soldiers, sailors, and marines summoned by the president would hardly be numerous enough to quell the battleground.

But then it started raining. It started raining, and the rain did not stop until every man in the city had lowered his gun, sheathed his knife or just shoved his fists back into his empty pockets and gone home. Rain laid low the gunfire and dispersed the mobs. Then it washed the blood from the streets and walls.

In the morning, Washington awakened to the exposure of its racial hatred. As *Leslie's Weekly* reported, "That race riots should have broken out in Washington, a city where a large proportion of the white population shares the antagonistic feeling of the South against the negro race, caused only mild surprise throughout the country," but that black residents so swiftly armed and defended themselves was revelatory.[16] James Weldon Johnson, the NAACP's field secretary, predicted further racial violence around the nation, warning that "the colored men will not run away and hide as they have done on previous occasions of that kind. The experience here has demonstrated clearly that the colored man will no longer submit to being beaten without cause."[17] Black Washingtonians' armed resistance was imitated in Chicago one month later when African American snipers held rooftop positions against white swarms. "In previous race riots they have run away and have been beaten without resistance," Johnson cautioned, "but now they will protect themselves."[18]

Over the coming weeks, Washington cooled. Streetcars and sidewalks filled again with residents aware that little had changed. Their lives and city soon buzzed anew. Unemployed drunks black and white slept and begged again and congressmen and presidents continued to arrive and depart with little regard for the citizens hosting their offices. The Justice Department blamed "Russian soviet interests" for "sow[ing] discord among the negroes," and a prominent local white preacher blamed Prohibition for causing the "Bolshevism" that caused the "race riots."[19]

In his opening prayers in the House of Representatives on July 22, the Reverend H. N. Couden, Congress's blind chaplain, tore through the political gauze when he beseeched the Lord to deliver Washington from "the hateful thing we call race prejudice."[20] As soon as the reverend ended his prayer, congressmen blamed the riot-war's violence on communist Russian agitators and refused to investigate why the Metropolitan Police Department had left black citizens to fend for themselves against lawless slaughter.[21] President Wilson continued to give speeches about freedom and democracy, while the Washingtonians killed in July's mayhem awaited burial in segregated cemeteries.

3

No Tea for the Feeble

DEAN CHARLES HOUSTON SEIZED the helm of Howard Law School's day program with the fervency of a man answering a calling. He brooked no moderation. That the nation's premier school for black attorneys lacked accreditation was an affliction that black people no longer could suffer in the face of their dire need for lawyers. "Experience has proved that the average white lawyer, especially in the South," Houston wrote, "cannot be relied upon to wage an uncompromising fight for equal rights for Negroes."[1]

Professors who had grown comfortably lackadaisical at the law school were fired or resigned under pressure. Houston replaced them with gifted attorneys who, but for racist hiring policies, would have been teaching at America's top-tier law schools. Without compunction, Dean Houston placed academia's racism at his employ.

First among these equals was William H. Hastie, his cousin and close confidant. Like Houston, Hastie had graduated with highest honors from Amherst College and Harvard Law School, where he too served on the law review. When his cousin asked him to join the faculty at Howard, the country-born lawyer, who later would earn a Doctorate of Juridical Science from Harvard just as Houston had done years ago, could scarcely say no. Hastie was a man of conscience and unfailing urbanity; even the closest observer never would surmise that he had grown up on a Tennessee chicken farm. The years would soon find him sworn in as the nation's first

African American federal judge. Where Houston was "Charlie," Hastie was "Bill," and, according to a mutual friend, "Charlie was the earthier of the two."[2] Hastie's cool congeniality reflected itself in his handsomely reserved demeanor—a triangular mustache tapered at the corners of his smile, just above a necktie that would remain knotted until the day's demands were behind him.

William Hastie was nine years younger than the cousin he so admired. But unlike his cousin, he had neither enjoyed a childhood sheltered from the white people who despised him nor been hurled into a brutally racist army regiment to serve with them. Accordingly, Hastie did not labor beneath the bridled fury that was both master and servant of his cousin's brilliance.

Leon A. "Andy" Ransom stood just a hair shorter than Houston and would grow to be a bear of a man as he approached middle age. His mind was indomitable. After graduating first in his class from the Ohio State University School of Law, Ransom eagerly brought his photographic memory to Howard Law School.

These professors prepared for their classes and challenged their students with verve. They believed in Dean Houston's aspirations for the school: One out of every four African American law students was attending Howard, and if they were to benefit their country and their race, the law school must, as Houston explained, "equip its students with the direct professional skills most useful to them." Howard would perform the "distinct, necessary work for the social good" by graduating black lawyers who accepted the task that injustice had set before them.[3]

In a memorandum to the faculty, Houston informed professors that he was "planning to make a study of the entire curriculum for the purpose of co-ordinating the subjects and eliminating waste." For example, there was little need for a class devoted to juries because that material "could properly be handled in Criminal Procedure, Criminal Law Laboratory, Common Law Pleading and Moot Court."[4] So that Houston could conduct the thorough examination he deemed necessary, professors were asked to submit lists of their assigned cases and text materials, "grouping them by chapter and section," and to submit "an informal short memorandum of [their] opinion [on] how much work can profitably be covered in the semester, and the best way to cover the same." The vice dean asked to receive the information in the next five days.[5]

In addition to his considerable administrative duties, Houston taught a full load of courses and thereby set an example of exhaustive preparation for his fellow professors. To first-year students he taught History of Law, Legal Bibliography and Argumentation, Evidence, and Criminal Law Laboratory; he taught second-year students Common Law Pleading and instructed third-year students in Conflict of Laws and Municipal Corporations. It was in teaching these demanding classes that he earned what Thurgood Marshall termed "the affectionate nickname 'Ironshoes.'"[6]

After purging the faculty, Houston raised admission standards. No longer would the law school accept applicants who had graduated from unaccredited colleges. For an unaccredited law school, this was quite a proclamation. The announcement triggered a dramatic decline in enrollment. By now, the board of trustees had become concerned with the swift and serious changes sweeping the law school. Its members were hardly prepared for Dean Houston's next request, which university president Mordecai Johnson delivered in early 1930.

Houston sought permission to eliminate the night school. Doing so was the only way for administrators and professors to focus their energies on developing a full-time day school worthy of being accredited by the Association of American Law Schools and the American Bar Association. His request was fraught with impact: Most African American law school graduates had earned their degrees from Howard's evening program. When few black adults could devote the workday to study, the night school provided the path to a profession. Indeed, Houston's own father, William, one of the most prominent and respected lawyers in black Washington, had attended the night school while working as a government clerk to support his family. If he was so intent on meeting black folks' national need for lawyers, why did Dean Houston want to shut down the institution most directly devoted to meeting that need?

Mordecai Johnson explained to the board that black people needed more attorneys of the first order, and, frankly, the evening program was not producing them. Yes, Houston had made significant qualitative changes in the faculty, but these limited resources would be best spent on students who were willing and able to attend classes full-time. Persuaded again by Howard's president, the board of trustees voted to abolish the evening program after its current students graduated.

The decision met with immediate condemnation from outraged alumni. "Among the two groups," an alumnus protested in a newspaper article, "those who pursue their law study in the day and those who take advantage of the evening possibility, the latter are in most cases more conscientious."[7] African American members of the bar nationwide debated the new vice dean's attempts to "Harvardize Howard." Even those who supported Houston's vision wondered whether the small law school might buckle beneath the weight of his demands.

Upon learning of the university's decision to close the night school, all its white professors resigned.[8] They were equally livid and incredulous that President Johnson had taken Dean Fenton W. Booth's duties and reassigned them to Vice Dean Houston. As chief judge of the U.S. Court of Federal Claims, Johnson countered, Booth was unable to devote most of his energies to Howard. The professors' primary concern was that Houston was "engaged in a general reorganization of the law school." None of Howard's African American faculty members would comment on their white colleagues' collective resignation, but most of them had also opposed closing the night school.[9]

Derided as a gifted but misguided elitist, Houston labored undaunted. He purchased volumes for the law library and hired a full-time librarian. Consulting with the country's leading African American lawyers, he developed a bond with a tough Texan litigator named James Nabrit, Jr., who one day would become president of Howard University. Nabrit maintained a wily, successful civil rights and commercial litigation practice about which the Texas Ku Klux Klan was apoplectic. From attorneys like Nabrit, who had graduated from Northwestern Law School, Houston received encouragement to continue along his chosen path of considerable resistance.

As the date of the accreditation inspection grew near, Dean Houston issued a "Faculty Bulletin" reminding professors, among other duties, to "please make special effort to have the 8:30 classes begin on time. Do not permit the students to straggle in late." Instructors should "report persistent tardiness" to Houston's office, "where it will be promptly corrected." Full-time professors were instructed to submit "immediately a definite schedule of office hours during the week, so that a consolidated list may be published on the bulletin board." Finally, Houston asked the teachers to "make it a point to do a little work, at least, in [Howard's] own library, by way of inspiration to the students." His reason was optimistic and plain: "Nothing encourages a student to work more than to see his teacher working near him."[10]

CHARLES HOUSTON'S CONTROVERSIAL EFFORTS at the law school were vindicated in the spring of 1931, just two years after he became vice dean. The American Bar Association awarded Howard University full accreditation and approval. That winter, the Association of American Law Schools admitted Howard to its membership. The occasions were victories for the school's staff and students alike.

For Dean Houston, however, Howard's accreditation only marked commencement of the true work. Armed with the school's hard-earned credentials, he directed the law school to redouble its efforts to graduate lawyers fit to effect social gain. He extended the academic year to the middle of June and required students to spend at least eighteen hours in class each week. Many students dropped out. Houston's new requirements combined with the Great Depression to collapse enrollment by half.

To some, Houston appeared to relish the shriveling student body as proof of stripping the wheat from the chaff. "Look to your left and look to your right," he commanded first-year students. "Next year one of you won't be here." If he learned that a student was holding a job, he encouraged him to quit the job, telling one such young man, "You can't work and go to law school. Don't get any notion that you can."[11] Students who visited his second-story office to express concern about the countless hours they spent briefing cases in the first-floor library were told that there was "no tea for the feeble, no crepe for the dead." It was a refrain Howard's students and professors had grown wearily accustomed to hearing from their vice dean.

Despite his rigid exterior, however, Houston empathized with his students. The Depression ravaged Americans of every race, but black workers were hit particularly hard and Houston understood that his insistence on Howard Law students' attending classes full-time deepened their financial struggle. The dean regularly slipped money to students in need of a little help and invited them to dinner at his and Mag's home. "He was a sweet man once you saw what he was up to," Thurgood Marshall later recalled. "He was absolutely fair and the door to his office was always open."[12]

Dean Houston brought sandwiches and coffee to his secretary, a 1921 Howard Law graduate named Ollie May Cooper, one of only about twenty-five black women licensed to practice law in the United States. With Isadore Letcher, Cooper had opened the nation's first law firm owned and operated by black women. As a professor, law clerk and secretary to at least ten law school deans, Cooper served her alma mater for over forty-three years. By the time Houston eliminated the evening program and became dean of the entire law school, Ollie Cooper's institutional knowledge had already proved invaluable. Not for idle flattery did he address her as "Dean Cooper" when he placed a fresh cup of coffee on her crowded desk.

There was no denying, however, that Houston was, as Marshall also described, "hard crust." He countenanced no impediment to Howard's ability to graduate attorneys who were, in his words, "not only good but superior, and just as superior in all respects as time, energy, money and ability permit." Students who failed to brief assigned cases and prepare fully for class could expect "disciplinary action" that would "be swift and severe." Indeed, Dean Houston's quips could border on the pugnacious: "The only thing I love is to flunk valedictorians and smart people," he would bluster to a class of black men with fraternity keys Alpha and Omega shoved into trouser pockets. "It doesn't do me any good to flunk dumb people, because dumbs are dumbs and it doesn't mean anything."[13]

But to suggest that Houston was, as one former student recalled, "more of a machine than a man," was to mistake his purpose. He did not demand from his students and faculty all that they could give; he exacted from them all that he deemed necessary to prepare them for what lay ahead.

And the tall and proud man knew what lay ahead because he had experienced the virulence of what had been. Little had changed since he served in the Great War, and since the nation's capital burned in a race war. The army had introduced him to the America beyond the confines of Northwest Washington, D.C. The army had stripped him raw, and raw he remained: There can be little doubt that serving as an army lieutenant in

Europe during World War I was the crucible of Charles Hamilton Houston's life.

WHEN THE UNITED STATES entered the world war in 1917, Charlie Houston was a twenty-one-year old English instructor at Howard University. His father had procured him the job two years earlier out of fear that his son might commit himself to a career as a concert pianist. As much as William Houston enjoyed classical music unfurling in their parlor, he and Mary had not exhausted their savings on Amherst's tuition for their son to while away his life on a piano stool. Charlie also spoke of becoming a diplomat and had studied French, German and Spanish, but William put little stock in this ambition; Woodrow Wilson's State Department might close its doors before allowing a young black man to take a diplomat's oath.

Howard University, conversely, was an institution keen on hiring a Phi Beta Kappa graduate of Amherst College. William by now had grown to some influence in the black Washington that lived north of K Street NW. The son of an escaped slave who became a preacher so renowned that his Maryland funeral drew over a thousand mourners in the walking days of 1895, William understood that it took generations for a black man to grow old with soft hands. Charlie was gifted and educated, but he nonetheless remained just one generation removed from being legally owned by another man.

That escaped man's son William became a lawyer and dreamed of his child becoming a lawyer. He named Charles for the attorney who years ago had encouraged him to go to law school. While his son studied at Amherst, William Houston watched the District devolve into a city as virulently racist as any north of South Carolina. Woodrow Wilson's reelection in 1916 ensured unabated deterioration. Despite his impressive academic record, neither the public nor the private sector could be expected to welcome Charlie to the workforce. William learned that a Howard English professor was leaving the university, and he persuaded the board of trustees to hire his nineteen-year-old son.

Two years later, Charlie was one of the most dynamic instructors in the Commercial Department, a junior college–like segment of Howard that offered courses in math, English, typing and history. Students who excelled in the Commercial Department could earn enrollment in four-year colleges. Eager to prove that his position was based on merit, Charlie demonstrated both hard work and academic creativity. He swiftly earned the respect of both his students and fellow faculty members.

ALL OF HIS CLASSES were informally canceled a few weeks later, along with most other classes on campus. Howard University was swallowed whole by a student-led movement in 1917. Male students registered their claim by marching and conducting precision drills in their school clothes. Women sold campaign-style ribbons and tags espousing the cause.

Black students were demanding an officer training camp so that they could command soldiers in the U.S. Army. The call was at once daring and meek. It did not ask that qualified African American candidates be admitted to existing officer training camps where they might study and drill with white inductees. The students sought only what seemed possible: that black men who had attended college be commissioned as officers to lead black soldiers. Graduating seniors and junior faculty alike knew that establishing a segregated officer training camp was their only hope of escaping the enlisted ranks that treated black servicemen so poorly. If they became commissioned officers, they would command soldiers in battle; if they waited to be drafted as enlisted men, they would cook for and clean after white men of their same low rank. "New England Negroes opposed it as spreading segregation," Charles Houston later wrote. "But the Howard men took the position that, while they were opposed to segregation the War Department was going to put them in separate units anyway and if they had to be segregated they were determined to fight all the harder for Negro officers over Negro units."[14]

That the army should establish an officer training camp for black inductees was an idea first espoused by a Jewish cofounder of the NAACP who would rise in the army to the rank of lieutenant colonel during the war. One hardly could question Joel E. Spingarn's commitment to improving the lives of African Americans, but his serving as chairman of the NAACP's board of directors seemed to some incompatible with his call for a separate but equal officers' academy. After a year of beseeching the War Department to admit black college graduates to an existing officers' academy, however,

Spingarn resorted to calling for a separate camp for black candidates. This tactical bow to pragmatism foreshadowed the compromises awaiting NAACP leaders in the looming decades.

Spingarn exchanged the ideal of integration for the task of honest seg- regation. The hideous truth was that an all-black officers' academy was a viable proposition and would graduate more black officers than would a white camp sprinkled with a few earnest and unwanted black candidates. Spingarn encouraged Howard's draft-eligible men to form the Central Committee of Negro College Men to lobby elected officials and public opinion in support of an officer training camp for black college men. As Houston remembered decades later, Joel Spingarn "was concerned to see that Negroes should have their fair share of opportunity for leadership in the armed forces."[15]

The War Department relented in 1917 and established a training camp for black officer candidates at Fort Des Moines, Iowa. Instruction would commence on June 15, 1917. Charles Houston was the last man accepted into the program.

IN THE FINAL DAYS before the men left for camp, Washington effervesced with toasts and parties celebrating the new training camp. Black officers soon would command black soldiers in a world war because black Washing- ton had refused to accept otherwise. Proud families chartered a train not only to carry their sons to Fort Des Moines, Iowa, but to chug through Pittsburgh and Chicago en route and ferry those cities' registered candidates to the heartland. Though their triumph was modest, it was a drop of water fallen on the rock of inequality. Myriad more could bore a hole.

HOUSTON ESCHEWED THE REVELRY. In part because he was the last man ac- cepted into the camp, he intended to be one of the first to arrive. He boarded an earlier westbound train. Fort Des Moines was something just shy of deserted when he disembarked from the train, dust and duffel bag– laden. He milled about for a while, gray eyes cast toward gray-dusted clus- ters of enlisted black men working the camp into condition. These soldiers had been uniformed years before war, before college boys had chosen to become officers and willed the choice to exist.

That afternoon, he happened upon a high school classmate and fellow

Amherst alum. Francis Dent had arrived at Fort Des Moines even before Charlie. He had been training with white army candidates at Fort Myer, Virginia, just across the Potomac from his family in the District, when the army ordered him to Iowa. At Fort Myer, the army had ordered Francis to eat alone, to sleep alone, and even to drill alone. After Dent performed the same drills and the same exercises in the same uniform for the same pay as the white recruits, the white instructors refused to return the salute they'd taught him. Charlie's familiar face was as welcome to Francis as cooked food to a waking man. Francis Dent later would become an accomplished attorney in Michigan, but for now he contented himself with helping his old friend complete his induction paperwork and prepare for life as a member of Company Five, Seventeenth Provisional Training Regiment, Fort Des Moines.[16]

Company Five was composed mostly of Washingtonians who, like Houston and Dent, had excelled on cadet drill teams in high school. While their juvenile marches had been for awards and "side bets," their Iowan drills instilled discipline for combat. Their formations moved like fresh-wound clockwork. For the first month the men trained for general infantry service and the long summer days swiftly passed.

The second month was scheduled for specialized training but the general infantry instruction continued unabated. When the candidates asked why their specialized training was delayed, the instructors replied that it wasn't; it was canceled. War Department officials in Washington had decreed that the Fort Des Moines recruits could train only for infantry. As Houston described it, "field artillery required a better educated soldier than infantry," and army officials at the highest levels had determined that black officer candidates were unfit to lead any but an infantry unit. Instructors advised candidates that a recruit could register his disagreement with the policy by resigning, and take his chances with the draft.[17]

The men steamed with rage. None would serve in the engineers' corps or in field artillery units. Neither would any resign; "it was better to go to war as infantry officers," Houston explained in a series of articles published in the *Pittsburgh Courier* in 1940, "than to be drafted as privates into labor battalions."[18]

Training at Fort Des Moines trudged toward September 15, when its candidates were scheduled to be commissioned as army officers. The importance of their becoming officers was inspiration sufficient to maintain a measure of morale. Shortly before their date of commission, the War Department extended their training by another month. No reason was provided but none was expected. Houston vividly remembered learning the news: "This was a heavy blow. Many candidates resigned in disgust, stating they had lost all confidence in the Government's intention to give the Negro a square deal. Others of us argued against quitting in the middle, on the ground that it would play into the hands of those officers in the army who never wanted to see Negroes as officers in the first place."[19]

Most Fort Des Moines men remained, but so many left the camp that companies were consolidated; Company Five became Company Two. On October 15, 1917, the Fort's 639 African American men were commissioned as officers in the U.S. Army—106 captains, 329 first lieutenants and 204 second lieutenants, in rank order highest to lowest. The army commissioned Houston as a first lieutenant.

The men waited in little suspense to learn their regiment assignments. Because they had trained only for infantry duty, they knew that it was in the infantry that they would serve. They were flabbergasted when dozens were ordered into field artillery units. Even more staggered were the scores of men delegated to the engineers and field signal battalions. They had received no training in these areas; on the battlefield, their ignorance could cost lives. As these black officers would be restricted to commanding black enlisted men, their assignment laid bare the army's indifference to the lives of its African American soldiers. One of the young black captains, racked by one senseless defeat too many, killed himself, Houston recalled, "in protest at the treatment meted out to Negro officers."[20]

The officers vigorously protested their assignments. They requested transfers to infantry units, to the positions for which they had studied and trained. English majors designated for the engineering corps sought out black officers of the same rank who might have taken engineering courses in college; together the men offered the army a mutual exchange of service, even volunteering to pay their own transportation costs between camps. On every count the War Department refused.

As the technical units drilled for war, the black officers' lack of training was obvious. It was clear that their being placed in theater would undoubtedly cost American lives. Army officials attributed their failures to a lack of aptitude and ability. Black officers were unfit for any regiment but infantry, they reported, and they had the field tests to prove it.

From the beginning, Lieutenant Houston was assigned to the infantry. He served in the 368th Infantry, but, undeterred by the experiences of other African American officers assigned to the technical units, he "was keeping up a constant agitation to transfer to the Field Artillery, to the irritation of all [his] superior officers." Deployment marched near. Without warning, he and other interested black officers were invited to take the field artillery entrance examination, which, according to Houston, "was fairly easy."[21] He and his fellow officers could hardly feign surprise that they never learned their grades.

Pleasant surprise did arrive in the form of an order to serve as an army judge advocate. Assigned to investigate and prosecute two black enlisted soldiers accused of disorderly conduct and insubordination, Houston understood the mission as the pursuit of justice. He examined the allegations, investigated the facts and issued his report to the white ranking officer; all the available evidence was grossly insufficient to procure a conviction against the soldiers. The superior officer excoriated him. Never again would he serve as a judge advocate because he was "no good" at the job. Were he a worthy judge advocate, he would have tried the cases and secured convictions, just as another advocate had done in a companion case. Under facts nearly identical to Houston's two cases, an African American sergeant was found guilty of disorderly conduct and insubordination. The army sentenced the sergeant to one year of hard labor, loss of rank, and ordered him to forfeit most of his pay. Lieutenant Houston was appalled. As he later recalled, "[I vowed] that I would never get caught again without knowing something about my rights; that if luck was with me, and I got through this war, I would study law and use my time fighting for men who could not strike back."[22]

THE NINETY-SECOND DIVISION, to which the newly commissioned African American officers were assigned, received its orders. Houston passed his final physical exam and packed his duffel bag for overseas duty. He had submitted his baggage and effects for processing when he received an order from divisional headquarters; the army was removing him from the 368th Infantry. He was ordered to report to field artillery school. The victory was as abrupt and happy as any he ever would know.

At Camp Meade in Maryland, Lieutenant Houston joined ninety-six other black officer candidates in field artillery training. Because he already was an officer, military regulations prohibited his fraternizing with the candidates. His fellow officers, all of them white, were loath to socialize with him, and Houston relaxed easier around the black candidates anyway, so he retrieved his officer candidate's uniform from his bag and wore it every day. He bonded closely with the men. Decades later, knowing the company of Supreme Court justices, congressmen and the president of the United States, Houston maintained, "The men in the [field artillery] school were some of the finest men I have ever been privileged to associate with."[23]

White enlisted men and officers at Camp Meade laid raw their disgust at belonging to a division that included black soldiers. White officers refused to meet with their African American colleagues. As deployment drew near, the army ordered the Ninety-second Division to select, as every division had done, a symbol to represent its soldiers; the emblems would be sewn onto the left sleeve of each man's uniform. The division selected the buffalo, which, in a breach of discipline inexplicably tolerated by their superior officers, the white enlisted men and officers promptly refused to wear. Instead, they sewed swastikas onto their uniforms for good luck.

SCATHING THOUGH IT WAS, the racism Lieutenant Houston thus far had encountered in the army was mostly institutional. The military was a bigoted organization and operated in bigoted fashion. African American enlisted soldiers and sailors were confined to subservient labor; they cooked, they cleaned, they dug ditches and moved heavy objects, all the while subjected to discipline of a severity unfamiliar to white men of similar rank. As a commissioned officer, Houston expected to escape the ardor of domestic labor and brute toil, and, for the most part, he did. The first lieutenant was not ordered daily to scrub latrines or subjected to the whims of any given white sergeant.

He was, however, governed by a War Department reluctant to place any tool save a shovel, spatula or mop in the hands of a black soldier. His charge was to lead men into battles from which their return was not promised, but his orders continually isolated him from both command and conflict. As he boarded the ship that at last would ferry him across the ocean and into war,

Houston hoped that the awaiting fates of a distant shore would "answer the question what it meant for a Negro to wear the uniform of the United States."[24]

AFTER THE "GRAND VACATION" of a voyage across the Atlantic, Houston's contingent landed in France at Saint-Nazaire and soon traveled to Camp Mençou, in the ancient hamlet of Vannes. The ninety-seven African American field artillery soldiers were the only black servicemen at the camp; indeed, they were the only black people for many miles surrounding the town. The townspeople, however, greeted the African-appearing American soldiers as warmly as they did all arrivals decked in American fatigues.

The citizens' welcome contrasted sharply with the reception the soldiers received from the men of Camp Mençou. Years later when Houston first ventured into the American Deep South, it was but a return visit, because the Deep South's racist culture was on full display at Camp Mençou. Jim Crow ruled the base; officers and soldiers alike were classified by neither rank nor character, but by race alone. By now he was beginning to suspect that he might never see combat, but, as he later declared, life at Camp Mençou "destroyed the last vestiges of any desire I might have had to get in the front lines and battle for my country."[25]

As night shrouded their first day at the camp, Lieutenant Houston and his fellow officers followed the line to the officers' mess for dinner. They were refused at the door, ordered to turn back. The officers' insignia stitched on their uniforms might mean something to the desk warmers back at the War Department and might make their high yellow girlfriends swoon and their black mamas proud, but here at Camp Mençou there was order to keep. The officers' mess was for white officers.

Where were they to eat, then? Army regulations prohibited their eating in the enlisted mess.

The officers ate dinner off their laps, huddled on benches in an abandoned kitchen.

A few days later, they received orders to attend yet another field artillery training class, this one to be taught by both French and American instructors. The fairness with which the French teachers instructed the class contrasted sharply with the American teachers' determination to make a circus out of the black officers in the class, taunting them by insisting that they were wrong even when they had answered correctly. Conditions became so obnoxious that one of the African American lieutenants, Sylvanns Hart, who later would practice law in Jacksonville, Florida, took the risk of reporting the blatantly racist practices to the school's commanding officer. If only because poorly trained American field artillery troops of any race could endanger the lives of Allied forces, the commander reassigned the two most offensive instructors.

The black officers, in violation of army regulations, were ordered to sleep in the enlisted men's barracks. After several white enlisted soldiers registered protest over their integrated quarters, certain showers in the barracks were designated as COLORED. One afternoon, some German prisoners of war working the latrines asked aside a few black officers to tell them that white American soldiers had told them that the black officers were merely enlisted men "dressed up in officers' uniforms."[26]

Adding injury to this parade of insults, Houston suffered a hernia and a debilitating bout of influenza due to exposure. Both troubled him for his entire stay in France. After he returned to the States, his condition worsened and eventually morphed into a minimal lesion in his left lung and a case of active tuberculosis.[27]

As OFTEN AS THEY COULD, the African American officers escaped their camp for the aged roads of Vannes. The more time they spent in town, the more the residents seemed to favor them in whatever small ways were still permitted by white American soldiers who already had threatened most of the hotels and restaurants into refusing the black officers lodging or service. More than a few of the black officers spoke French and enjoyed laughing through cigarette smoke with the shop and tavern keepers.

Two white army captains, who outranked Houston and his friends, enjoyed in Vannes the company of two "sporting girls." By the Great War's twilight, sporting girls were as ubiquitous as aspiration itself; they flocked to officers in Europe as they did to boxers back home in the United States. Beneath felt-brimmed hats and double-poured liquors they plied a trade between prostitution and courtship.

On this Saturday night, the two captains were strolling with their two favorite women when a particularly handsome black lieutenant happened to pass. Being sporting girls, the women were already familiar with and fond of the lieutenant, who spoke French fluently. They abruptly became bored with the company of two captains, who spoke only whiskey-slurred English, so the sporting girls broke rank to join the lieutenant. Words sharp and loud pierced the still town square.

Charlie and his friend Mortimer Marshall were returning from the cinema when they stumbled upon the ominous scene: One black lieutenant, with a white woman at each side, exchanging words with two white captains. Sensing a disturbance greater than the usual drunken quarrel, the townspeople pulled their shutters tight.

One of the two captains sent word for Camp Mençou's white enlisted men to join their superiors at the town plaza. In the night's near distance a lynch mob soon formed like a funnel cloud and trundled forth. Enlisted soldiers spat hate to the wind. Officers or not, these boys had to be put in their place. The white solders declared, as Houston recalled, that America wouldn't "be a safe place to live when they [got] back" unless they dealt with this problem now.[28]

In vain the lieutenants tried to reason with the captains but the leash had come undone. White men in American uniforms blocked their path. A French guard squad marched across the square, oblivious to impending murder.

The three black officers stared at their white colleagues. Wind lapped at the lapels of their uniforms. The men stood their ground.

Then: "ATTENTION!" The captain of the military police stormed through the uniformed throng, ordered all enlisted men back to their quarters and harangued both the white and black officers for disgracing the American uniform with "a public street brawl."[29] The men wordlessly dispersed. Whether he knew that he had averted much more than a brawl the captain never confessed.

IN APRIL OF 1919, Lieutenant Houston left active duty. He accepted a commission in the Field Artillery Reserve Corps because, as he explained, "we had had such a hard time getting Negro field artillery officers that I wanted to keep a foot jammed in the opening in case war ever threatened again." Black officers would not be railroaded into the infantry if he could help it. "But basically," he wrote, "I was through with the Army and never wanted to see it again."[30]

He had volunteered to join the army for three reasons. First, he "was 21, single, healthy, with no dependents, and [he] figured [he] would be drafted anyway." Second, he had been active in the Central Committee of Negro College Men, which publicly had led the struggle for the army to induct black men as officers, "so when we got the chance we were clamoring for, there was nothing to do but take it." Finally, Houston had determined that he "was going to have something to say about how this country should be run and that meant sharing every risk the country was exposed to." The military rigor did not faze him and he had "no complaint about the army being tough." Indeed it was in the army that he learned the mantra he later would inflict on anyone who walked through Howard Law School's front door: "No tea for the feeble, no crepe for the dead."[31]

But World War I, he believed, "was just not my fight." The scorn hurled at black officers by the army and its white soldiers convinced Houston that "[his] battleground was America, not France." He arrived home to learn that his job at Howard was no longer available, so he taught high school English. A few months later, Washington erupted into a race war masked as a riot. Charles Houston stood in the smoldering aftermath an embittered man in an embittered hometown. His father had long encouraged him to become a lawyer. At last he considered the profession, the education, the tools.

In later writings about his military years, Houston professed gladness that he had not sacrificed his life for his country. But in the end this is exactly what he would do. Houston met the toil and ardor of the coming years with what his cousin William Hastie called "a soldier's faith." The army forever was with him.

4

THE SOCIAL ENGINEERS

NEARSIGHTEDNESS HAD NOT YET befallen the young man's eyes, so he glanced easily from his assigned cases to the landscape scrolling by the train's window. By now the miles between Washington and Baltimore were littered with landmarks telling Thurgood he was almost home or was nearing Washington. Woods and clearings blended but did not blur. He returned to his reading, determined to outline a brief of the case before the train reached home. "All of my notes I would take down in the book by hand and that night I would type them up after I rode back to Baltimore."[1] The train rumbled like the world's largest empty stomach and still offered more spans of quiet than he could expect at home.

Thurgood Marshall lived in his parents' house with them, his wife, brother and sister-in-law. Life behind 1828 Druid Hill Avenue's front door was loving, involved and loud. Their home roiled with affection and acrimony. Everyone worked to bring in money; his wife, Buster, worked at a nearby boutique to help pay her husband's law school tuition. The family argued politics at the dinner table, with Thurgood and his dad habitually working themselves into a lather. "I got the idea of being a lawyer from arguing with my dad," he fondly remembered.[2]

His father, Willie Marshall, was a study in clipped hope. With only an elementary school education, he had worked as a railroad porter to save the money for the three-story, five-bedroom row house in which he raised his family. He left the railroads to become head waiter at the Gibson Island

Club. His skin was whiter than that of some members of the all-white club; he wore his wavy black hair combed back and sported a tapered mustache, which his son Thurgood imitated as soon as puberty allowed. That Willie sometimes drank at work, reddening his face and loosening his tongue, was for now not much of an issue. His drinking fueled dinner table discussions and Willie Marshall was enamored with the law. Baltimore's judges often found him sitting in the back row of their courtrooms watching the proceedings.

Perhaps because she had spent her life with a man of hobbled possibility, Norma Marshall drove her two sons, Aubrey and Thurgood, to academic achievement. Her work as a substitute teacher in Baltimore's segregated schools exposed her to the cracked walls and curled paint that Jim Crow allotted black children. Despite the odds, she would see to it that Aubrey became a doctor and Thurgood a lawyer or perhaps a dentist. Thurgood waited tables with his father during the summer after graduating from Lincoln University but by autumn had not earned enough money to enroll in Howard Law School. He resigned himself to another white-coated year at the Gibson Island Club, but Norma Marshall pawned her engagement and wedding rings, handed her younger son the money and sent him on the train to Washington. When he opened his Baltimore law practice a few years later, she would pull the rug from their family's living room and insist that he lay it in his stark office.

Aubrey indeed became a physician, but, like most of Baltimore's African American doctors during the Depression, his practice existed largely in name. The recent Howard Medical School graduate spent most of his time working at the local clinic. Although the brothers shared an alma mater and a fraternity, their relationship was one of strained distance. Aubrey was a reticent man of fierce ambition. His college life was marked by achievements academic and social, but, with the exception of his courting the young Baltimore beauty he soon would marry, they were quiet years. Aubrey endured Alpha Phi Alpha Fraternity's rigorous pledge process only to spend most of his free time away from campus.

In 1925, Thurgood enrolled as a freshman as Aubrey began his senior year. The 285 students at Lincoln University were men united by an array of hazing rituals varying in humor and brutality. Even after Thurgood sustained the beatings and pranks commensurate with freshman year and fraternity pledging, the brothers could find no bond. One classmate recalled, "The dislike between Thurgood and Aubrey was so intense. I've never seen it in any two brothers that I know who came from the same parents, same background and everything else."[3]

Now the brothers found themselves living with their parents and wives in one house. Thurgood had had to forgo law school for a year because the family could not afford to have both sons simultaneously attending graduate school. Once enrolled in law school, he held faith that education could protect him from the frustration that clenched his father, but every day he watched the same frustration wrap itself tighter around his brother. Aubrey's medical degree had failed to shield him from the Depression; his ashen face, to Thurgood, resembled promise broken.

Neither years nor mutual success brought the brothers closer. After Thurgood was confirmed to the Supreme Court of the United States, Aubrey's wife would tell friends that she and her husband were spending the weekend with Thurgood and his wife, but they never did. Aubrey instructed his son "to stay away from" his uncle Thurgood.[4]

IN CONTRAST TO HIS HOME'S TUMULT, Thurgood savored the unrelenting order Dean Houston imposed at Howard. Fervent study became for him its own ambition. In the library and on the train, each turned page demanded the next's turn until he knew the case, the law, and the book could be put away. He studied feverishly. His mother's pawned rings and his wife's long hours at the clothing store inspired his murmuring, scribbling, memorizing vigil. "When I was in law school in my first year I lost thirty pounds solely from work. Intellectual work, studying," he recalled, "and that's how you get ahead of people."[5]

His book-laden trudge from the law school to Union Station each evening wound through a tableau of the Great Depression, sidewalks littered with men collapsed and broken like something had fallen on them. Businesses sat shuttered and sullen while their peeling painted signs advertised nothing anyone still wanted or could afford. Children scampered barefoot through alleys so fetid with human waste and refuse that a West Virginia congressman introduced legislation to close the District's countless alleys, shocked that "such conditions could exist in a civilized community."[6] Increasingly common suicides did not always happen indoors. A *Washington*

Post editorial called the police department "undermanned and underpaid"; officers' salaries were set by congressmen who lived in the city for just a few months each year.[7] The nation's capital was sinking into its own worst possibilities in 1930, and Baltimore, where one elderly couple was found lying in bed with their throats slashed next to two bloody razors and a suicide note describing their destitution, fared no better.

On each day's slog through this morass Thurgood peered into poverty's yawning pit. His working-class family had never been truly poor, but earning and saving enough money for tuition had troubled him since his senior year of high school. Moreover, in its first year as a full-time day school, Howard Law was no longer a "dummy's retreat." By May, half his classmates would be asked to leave; he could not be one of them. He could not be condemned forever to a job where the boss called him boy and patrons sometimes called him worse. After all her sacrifice, he could not tell Buster that they had to live with his parents indefinitely because Howard had turned out to be a real law school and it had conquered him. The twenty-two-year old had no alternative plan.

AT THE END OF THE SCHOOL YEAR, Marshall ranked first in his class. The accomplishment vindicated the grueling scholastic demands he had imposed on himself. As he returned to waiting tables at the Gibson Island Club for the summer, he felt relieved to know that if he worked hard enough, he could succeed in law, could move with Buster into a home of their own and start a family.

In September, Marshall's ranking at the top of his class garnered him a job as the law librarian's student assistant, welcome income to help pay tuition. More important, the job allowed him to work for the first time with a man he already had grown to idolize. Dean Charles Houston was all but building the law library from nothing and he welcomed Thurgood's help. Their most immediate goal was obtaining books. The American Bar Association's accreditation committee would condemn the law school based solely on its meager collection of volumes. Hunched over his typewriter and sporting an accountant's green visor, Houston feverishly typed letters imploring acquaintances and colleagues to donate law books to the library. By the time the accreditation committee inspected it, the library boasted over ten thousand volumes.

In Houston's presence, Marshall sparked like a match touched to flame. He admired the dean's singular devotion to excellence, his contempt for good enough, and this admiration kindled within him those same traits. Houston spent most of his waking hours in the law school and Thurgood now was right there with him. Most nights they worked until ten o'clock, sometimes together on library business, often on their own separate projects but comfortably within each other's company. "We've got to turn this whole thing around," Dean Houston would tell him. "And the black man has got to do it; nobody's going to do it for you. You've got to go out and compete with the other man, and you've got to be better than he is. You might never get what you deserve but you'll certainly *not* get what you *don't* deserve."[8]

The starched dean enjoyed working with his brash and gifted student; Houston began to spend less time in his third-floor office hunched over a desk mountained with paper, and more hours in the library mentoring a pupil whom classmates called Turkey on account of his gobbling strut. The two men had contrasting temperaments: Where Marshall celebrated ribaldry and revelry, Houston, according to Professor Nabrit, "did nothing with levity." Houston's work "was his only real interest in life," while Marshall was by nature an unapologetic bon vivant.[9] The two men were brought together by a fervent faith in the law—or, more accurately, in a shared belief that they could mold American law into what it purported to be.

Thurgood began to appropriate his mentor's sayings and was especially fond of Houston's only professional foray into loose grammar: Whenever a student questioned one of his school regulations, Houston snapped, "Rules is rules!" Five decades later, Associate Justice Thurgood Marshall sometimes encountered sympathetic appellants whose lawyers had submitted briefs that failed to conform to the Supreme Court's myriad procedural demands. His clerks' pleas for him to vote with Justice William Brennan to grant certiorari were met with Houston's echo. "Rules is rules!" Marshall thundered, and indeed the Court's liberal lion enjoyed a reputation for an intransigent adherence to the Court's rules.[10]

As a law student he had yet to represent a client, but Marshall also enjoyed repeating Houston's maxim "Lose your temper, lose your case." It was woefully necessary advice for African American lawyers in an era when white judges, witnesses and opposing counsel did not always treat them with professional respect. Thurgood would later caution NAACP lawyers with the same words, "Lose your temper, lose your case."

HOWARD LAW SCHOOL'S ENROLLMENT continued to decline. In 1931, Dean Houston released a "Student Information Bulletin" noting that "average law school attendance throughout the country has dropped about 19% since 1928." That Howard's enrollment had decreased by more than 50 percent during those years was "neither surprising nor alarming" and was attributable to three factors:

1. marked increase in standards of scholarship;
2. elimination of 50% of the colleges from which students may be accepted into the School;
3. the acute economic depression among Negroes.

Houston was sanguine about the coming years. "Unless a new economic crisis intervene[d]," he expected enrollment to rise.

The students who remained were receiving an education that was as philosophical as it was practical. By now they understood that their collective ambition was to become social engineers—to use the law to change the law. Edward P. Lovett, an unassuming but gifted student, recalled: "In all our classes, whether it was equity or contracts or pleadings, stress was placed on learning what our rights were under the Constitution and statutes—our rights as worded and regardless of how they had been interpreted to that time. Charlie's world view was that we had to get the courts to change—and that we could and should no longer depend upon high-powered white lawyers to represent us in that effort."[11]

Perhaps more than any other, Lovett's description asserts the radicalism of Houston's mission at Howard. To this day, American law schools teach the law; indeed the essence of attending law school is that one learns what the law is and studies how to apply it to a multitude of hypothetical fact patterns. By doing this, students learn what it means, as every first-year law student hears repeated ad nauseam, to "think like a lawyer."

Learning the law and learning to think like a lawyer were but the elementary steps in becoming a social engineer. The third step, described by

Lovett in his recollection, was the most critical: In order to give meaning to steps one and two—if they were to be anything but "parasites" on their society—African American lawyers were obligated to know what the law *should be.* They had to know the Constitution better than the Supreme Court had allowed it to be known and trust its precepts more than the framers had themselves. Despite what settled case law mandated, the Constitution did not allow for a nation divided separately but equally by race. As surely as it forbade slavery itself, the post–Civil War Constitution forbade the discrimination that inevitably dehumanized both races. For all his Ivy League education and conservative mien, Dean Houston's teaching law in this manner was as audacious as the arguments he and his former students would soon begin presenting to courts across the country.

So that they might understand the significance of their charge, Houston bustled his students all around Washington, D.C. He ushered them on field trips to the United States Attorney's office, the local jail, the FBI's headquarters, various courtrooms and even police precincts. The dean impressed upon the young men that behind the cases they read each night were lives lived by people who went on living after their cases were decided and justice done or undone. "Doctors can bury their mistakes," he quipped in his fedora and trenchcoat, hands pocketed against the wind. "Lawyers cannot."[12] Social engineers were obligated to improve their clients' lives by perfecting whatever little piece of the world those plaintiffs and defendants called their own.

THURGOOD MARSHALL was a second-year student when Howard Law School won accreditation from the American Bar Association. Like all students and faculty, he savored the victory. He and his classmates by now understood and believed in what Dean Houston was doing with them and their school. Oliver W. Hill stood a little taller than Thurgood and was ranked second in their class, one spot behind the friend and rival with whom he would work on landmark desegregation cases a few years hence. Before he died at the age of one hundred, Oliver Hill would receive the Presidential Medal of Freedom, greet the queen of England and watch as the Commonwealth of Virginia's Supreme Court of Appeals building was named after him. He remembered his law school days as rigorous years shaped by a rigorous dean. "Oh, he was a *tough* disciplinarian," Hill said of

Houston. "He kept hammering at us all those years that, as lawyers, we had to be social engineers or else we were parasites."[13]

By their third year, 1933, Houston's intensity would reduce Marshall and Hill's class from thirty-six to just six students who were as competitive with and endeared to each other as any could be. They had earned their dean's respect. When Houston agreed to defend the accused murderer George Crawford in Loudoun Country, Virginia, he asked Marshall to help him prepare the case. Lovett assisted in the courtroom. The case's remarkable conclusion thrust Houston into the national spotlight, and his students had never been more proud of their dean or grateful for the painful miracle he had worked at their school. That they would earn diplomas from an accredited and suddenly famous law school was celebrated news.

SOUTH JOURNEY CHILDREN

IN SPRING OF 1933, Thurgood Marshall graduated as valedictorian from Howard Law School. He and salutatorian Oliver Hill, as the latter remembered, "went to a nip joint and booted up a few."[1] For the first time in his life, Thurgood had attractive options to consider. Harvard Law School's dean Roscoe Pound offered Charles Houston's favored student a scholarship; at no financial cost he could earn a doctoral degree in the law just as his mentor had done ten years earlier. Thurgood relished the invitation for reasons beyond its obvious benefit. The University of Maryland would not have considered admitting him to its state-run law school, but here was the nation's oldest university offering to pay his way into its classrooms. Harvard Law had graduated Professor Hastie and Dean Houston, men he admired not just for their towering intellects but also for their lives of financial comfort. Neither was wealthy, but neither did they labor under the economic angst he had known for so long. Accepting the scholarship offered by Dean Pound would admit him to their coterie.

Working on the George Crawford murder trial, however, had awakened Marshall to the thrill of real case work. Spending late library nights proposing and challenging theories, researching case law's diamonded facets, straining his eyes and mind to save a man's life—it was too exciting and meaningful to be disregarded easily. He had just spent three arduous years being trained to affect society. Enrolling in another school to devote more years to study struck him as something of a retreat. Instead he could open his own law office in Baltimore, begin representing clients and, finally, be-gin earning some real money.

Deciding between Harvard and a legal practice was more pleasant than it was difficult. He wanted to practice law and decided to open his own office in Baltimore. Before then he would have to study, apply for and take the Maryland bar examination. This required money, and summer was the busy season, so back to the Gibson Island Club he went. The white jacket did not bother him at all now and he kept his schedule flexible. When Houston invited his protégé to join him on an NAACP-sponsored fact-finding mission into the Deep South, Marshall happily accepted, convinced that the post-graduate study he needed lay in Alabama, not Massachusetts.

CHARLES HAMILTON HOUSTON and Thurgood Marshall took to the open road of the American South. The NAACP was considering a legal challenge to segregation in public schools and Houston and Marshall were tasked with documenting the gross inequalities between schools for black children and schools for white children. Their later correspondence does not make reference to this first trip, but the venture surely was a turning point in their relationship. No longer were they dean and student; they were lawyers and mutual protectors in hostile hinterlands, still mentor and pro-tégé, but abruptly, happily, colleagues. And now that Thurgood had gradu-ated, the two fraternity brothers could become friends. In each other's company, Ironshoes softened his kick and Turkey swallowed his strut. But their contrasting personalities remained a constant, opposite sides of a coin more valuable than either man then knew.

Twenty years before construction of the Eisenhower interstate system, Charlie and Thurgood sped down rural roads in Houston's trusty Graham-Paige, its six-cylinder engine rumbling behind bug-eyed headlights. From Washington they rode all the way down to New Orleans, through South Carolina, Georgia, Alabama and Mississippi, lodging with families and eating whatever food they could pack with them from their hosts' kitchen. Barred from the South's restaurants, they loaded the car with bags of fruit, and, as Marshall remembered, "most of the time, we'd just eat the fruit."[2]

IT WAS NO SMALL ACT of courage for them to venture down into the Deep South. In 1933, southern trees witnessed many a black man's moonlit torture. Perhaps the man fell victim for nothing more than accusing his white landlord of theft, asking why rows of his crops had gone missing from behind the fence; or maybe he had conspired with a fellow share-cropper too obsequious to keep to himself a proposal that they sell their harvests together at an agreed-upon price so that both their families might end the winter with teeth and food in their mouths. However he had drawn the mob's ire from its brimming well, it was unlikely that his of-tense involved a white woman. Contrary to popular belief, most lynchings did not result from allegations of black men assaulting or even flirting with white women. Only 16 percent of lynching victims were accused of sex crimes; the remaining thousands were accused of "crimes" varying in seriousness from murder to breaching one of the South's countless rules of racial etiquette.[3] Proof positive of this fact were the black women mas-sacred at the rope, women like Mary Turner, who was seized in the Geor-gian night, strung up a tree by her ankles, sliced open with a buck-knife and forced to watch upside down as the men pulled her unborn baby from her screaming insides and killed it first.[4]

Houston testified to this very point before the U.S. Senate's Judiciary Committee a few months after returning safely from his and Marshall's journey: "The truth of the matter is that lynching is not to protect Southern women but Southern profits," he told the senators, "to continue the ex-ploitation of the Negro and to terrorize him to the point that he dare not make any resistance or protest."[5] The mobs' behavior comprised a calcu-lated rage, rational savagery. Oppression fed on order, and order would be maintained. "In 1933['s] lynchings the most striking feature of nearly every press photograph is the number of women and little children present at the festivities." Houston told the assembled senators that lynching unavoidably "brutaliz[ed] the white population" as well as the black.[6]

The danger of Houston's and Marshall's falling victim to a white mob was real. They were traveling with typewriters and cameras and inter-viewing African American students and parents to document the awful state of the South's segregated schools. Black men had been slaughtered for far less.

THE CONDITION OF THE SCHOOLS they visited was even worse than they expected. They photographed the school buses and one-room schoolhouses and recorded their findings in staccato notes they typed in the car. "The student body. 68 pupils packed into one room, 20×16 feet, on seven benches. No tables, no desks, no stove. One chair, one open fireplace." Meanwhile, the same county's white children learned in a school with "six rooms, six teachers. Assembly hall, piano, individual desks. Three buses to transport children. Two Negro women janitresses clean entire building and make 6 fires daily for wages of $4.00 per month each."

When they needed to relieve themselves, the black children had "to cross railroad and highway to get to the woods."[7] Compulsory attendance laws were not enforced in schools for black children, resulting in collapsed enrollments until "after the crops were in." In one rural county, an abandoned school for white students sat shuttered about one mile from a school for black children that had "no desks, no chairs, one old piece of blackboard" while the students sat "crowded together on benches." In the derelict school for whites, there were "curtains still at the windows" and the building was "full of desks and other school equipment not in use." Houston verified that the local authorities would "not permit the Negroes to use either the abandoned building or the abandoned equipment."[8]

Upon returning North, Houston and Marshall reported to the NAACP, which had funded the trip, that the segregated schools in the Deep South were separate and manifestly unequal. White southern politicians condemned black children to classrooms so wretched they mocked purpose. The poverty was leagues deep. Decades later Marshall remained struck by a little boy he met in the dirt lot outside a Mississippi school. The boy kept staring at the fruit in Marshall's hand until he offered it to him. The boy "had never seen an orange before. He just bit right through [the skin] and enjoyed it."[9] Sons of the borderlands, Houston and Marshall were strangers to their people in this valley of despair. Dew-dropped blades of grass bent each morning beneath the bare feet of black children who were either scampering to bookless schools or trudging into the fields, for the school year ended when the strawberries grew fat.

THE LAW OFFICES
OF THURGOOD MARSHALL, ESQ.

S TUDENTS AT HOWARD LAW SCHOOL began to take umbrage at the
amount of time their dean was spending away from the school. Dean
Houston had tried the Crawford case while on an official leave of absence,
but after he returned to Howard, the extracurricular demands on his time,
particularly with the NAACP, only seemed to multiply. In addition to his
trip through the Deep South with Marshall, Houston wrote articles for
the NAACP's widely read magazine, the *Crisis*, defended the radical International Labor Defense's white lawyer against charges warranting disbar-
ment, testified before Congress on behalf of federal antilynching legislation
and traveled the country speaking to groups like the Young Women's Christian Association and the Commission on Interracial Cooperation. It appeared
that the man who had demanded so much of his students' time, who had
forbidden them from holding jobs, had become a part-time dean.

He was corresponding several times a week with NAACP secretary
Walter White, who sought his advice on everything from legal matters to
scheduling meetings. White was the savviest of social and political operators,
almost certainly the first black person to become a regular White House
visitor, and by 1933 he valued Houston's opinion perhaps more than anyone else's. On whether he should take a trip that autumn, White wrote, "I
wish you would wire me your opinion . . . If I go to Alabama I will go on
there from Washington. I should like to have your opinion so I can make

my plans accordingly."[1] Houston was intimately involved in setting the itinerary and priorities of the NAACP's senior officer and, accordingly, of the
nation's premier civil rights organization itself.

As secretary of the NAACP, White received scores of letters every day
from citizens across the country seeking help in fighting myriad injustices. White forwarded many of these entreaties to Houston's office at the
law school, asking: "Have you any suggestions or comments to make? If
so, let me have them by return mail."[2] Houston's files soon burst with papers because White "wanted [him] to have the enclosed copy" of a letter
from this or that activist or victim.[3] In a typical instance, a man named
Louis Campbell wrote to White from Bondtown, Virginia, where Campbell had read in the *Chicago Defender* that the NAACP was working "to
defeat the Poll Tax Amendment to the Constitution of West Virginia. Let
it be hoped that they succeed. 'Subterfuge' is a more befitting name for
such an amendment." Campbell then informed White that "they have a
Poll Tax voting law in Virginia. Believe me, it make[s] a complete job of
disfranchising the voters." Campbell paid his poll tax but still had great
difficulty in securing his right to vote. It was only with determination and
the help of "a professional man" that he succeeded. He was convinced
that "poll tax (or subterfuge tax) laws ought to be fought down in all
states."[4]

White forwarded the letter to Houston, asking in a rapid succession of
dictated thoughts: "Has the legality of the poll tax ever been attacked in the
courts? Is not that class legislation which penalizes a man who does not
have the price of the poll tax? This is at least an interesting slant, don't you
think so?"[5] It was no wonder that Houston, when he was "swamped with
school work," replied, "Have not had chance to go through N.A.A.C.P.
correspondence this week but will get on it tomorrow and Sat."[6]

Rare was the occasion when Houston begged off White's request for
advice or assistance, however, and soon Howard's law students objected to
their dean's "absenteeism."[7] Many of them had enrolled because they were
excited about Howard's new accreditation and rigorous curriculum. Now,
while they were studying, the dean about whom they had heard so much
was busy with activities like planning a silent street protest against a Justice
Department conference whose agenda excluded a discussion of lynching.

The protests, consisting of suited, stoic men and women standing with nooses around their necks, successfully drew attention to the issue. The conference addressed lynchings and the federal government's role in ending them. Howard Law students participated in the dramatic antilynching demonstration before turning their outrage inward: To protest their "absent" dean, they commenced organizing a strike.

FORTY MILES NORTH IN BALTIMORE, Thurgood Marshall learned of the law students' planned strike and knew the embarrassment it would cause his mentor. From his Baltimore office, he coordinated with fellow alumnus Edward Lovett, who was practicing law in Washington, and together they persuaded the students to call off the strike. Marshall promised Houston in a letter that he would "give anybody *hell*" if Houston sent the word.[8]

By now Marshall had been in private practice for about a year, the sole practioner in a tiny office on the sixth floor of Baltimore's Phoenix Building. THURGOOD MARSHALL, ATTORNEY & COUNSELLOR AT LAW read his letterhead. He would later recall that his one-man shop "was a complete general practice, ranging from representing business corporations, building associations, negligence cases, criminal cases, probate cases and so forth, the general practice of law in the State and Federal Courts in Maryland."[9] But with the Great Depression that had so haunted his law school years still raging in the streets below, he spent a great deal of time working for free or not working at all. Paying clients were scarce and his practice was losing money. He supplemented his meager lawyer's income by working as a clerk in Maryland's Bureau of Communicable Diseases.

He and his secretary held the faith. "One day, I'd bring two lunches and the next day my secretary would bring two lunches and sometimes we'd be the only two people in that office for weeks at a time."[10] The islands of paying work were occasions for celebration. "Once in a while, I got a good fee. Then my secretary would immediately take the check to the bank. She'd call her husband and I'd call Buster and we'd get the biggest steak in town to celebrate."[11]

He and Buster were still living with his parents, his brother, his sister-in-law and their son Aubrey, Jr., in the house on Druid Hill Avenue. The sound of his new nephew's crying was a wailing reminder of his and Buster's inability to conceive. Like his mentor and friend in the dean's office at Howard Law School, Marshall had a stressful life at home and at work.

So when Houston invited him to hit the southern road again on more fact-finding missions for the NAACP, Marshall leaped at the chance. Through the states, days and nights they sped and talked, laughed and argued. Along thicket-lined roads in Virginia, Missouri, Tennessee, Kentucky and back down through lowlands of the Carolinas and Mississippi, the two lawyers exchanged the trials of home and family for the dangers of the road. When they reached Mississippi, the NAACP's state president assigned two riflemen to protect them as they investigated the shoddy shape of the segregated schools.[12] Through the open window Thurgood smoked one cigarette after another.

Ever the educator, Charlie employed the god-awful conditions of the schools they visited as instructional exhibits in explaining to Thurgood that integration was the only means by which to guarantee that black children would receive educations equal to white schoolchildren. In fact, integrating the nation's public elementary schools was a necessary step in ending American racism; as children interacted in schools, they would be inoculated against racist stereotyping. If allowed, the children would lead. Houston's was a revolutionary prospect whose truth would be affirmed three and four decades later in the wide-eyed rants of white parents yelling that integrated public elementary schools would end their segregated way of life. They were correct and that was the point.

Marshall returned safely to Baltimore more convinced than ever that the laws segregating American citizens by race were unconstitutional. Embracing his responsibility to act as a social engineer, he began to provide free legal assistance to the NAACP's venerated Baltimore branch. Although his firm still struggled financially, he was earning a reputation among Maryland's bar and judges as a conscientious and able advocate. Uncle Fee helped him buy a car so he could travel around Maryland more easily. On behalf of African Americans prominent and meek, Marshall argued motions, observed criminal trials, organized black workers and reported back to Houston.

THE OPENING OF THE SCHOOL YEAR 1934–35 found Dean Houston absorbed with his most ambitious mission yet. One evening in his office above the library, he clacked furiously as ever at his typewriter, but he was drafting neither an examination nor a letter to his professors. Rather, he was composing a proposal solicited by the NAACP, a memorandum setting forth a legal plan to attack racial segregation nationwide, in schools, buses and trains. It was a plan both audacious and prayerful. It was firmly rooted in a belief that the Constitution did not allow America to remain as it was.

The NAACP enthusiastically received Houston's report and soon thereafter asked him to become their special counsel, to enact the battle plan he had designed. He accepted the position but, because the school year was in progress, agreed to serve only on a part-time basis until he could procure a leave of absence from Howard at the school year's end. That he was working for the NAACP only part-time might have surprised many of Howard Law School's students, who began to see even less of their overextended dean.

One student, who was otherwise "friendly to the administration, in general," excoriated Dean Houston in a column published in a weekly Washington newspaper.[13] Frederick S. Weaver blasted Houston for " 'utter neglect' of his duties at the school by taking time out to argue cases like the George Crawford case and for carrying on other investigations for the N.A.A.C.P." Weaver's criticism earned the attention of the national black press.

"In one charge," the *New York Amsterdam News* reported, "the young columnist compared Dean Houston to Huey P. Long as a publicity seeker."[14] University president Mordecai Johnson's administration responded by putting the student "on trial," with law school faculty members sitting in judgment of whether the student should be disciplined. Weaver secured counsel, one of Houston's fellow members of the D.C. School Board, but by the time the hearing was held in the late autumn of 1935, Houston had already left Howard on a one-year leave of absence.[15]

Up in Baltimore, Marshall was growing weary of working for free. "You don't pay me a goddamn nickel," he reminded the Baltimore NAACP's branch president when she chastised him for his nightclub drinking, "then you want to run my life."[16] As much as he enjoyed working for the NAACP, none of the association's cases sought integration as legal relief. If integration was their goal, integration they should seek. Just as frustration was taking root in the young lawyer's ambition, he received an early gift during the Christmas season of 1934; Marshall bypassed the intrusive Baltimore NAACP branch president and approached Houston directly with the name that would become the case that would become the first battle in a legal campaign that would continue for decades to come: *Donald Gaines Murray.*

MURRAY V. MARYLAND

TO LITIGATION THERE IS A RHYTHM, a lolling swell and collapse. Research, planning, drafting, questioning and answering—good lawyers learn the cadence; they intuit the best arguments against their own. Great lawyers master the rhythmic triumphs and travails of each case like captains at sea holding the wind at bay by employing it for propulsion.

A lawyer's case is his ship; his wind is the law that he must put to his command. Gifted attorneys sometimes persuade courts to extend existing law but rarely to reverse it. While often heralded as a reversal of long-standing jurisprudence, the Supreme Court's decision in the cases gathered as *Brown v. Board of Education* was in fact an extension of the Court's earlier decisions. *Brown* expanded existing law and the ship launched by Charles Houston twenty years earlier at last reached uncharted shores.

In 1935, however, the wind blew steadily in the opposite direction. Separate but equal schools and buildings were constitutionally permissible under the Supreme Court's *Plessy v. Ferguson* decision. To challenge *Plessy*—to set sail into the wind—would be the mission of a doomed fool.

So when Walter White asked Houston to present a plan by which the NAACP could launch a sustained legal campaign to end segregation, Houston charted a novel course: To defeat the law of separate but equal, he would argue for enforcement of separate but equal. In southern states he would argue that segregation's mandates needed to be met. He would seek to end segregation's scourge by arguing for fulfillment of its promise.

HOUSTON NOTED IN HIS REPORT that his scope was limited by the funds available: "On a budget of $10,000.00 it is exceedingly difficult to execute an effective program on a national scale on two issues as large as discrimination in education and discrimination in transportation. Isolated suits mean little unless the communities and persons affected believe there is an unexpended reserve available to sustain a persistent struggle. This calls for concentration of effort."[1]

He favored concentrating the fight against discrimination in education on two fronts: against the race-based unequal allocation of public school funds and against differentials in teacher salaries in the schools for white and black students. Houston aimed "(1) to arouse and strengthen the will of the local communities to demand and fight for their rights; (2) to work out model procedures through actual tests in court which can be used by local communities in similar cases brought by them on their own initiative and resources."[2] That is, the lawyers would ask the courts to enforce the law of the land—to make "separate but equal" truly equal. As he and Marshall documented on their travels through the South, schools for black students were horribly inferior to those attended by white students. Houston was convinced that seeking to enforce segregation was the most viable path to integration: Because the segregated cities, counties and states could not afford to equalize their facilities, they were unable to fulfill the mandate set forth by the Supreme Court in *Plessy v. Ferguson*. The states would be ordered to integrate because it was the only way to provide equal schools and facilities to black and white Americans.

MEANWHILE, up in Baltimore, Thurgood Marshall had grown anxious at wind of a rumor. For about a year now, his and Houston's fraternity had been working on plans to file a lawsuit to integrate the University of Maryland. Led by its assistant general counsel, Belford V. Lawson, Jr., Alpha Phi Alpha had asked for and received help from the NAACP's Washington chapter in conducting research and searching for a suitable plaintiff.[3] Although Lawson was a prominent and respected lawyer, Marshall believed his dean would better handle the case.

Neither Maryland nor the university had laws or rules mandating that the college be segregated. The university's racist administration excluded African Americans as a matter of policy.[4] That the case was winnable accentuated the imperative that it be won. Between 1933 and 1934, nine black applicants had been rejected—nine potential plaintiffs from whom Lawson soon would have his client. Swarmed with work at the law school and for the NAACP, however, Houston had not responded to Marshall's entreaties about filing a case against the university.

By the opening months of 1934, Thurgood's tone had become stressed: "Dear Charlie, Trust you had a good Christmas, etc. I hate to worry you so much about this University of Maryland case. When are we to get together on it? Things are very slow just now and I would like very much to get started as soon as possible."[5] A few months later Alpha Phi Alpha allocated sufficient money to try the case. As Lawson began to conclude his preparations, Marshall implored Houston: "What about the University of Maryland case? B.V. Lawson has been writing me and seems to think that the fraternity is going to try the case along with the local branches of the NAACP. I am up a tree as to just what is going to be done."[6]

As if sensing his fraternity brother's anxiety, Lawson invited Marshall to a strategy planning session in Washington. Houston was in Augusta, Georgia, on an NAACP mission. Marshall reached him by telegram. ATTEND LAWSON'S MEETING, Houston replied by wire. GET FACTS BUT BE CAREFUL ABOUT COMMITMENTS.[7] Marshall would be more than careful; he refused to commit himself or the NAACP's Baltimore chapter to Lawson's case because he did not want to be a sailor on Lawson's ship and his Baltimore branch was irked that the Washington branch would file suit in Maryland. Intra-organizational politics it was, but Marshall's primary concern was that the case be won. Belford Lawson was a formidable attorney but he was no Dean Houston. Truth be told, as far as the younger attorney was concerned, Lawson was no Thurgood Marshall either. Marshall disregarded Houston's advice and respectfully declined to attend the meeting.

A week after his Washington strategy meeting, Lawson identified his plaintiff. Donald Gaines Murray was an eminently qualified recent graduate of Amherst College and the scion of a widely respected Baltimore family. He wanted to attend the University of Maryland School of Law. Lawson agreed to represent him and would proceed without the NAACP.

Or so he thought. With an impeccable plaintiff now identified, Houston gave Marshall the word; the NAACP would try the case. Lawson's in-
tentions and efforts were laudable but, even supported by the nation's
oldest black fraternity, he was outmatched in resources and experience.
Houston and Marshall took over the case, Murray signed on to be their
client, and Lawson angrily became one of the first activists to learn of
Houston's and Marshall's resolute belief in both the cause and their superior ability to effect its victory.

NEARLY EVERY BIOGRAPHICAL ACCOUNT of Thurgood Marshall's life de-
scribes him as lead counsel for the plaintiff in *Murray v. Maryland*. This
nearly unanimous misrepresentation ignores Marshall's own account. "I
worked the case out on the ground and I drew the pleadings since there
was some intricate old Maryland common law involved, but outside the
legwork I did very little. The court presentation was [Houston's] doing.
The fact is, I never was chief counsel in a case that Charlie took part in."[8]
The *Chicago Defender* concluded its trial report with this note: "Assisting
Attorney Houston in the Maryland University case was Attorney Thurgood Marshall of Baltimore."[9] These accounts buttress the recollections of
others who practiced with Houston; Old Ironshoes was not a lawyer given
to second chair. When the time came for an appeal, Houston instructed
Marshall to "be sure to look up biographical data on all the judges of the
Court of Appeals with special reference to the places and schools where
they took their education. I am anxious to know how many attended
unsegregated schools."[10] Such was the sort of detailed preparation that
would see Marshall to and through where Houston by now believed he
could go.

Armed with counsel, Murray applied to law school at the University of
Maryland in 1935; the registrar promptly returned his application and ac-
companying fee. "President Pearson instructed me today to return to you
the application form and the money order, as the University does not accept Negro students, except at the Princess Anne Academy."[11] Princess
Anne Academy, on Maryland's rural Eastern Shore, was more high school
than university, and it had no law school. The state of Maryland, therefore,
offered no legal education to its black citizens. There were no separate law
schools by which even to reach the question of equality.

On April 20, the *Washington Post* reported, "Donald G. Murray, Negro graduate of Amherst college, filed mandamus proceedings [in Baltimore] today in an effort to compel the University of Maryland Law School to admit him as a student." The complaint filed by Murray's "Negro attorneys" asserted that "alleged refusal of the institution to accept Murray as a student was not supported by the law or the constitution of Maryland and it violated the fourteenth amendment to the United States Constitution."[12] The lawyers filed suit against university president Raymond A. Pearson, but the case would become famous as *Murray v. Maryland.*

It was Judge Eugene O'Dunne's turn to be incredulous. In all his years on the bench the colorful jurist had seen many a law school professor move to have one of his students admitted to the bar of the state of Maryland for the purpose of trying a case; *pro hac vice* was the term, meaning "for this particular occasion," and a member of the D.C. bar, like Houston, could be admitted to practice in Maryland for the purpose of litigating a specific case.[13] This June morning in Baltimore City Court was the first time, however, that Judge O'Dunne had ever seen a newly minted lawyer move to admit his former law school dean *pro hac vice.* The meager courtroom crowd enjoyed a laugh at the judge's observation, with the heartiest coming from veteran trial observer Willie Marshall, who arrived proud and early with Norma to watch their son's first civil rights trial. The courtroom was nearly empty, however, because, as Marshall described it, "Negroes did not take more interest in the case because they felt it was hopeless."[14]

Houston rose to deliver the plaintiff's opening statement. His deep voice resounded against the wooden chamber's walls. Plaintiff Donald Murray had applied to the University of Maryland School of Law with an academic record far exceeding the school's admission requirements. And the school had rejected him for the sole reason that it did not accept Negro applicants. The University of Maryland thereby violated the rights guaranteed to Murray by the Fourteenth Amendment to the U.S. Constitution. Neither state law nor the university's charter enjoined Murray's enrollment. Only the "race prejudice" of the school's administration stood between Donald Murray and a legal education.[15]

Maryland assistant attorney general Charles T. LeViness III rose to offer the defense's opening statement. Before he uttered his first word, however, Judge O'Dunne had a question.

Was the plaintiff's race the university's acknowledged reason for rejecting his application?

Yes, Your Honor; it was a matter of public policy.

What did this public policy have to do with the state of the law?

Well, the state of Maryland presented its colored citizens with a sophisticated array of educational options, including a junior college and over two dozen two-hundred-dollar scholarships for colored students to attend colleges outside the state.

Suppose, the judge wondered, a Negro student didn't want to leave the state to pursue his studies?

LeViness bristled. Your Honor, one must be practical about these sorts of things. The state could not be expected to build a new separate graduate school every time a young Negro got the notion to become a professional.

Was the state willing to stipulate for the record that, but for his race, the plaintiff was qualified to be admitted to the law school?

Yes, Your Honor.

Houston and Marshall managed to mask their elation. Although his academic record should have placed it beyond dispute that Murray was qualified for admission to the law school, they had been prepared to spend hours litigating that very point. Murray's qualifying for admission was a question of fact, and if the court found that he was not qualified, his case would be moot. That the state's counsel conceded the point in the trial's opening minutes was a welcome surprise.

Judge O'Dunne allowed the state to present its opening argument before instructing the plaintiff to call his first witness. Houston called his client, Donald Gaines Murray. The plaintiff stood about average height, shorter than both Houston and Marshall, and wore a tapered mustache similar to Thurgood's. That he leaned back so comfortably on the witness stand was as much a testament to his self-assuredness as it was to his having been well prepared by his attorneys.

How long had Mr. Murray lived in the state of Maryland?

All his life. Murray answered his lawyer's questions to describe his desire to become a lawyer, his academic record, and his attempts to gain admission to the University of Maryland's law school. The testimony was purposely dry; with Murray's testimony Houston was entering facts into the record that he deemed critical for the appeal already anticipated by everyone in the courtroom. His witnesses were mouthpieces for facts he wanted on the record, and any witness reluctant to accept such a role was likely to express his truculence by being evasive or argumentative.

And so Houston called university president Raymond A. Pearson as a hostile witness, which in practical terms meant that Houston could "lead the witness"—ask him yes or no questions. Watching a masterful trial attorney like Charles Houston question a hostile witness was like seeing a tomcat paw a cornered mouse.

The plaintiff, Mr. Murray, had applied through the proper channels and submitted all necessary paperwork for admission to the law school, hadn't he?

Yes, he had.

And, just to confirm, had he been a white applicant, Mr. Murray would have been admitted?

In all likelihood, yes, but because Negroes were not eligible for admission to the University of Maryland, the state provided them with scholarships to out-of-state institutions.

These scholarships were not available when Mr. Murray applied to the law school, were they?

No.

In fact, the state created them only after Murray's application was rejected, correct?

Yes.

And in fact the funds allocated for the scholarships had already proven insufficient to meet the demands of Maryland's colored citizens?

Yes, but this was why the state offered higher education to Negroes at the Princess Anne Academy.

Did the two-year course at Princess Anne Academy for Negroes offer the same caliber of education as, say, just the first two years at the University of Maryland?

Yes, of course, and even the faculty members were comparable "in some instances."[16]

But wasn't it true that the faculty at Princess Anne had only one instructor with a master's degree and did not have even one professor with a doctorate degree?

Well, yes.

Was Dr. Pearson aware that the biology and chemistry lab at Princess Anne consisted entirely of one table, a few test tubes and a glass butterfly case?

Yes, he was.

Were these facilities adequate?

Of course they were.

They were?

Yes.

Then why did the University of Maryland's science labs offer so much more sophisticated equipment to its students?

Because the university offered more advanced classes than did Princess Anne.

With that admitted, Houston switched tacks and asked if Mexicans, Japanese, Filipinos and Indians were eligible for admission to the university's law school.

Yes, they were.

Then why were members of the plaintiff's race not admitted to the university?

President Pearson glared at his questioner. Negroes were not admitted because—he personally had no objection to their attending the university. It was not a matter of his imposing any sort of race prejudice on the school. It was a matter of state policy, you understand, beyond his control.

It was beyond his control even though he was president of the university and there was not a single law, rule or regulation requiring the exclusion of Negro applicants?

Yes. But this is why the state created the scholarships for them to attend out-of-state institutions.

The scholarships that were not created until after Mr. Murray's application had been rejected?

Yes, those scholarships.

Houston dismissed the witness after a withering hour-and-a-half examination.

Next he called to the stand Pearson's colleague Roger Howell, dean of the University of Maryland's law school.[17] Houston squeezed from Howell a series of valuable concessions. Yes, the University of Maryland's curriculum focused on Maryland state law, which made it unique among the nation's law schools. Of the school's eighteen faculty members, twelve were judges or otherwise prominent Maryland attorneys. The school's preeminence among members of the Maryland bar could scarcely be challenged.

Satisfied that his testimony elucidated the inequality between receiving a paltry scholarship to an out-of-state institution and studying law at the University of Maryland, Houston dismissed Dean Howell.

He called several more witnesses, all state officials, who described in detail the inequalities in the education Maryland provided to its black and white citizens. With the latitude granted by Judge O'Dunne, Houston elicited testimony regarding race-based differences in teachers' salaries, gross inequalities in the size and condition of the actual school buildings and the fact that the school year for Maryland's black students was one month shorter than that for white students, a fact that Houston's young cocounsel knew firsthand.

WITH NO SMALL AMOUNT of satisfaction did Thurgood Marshall work at the counsel's table in *Murray*. He had attended Maryland's abysmal schools for black children and for years was dismissed from the classroom a month earlier than his white friends. After college, his family had dissuaded him from applying to the University of Maryland's law school because it did not consider black applicants. Marshall watched the state's highest-ranking education officials answer Houston's questions under oath, answer for their having sent him to a high school that had no cafeteria, no library and no gymnasium, answer for sending him on a train ride to Washington for law school.

Charles Houston gave the closing statement to Marshall, the Maryland native who had known twenty-seven years of discrimination. In his hometown Baltimore accent that wasn't quite southern and wasn't quite not, Marshall declared that the Supreme Court of the United States had never ruled on a case such as this, where no separate school for blacks existed. He assured Judge O'Dunne that the latter would not contravene any existing precedent by ruling that the University of Maryland had to admit Murray to its law school, because it provided no other law school for him to attend. Instead, Judge O'Dunne should rule for Murray's admission, Marshall argued, because *Plessy v. Ferguson* demanded it. When it established a law school for its white residents, Maryland incurred a constitutional responsibility to provide a separate and equal legal education for its black citizens. By refusing to admit black applicants to its law school in the absence of a separate and equal state law school for them to attend, Maryland violated *Plessy's* well-settled constitutional demands. Marhsall returned to his seat filled with the fight of a man who had finally hit back.

Shortly after Maryland's assistant attorney general argued a closing that was by all accounts uninspired, Judge Eugene O'Dunne took the rare step of issuing his ruling from the bench. To the nearly empty courtroom he announced his decision to issue a writ of mandamus compelling the University of Maryland School of Law to admit Murray to its incoming class.

NAACP EXECUTIVE SECRETARY Walter White encouraged the newly enrolled student to "work hard; make the most brilliant record of which you are capable; conduct yourself with dignity and naturalness. By your very manner you will create, if you wish to do so, a new concept of the Negro in the minds of your fellow students and professors."[18]

The University of Maryland promptly appealed Judge O'Dunne's ruling. The *Washington Post* accurately summarized the state's points of appeal as follows:

> That Murray has no right to sue in mandamus to compel the university to admit him, but his remedy, if any, is by appropriate action to require the proper State officials to supply a law school for Negroes.

> That since education is exclusively a State matter, Murray has no right to admission merely because he is a citizen of the United States.

> [And t]hat private institutions may select their students arbitrarily without regard to the fourteenth amendment to the federal Constitution.[19]

As Murray prepared for classes, Marshall toiled on the appeal through the stifling summer. Sequestered with law books and treatises, he drafted, redrafted and drafted again a brief in response to Maryland's brief. Then he mailed it to Houston's office at NAACP headquarters in New York City.

Houston was unimpressed with Marshall's draft. The brief was burdened with case law quotations, and Marshall's response to the state's appellate contentions lay buried beneath them; research's purpose was to support an argument, not smother it. Houston wrote back that the brief "need[ed] to be thoroughly re-worked."[20] Marshall sieved the brief, sifted conclusion from quotes and the hours and nights revealed a brief polished by a burgeoning lawyer's scrutiny.

Houston instructed Marshall to address the unspoken issue at hand: "There are white women students in all the northern state universities and they go to school with Negroes without any difficulty."[21] While he did "not think it worth a great deal of bother to get the actual figures on the white women enrolled in the northern state universities," he did deem it worth Marshall's while to learn more about schools whose student bodies included both white women and black men.[22]

IN THEIR BRIEF and at oral argument before Maryland's highest court, Houston and Marshall explained why each of the state's arguments failed as a matter of law. The mentor naturally presented the more mature advocacy, but it was Marshall's passion that illuminated both the courtroom and the fundamental issue: "What's at stake here," he declared, "is more than the rights of my clients. It's the moral commitment stated in our country's creed."[23]

The court of appeals was persuaded that Maryland's appeal was without merit: By refusing to admit Murray to the law school on account of his race while failing to provide him with a separate but equal alternative institution, the state had violated his constitutional rights. Because "the erection of a separate but equal school [was] not an available alternative remedy," the court ordered the state to allow Donald Murray to remain a student at the University of Maryland School of Law.[24]

IN THE WAKE OF Houston and Marshall's appellate victory, their fraternity asked Houston to address its annual convention. Houston wrote to Alpha Phi Alpha's General President Charles Wesley and asked, "Would it not be possible for Thurgood Marshall to appear [instead]? There are many reasons why this may be more desirable than my own appearance . . . Thurgood is the real counsel behind the Murray case and I am simply associate counsel, giving it, perhaps, the weight of greater experience." Houston thought Marshall's appearing might inspire some of the fraternity's younger brothers: "The recognition to Thurgood would be an acknowledgment and recognition to a young man and would probably be an encouragement to other young men that if they go out and achieve, they will receive recognition and acclaim."[25]

Wesley agreed that Marshall could speak in Houston's stead, and the former dean immediately charged Thurgood, who was "very active in the Baltimore alumni chapter," with work to be done at the convention.[26] At the threshold, Marshall's chapter should seat him as a delegate, which would grant him the power to vote "at no expense to the chapter."[27] Houston then instructed Marshall on what he should tell Baltimore delegates about the *Murray* case and how to handle the fraternity's power brokers, including one of the organization's founding "Jewels," who remained irked at what they perceived as Houston and Marshall's usurping their case and client. Both men recognized that this was no simple squabble among fraternity brothers; Alpha Phi Alpha's membership bore might in the civil rights struggle and would for decades to come, drawing another Alpha brother, Reverend Dr. Martin Luther King, Jr., to address future conventions.

And so in a closed meeting at the convention, Marshall met with his fraternity's delegates and board members. He reported to Houston that many of them were "of the opinion that the Association, through you and me, had taken the thunder from them in initiating this fight, and that it was their original idea."[28] General President Charles Wesley scheduled Marshall's speech for the convention's first day but scheduled an official hearing on the *Murray* matter for "a little later date, because of the possible heated argument which might arise."[29]

Houston instructed Marshall to "handle the matter with tact and firmness . . . So far as you are concerned, you simply stand on the record and defend your position."[30]

Marshall performed as charged and, with Houston's permission, took the offensive. Now that Donald Murray was enrolled in the University of Maryland School of Law, the fraternity had yet to contribute a dime to keeping him there. The young man had tuition to pay and books to buy and scarcely the means to do either. Regardless of their understandable ire over the NAACP's handling the case, couldn't the brotherhood agree that everyone's best interests were served by keeping Mr. Murray enrolled? Marshall lobbied fraternity delegates for the scholarship just as he had congressmen and senators for antilynching legislation.

Less than two weeks later he and Houston received a letter from the Alpha Phi Alpha's Office of the Director of Education, greeting "Dear Brothers Marshall and Houston" with the news that, if they would "be good enough to have Mr. Murray fill out the enclosed application blank," the fraternity would send to him the first installment of his scholarship.[31]

Houston told Marshall, "good work at the convention," but certainly was more pleased than he let on.[32] He had sent Thurgood to the convention to brief the fraternity on the *Murray* case and to defend the association against brewing resentment; the young lawyer had returned not only having diffused the tension between the fraternity and the association, but having secured a scholarship for the association's client.

As DONALD MURRAY's first-semester exams grew near, Houston emphatically demanded that his client–law student be properly prepared. He implored Marshall: "For heaven's sake get hold of [Murray], check up on his notebooks and ship him over to Andy [Ransom] for review. If he is absolutely broke and without money," Houston would pay for him to travel to D.C. to be tutored by Ransom "in order to have him properly coached." Houston's near-frantic tone reflected the imperative of Murray's succeeding in law school. "Start working on this at once," he continued, "because whatever happens, we must not have this boy fail his examinations. We have got to teach him how to answer questions, too." Lastly Houston asked Marshall to relay a message to the first-year law student: "Impress upon Murray also that from now on, girls are nix until after his examinations."[33]

Murray excelled on his exams and enjoyed a year in law school without any friction with school officials or with his white classmates.[34] The following school year a second African American student enrolled in the University of Maryland's law school; Calvin Douglass's arrival on campus was heralded by the black press as proof that the "Legal Fight Conducted by N.A.A.C.P. Wins Lasting Results."[35]

In June 1938, Donald Gaines Murray graduated from the University of Maryland law school. "During the three years he pursued his law studies," one newspaper wrote, "he became one of the most popular students on the campus."[36] After graduation, he became a successful Baltimore attorney, winning several cases for the NAACP while working as partner in a local law firm. In 1985, one year before he died not far from where he was born, the law school honored him in a ceremony commemorating the fiftieth anniversary of the case that began with his handwritten letter to Dean Howell: "Dear Sir, I am writing you so that I may secure admittance to the Law School of the University of Maryland."[37]

DON'T SHOUT TOO SOON

B LACK AMERICANS GREETED news of Houston and Marshall's victory over the University of Maryland with such euphoria that, in March of 1936, Charles Houston published an admonition in the NAACP's official magazine, the *Crisis*. "Don't Shout Too Soon," the article's title admonished above a subtitle noting that "victory in the University of Maryland test case does not mean the battle for education equality for Negroes is over, warns the chief counsel in the legal campaign."[1] Houston's tone was plebeian and tailored to the message: "So far so good," he wrote, "but the fight has just begun."[2] In the wake of Murray's enrolling in the University of Maryland School of Law, public universities in Missouri, Virginia and Tennessee had rejected qualified African American applicants. "These students [had already] appealed to the N.A.A.C.P. for aid" but it had "cost the N.A.A.C.P. $2,000 and a lot of volunteer labor to get Murray inside the doors of the University of Maryland." The association now needed to "raise immediately not less than $6,000 to take care of these Virginia, Missouri and Tennessee cases," and "even so, money [was] not the sole answer."[3]

Legal realism's demand that judges and lawyers engage their cases knowing that these cases could shape the society from which they arose likewise demanded that judges and lawyers engage that society to prepare it for the outcomes of those cases. Because Constitution and judge declared it true did not make it so. The coming generation would learn this all too well in the *Brown* decision's gritty aftermath. Twenty years earlier Houston could

just as easily have been addressing the Warren Court or Eisenhower administration when he warned, "Law suits mean little unless supported by public opinion. Nobody needs to explain to a Negro the difference between
the law in books and the law in action." With time and appeals black applicants' lawyers could persuade judges to rule in their favor, but these rulings
would wither atop arid land without measurable public support. "The really baffling problem is how to create the proper kind of public opinion."[4]
He readied the *Crisis*'s enormous readership to "be prepared to fight, if
necessary, every step of the way." Along with the lawyers who would represent them, they had to "remain on the alert and push the struggle farther
with all [their] might."[5]

The segregated elementary and high schools littering the Confederacy's
remnants spurned even the suggestion of equality. In time, the NAACP
would file suit in these states and in time, Houston believed, it would
prevail—likely not at the state level as in *Murray*, but eventually, preferably,
in the Supreme Court. The road, however, still had to be paved: "For every
dollar the Association spends in litigation, it could profitably spend ten dollars in educational publicity and the formation of an enlightened public
opinion."[6] These years were, as one historian recorded, "a time of planting,
not harvesting."[7]

Houston understood that much work remained. He called on black
people and organizations to "redouble [their] efforts toward interracial
understanding."[8] The *Murray* triumph perhaps had come too easily, not for
the lawyers but for the public: A principal goal of his litigating civil rights
cases was to awaken and strengthen the will of local communities to fight
for their rights.[9] A county or town scarcely could be asked to demand and
fight for rights that appeared so easily won. The impatient attorney coun-
seled patience, perseverance. "Maybe the next generation will be able to
take time out to rest," he wrote, "but we have too far to go and too much
work to do."[10]

Houston knew that the rain would fall anew tomorrow and on the
morn following, even if black Americans heartbreakingly expected otherwise. There one day would be preachers to assure them that theirs was God's
side, but for now there were lawyers imploring their enduring dedication
despite a victory: "Shout if you want, but don't shout too soon."[11]

EVEN WHILE HOUSTON WARNED against too much celebration, Thurgood Marshall could not help but savor the triumph of *Murray v. Maryland*. Just as each child matures in a different family, each lawyer tries a different case; Marshall's *Murray* was a trial more personal than Houston's and the verdict a more intimate cause for elation. That his closing argument had emboldened the trial judge and persuaded the appellate court titillated Marshall with vindication. Had he not pestered Charlie to accept the case in the first place, Donald Murray might never have been admitted to the University of Maryland Law School.

At his Baltimore haunts Thurgood Marshall was now a man recognized in the fight for his people, "a Race man" in the day's parlance. In his hometown, he had fought and won. He became a sought-after speaker in and around the city and assured Houston unprompted that his speeches buttressed the theme set forth in "Don't Shout Too Soon." He wrote, "Dear Charlie: Your article for the Crisis is 'swell.' "[12] (Putting quotation marks around the adjective was a generational dig; Houston and Walter White consistently betrayed their age by praising Marshall's work as "swell.") In seriousness, Marshall explained that Houston's advising black Americans to recognize the long fight ahead "has been the theme of each of my talks here in Baltimore since the [*Murray*] case."

Winning *Murray* also earned Marshall heft in the NAACP's powerful Baltimore branch. *Murray* was unlike *Crawford* in two pertinent respects: First, it was a legal victory, not a moral one, and second, the win immediately benefited Maryland's black citizens. It was the very sort of triumph coveted by the association and its Baltimore branch. Membership swelled twenty times over and none could deny Marshall's indispensable role in the success.[13]

Houston was eager for Marshall to assume more of the legal office's "evangelist, stump-speaker" duties. Marshall needed no speech-coaching, but Houston did guide his preparation for events certain to garner press. When Marshall was asked to address the roles and restrictions placed on black policemen, Houston gave him a recent article from Oklahoma City's *Black Dispatch* newspaper on the topic and then offered several suggestions, which, like most suggestions he offered Marshall, involved time-consuming tasks that would leave him weary but exceptionally well prepared for his presentation.[14] Thurgood should "write immediately to the police chiefs in

Washington, Philadelphia, St. Louis, Cincinnati, Louisville and Charleston, West Virginia and ask their experience with Negro policemen." In fact, Houston continued, "You might work out a questionnaire and let them answer it. The questionnaire will direct their attention to the specific points you want and give you a uniform basis of information." Because his time frame was so short, it was important "not to ask a lot of questions requiring research," and it would be best to send "self-addressed, stamped envelopes to the police chiefs, air mail if necessary, and mak[e] it clear to them that you must have the information by Friday."[15]

So famous was the *Murray* victory that an independent party's power brokers implored Marshall to run for Congress in 1936. As Houston was drafting "Don't Shout Too Soon," Marshall sent him a letter asking for advice on whether to run. He was excited by the prospect of joining Alabama-born Illinois Democrat Arthur Mitchell, the only African American member of the House of Representatives, about whom *Time* magazine had recently marveled, "He is entitled to eat with [southern white congressmen] in the House Restaurant, sit beside them on the House floor."[16] After assuring Houston that the men recruiting him were not communists, Marshall wrote that he also was soliciting the advice of Carl Murphy, publisher of the *Baltimore Afro-American*.[17] Houston replied that Marshall should run for Congress but must "avoid communism and personal expense." Murphy advised against running for political office and pushed Marshall to build his law practice. The latter advice proved persuasive. Marshall eschewed a political run to focus on building a viable book of business.

Suddenly a player on his hometown's stage, he began receiving referrals, precious paying clients for his still-fledgling one-man law shop. Largely responsible for Marshall's newfound solvency was a man whose influence among black Marylanders could scarcely be exaggerated: Carl Murphy had earned a degree from Harvard and chaired Howard University's German department before becoming publisher and chief editor of the *Afro-American* newspaper in 1922. Murphy would lead the *Afro-American* for forty-nine of his seventy-eight years of life. In 1935, little happened in black Baltimore without Murphy's prior knowledge.

A bespectacled wisp of a man, Murphy was a deft political conductor who viewed unremitting protest as the right and responsibility of all black Americans. The son of a Maryland slave who fought for the Union in the

Civil War, Murphy was an active NAACP member; he orchestrated the
Baltimore branch's electing fiery Lillie Jackson president in 1935—a position she would retain until a year after his death in 1967. Murphy, or
"Mister Carl" as most residents addressed him, was a man soft-spoken for
confidence of being heard.[18] Grateful for Marshall's promethean pro bono
efforts on behalf of the NAACP, the publisher ensured that the young
lawyer obtained paying clients sufficient to sustain his practice.

The *Afro-American* avowed seven principles of "What the Afro Stands
For" and printed them in each edition. The newspaper's third tenet was
"equal salaries for equal work for school teachers without regard to color
or sex."[19] With his candidate elected Baltimore branch president and the
NAACP's membership rolls growing longer by the week, Mister Carl
thought now was the perfect time to fight for the *Afro-American*'s third
ideal. *Murray* had cleared the brush, but the path remained far from paved.
There were two black students in the University of Maryland School of
Law; there were thousands in Baltimore County's separate and unequal
public school system.

HOUSTON'S LEAVE OF ABSENCE from Howard University was also a leave
from his life in Washington. He had been living in New York City for eight
months by March of 1936, working as special counsel of the NAACP and
lodging at the 135th Street YMCA.[20] His workdays stretched to nights in
his office in association headquarters at 69 Fifth Avenue. Hours teemed
with dictating memoranda and correspondence, researching case law, conferring with executive secretary Walter White and planning Homeric trips
around the country to organize support and raise funds for the legal campaign.

Despite the furious pace, here in Manhattan he was happy. Amid his fre-
netic schedule he found a tranquillity that had been elusive at Harvard, at
Howard, at home. The controversies that had numbed the joy of his work
in the *Crawford* case and for Howard's accreditation faded to memory as
he roused enthusiastic crowds around the country to the work that history
had set before them. Speaking to civic groups, church congregations and just
about any other organization willing to hear him, Houston railed against discrimination in education and transportation. By year's end he would have
traveled more than twenty-five thousand miles in his trusty Graham-Paige,

subsisting on a three-dollar per diem and a four-cents-per-mile reimburse-
ment.[21] His gift for courtroom advocacy made him equally persuasive in
churches and parlors across the country. When visiting southern states like
South Carolina, the "field investigator, lawyer, [and] speaker" turned film-
maker and recorded the deplorable conditions under which black schoolchildren were expected to learn. For NAACP members back North, the
films brought to life ramshackle one-room schoolhouses several states and
worlds away. Houston believed that "motion pictures humanize and dram-
atize the discrimination which Negroes suffer much more effectively than
any corresponding amount of speech could do."[22]

He spoke in Memphis at the end of a three-week NAACP membership
drive and was greeted by "an unusually large crowd" excited to hear stories
of his "notable victories" on the association's behalf.[23] The African American fraternities and sororities that cosponsored the event lauded him as
"one of the greatest influences for progress that the race has ever had."[24] He
wrote an essay published in the *New York Herald Tribune* extolling the newspaper's recent antilynching editorial and arguing "the necessity for direct
Federal anti-lynching legislation giving the relatives of the lynched victim
a direct right to go into the Federal court" to seek criminal prosecution.[25]
Meeting regularly with the Associated Negro Press, Houston explained that
the devoted efforts of competent and conscientious lawyers were ushering
significant change in the nation. Amid the travel and bustle he assumed the
cheerful sanguinity of a man enjoying life.

Houston loved Howard but disliked academia's isolation; he loved
Washington but could not buy a lunchtime sandwich anywhere near his
office in the segregated capital; and he loved Mag, but their bond had finally buckled.

Houston's mother had first encouraged his interest in the demure Virginian whom she and his father had taken in on account of Mag's parents'
financial straits. Charlie was freshly starched in his army officer's uniform
when her beauty awakened him. He discovered the desire for a woman in
his life when he realized that one already was in his life. Charlie shortened
Margaret Gladys to Mag, and the young woman loved her new nickname,
which she deemed a vast improvement over "Buster," the day's common
moniker for blossoming young women. Everyone called her Margaret or
Buster, but Charlie called her Mag.

Their courtship was a strained affair. Although just as refined as he in manner, Mag was not his intellectual equal and the disparity sometimes fed his impatience with her. But his parents loved her and by now so did he. After he returned from his traveling fellowship, Charlie married Mag in Baltimore.

Like Thurgood and Buster, Charlie and Mag had long been unable to conceive. Their marriage was formal to the point of being distant even before this additional hardship. Charlie was still dean of Howard when the couple conceived a child. Their elation collapsed to grief a short while later when Mag suffered a miscarriage. Her physician's counsel was plain: Yes, they could conceive again but the pregnancy might permanently disable or kill her.[26] This news was nearly as devastating as the miscarriage. Charlie wanted his wife to be healthy but he also wanted a child. Mag flatly refused to risk her life on another pregnancy, and snow fell silently on their union.

By the time he began packing for New York City in 1935's midsummer, neither of them thought it better that she accompany him. In Washington they were living separately beneath one roof; his moving north would accomplish what they had been unable to for some time now.

MISTER CARL WAS ADAMANT. There wasn't one damn colored high school in all of Baltimore County, and that was an abomination.

Baltimore branch president Lillie Jackson didn't like all that cursing but she agreed with Murphy. The county's lack of a colored high school offended both God and the Constitution. White schoolchildren had eleven high schools from which to choose.[27] If a colored child wanted to attend school past the seventh grade, he or she had to pass an admittance exam to Frederick Douglass High School in Baltimore City. It was nigh a miracle that half the students passed the exam considering the conditions of the Baltimore County grade schools they attended. Rotted floorboards and sagging, seeping roofs were but the most obvious signs of failure of these dilapidated schoolhouses.

As a member of the NAACP's board of directors, Carl Murphy closely read each edition of the *Crisis*. In the October 1935 issue, the man recently hired as the association's special counsel set forth six goals necessary "to accomplish actual equality of educational opportunity for Negroes."

In an article titled "Educational Inequalities Must Go," Charles Hamilton Houston demanded:

a) equality of school terms;

b) equality of pay for Negro teachers having the same qualifications and doing the same work as white teachers;

c) equality of transportation for Negro school children at public expense;

d) equality of buildings and equipment;

e) equality of *per capita* expenditure for education of Negroes;

f) equality in graduate and professional training.[28]

Murphy wanted the NAACP to make Houston's claims in court on behalf of Baltimore County's black children. He already had published numerous stories in the *Afro-American* chronicling the students' horrid learning conditions. Only the lawyers could take it from there.

What they needed, Thurgood Marshall replied after much listening, was a good plaintiff, a request for relief that was attainable, and financial support from the NAACP's national office. For the last he could depend on Houston, whose warm working relationship with Walter White ensured the association's increasing financial commitment to legal struggle. By the first Marshall meant that they needed a female plaintiff; no lawyer this side of Sunday would argue in a 1936 southern courtroom for a teenage black boy to be admitted to a white high school because so much of segregation was built on southern whites' fixation on interracial sex.

Marshall's approach to finding a plaintiff revealed what relief he would seek. He and Houston in *Murray* successfully had argued that Maryland violated the separate but equal doctrine set forth in the Supreme Court's *Plessy v. Ferguson* decision because it provided no law school for black students. In *Murray* there was no separate and so there could be no equal. Baltimore County's refusal to provide a high school for its 10 percent black population seemed to present the same issue. By demanding the integration granted in *Murray,* Marshall and his cocounsel, Edward Lovett, Leon Ransom and Oliver Hill, hoped to jolt the county into constructing a high school for black students.[29]

Marshall by now knew better than to approach Houston without a plaintiff in hand. Like all great trial lawyers, Houston was a fact-specific man. Facts turned cases that moved law; no fact was as important as who sought relief.

The previous September, while Houston and Marshall were working on the *Murray* appeal and Murray acclimated himself to the arduous life of a first-year law student, two African American girls asked to attend Baltimore County's all-white Catonsville High School. The principal, David Zimmerman, refused to accept them.[30]

In January 1936, Marshall publicly "announced that he planned immediate court action" on behalf of the county's black high-school-age students.[31] The *Washington Post* reported that "Baltimore County Negroes" remained "[e]ncouraged by the action of the State Court of Appeals in ruling that qualified Negroes must be admitted to the University of Maryland Law School."[32] Thirteen-year-old Margaret Williams signed with her parents to be Marshall's clients. With both suitable plaintiff and recent precedent in hand, he convinced Houston to lobby Walter White for the national office's financial support while Carl Murphy urged his fellow members of the NAACP's board to support the Baltimore County litigation. The association agreed to finance the lawsuit as part of its campaign for equal education. *Murray* had proven Maryland fertile.

Marshall filed suit on Margaret Williams's behalf in March of 1936. He sued the principal of Catonsville High School, the Baltimore County schools' superintendent and the county's school board, asking the court to order them to admit Margaret to Catonsville High. The court set a hearing for May 23 but rescheduled it for late June after one of the county's lawyers fell ill.[33]

As he prepared for the Williams hearing, Thurgood Marshall took stock of his financial situation. Pro bono work for the NAACP was crippling him. As much as Carl Murphy encouraged him to build his practice and referred business cases to his office, the lion's share of his time and energy went to representing the NAACP on nonpaying cases. Researching facts and law, drafting and revising briefs and coordinating strategies with both the national office and the choleric powers of the Baltimore branch were taking a toll, both emotional and financial, on the young lawyer. His office received letters from livid creditors. Basic expenses of running a law office—legal texts, copious reams of paper, typewriter ribbon—became burdens too heavy. As he told Houston, every month was a struggle to "keep the wolf away from my door."[34]

And then there was home. He and Buster were still struggling to conceive in a house chafed by the day with friction. His father had been fired from the Gibson Island Club and his brother Aubrey, stricken with a terribly lingering flu, had taken leave of his medical practice.[35] The Marshall household needed more than Thurgood was able to contribute as a private practitioner. He inquired about a teaching job at Howard Law School, but was rebuffed on account of his closeness to the dean, whom some still resented for having "Harvardized" the school.

The Prentice-Hall book company was badgering him for overdue payments. After reminding him that he already had "been favored with an extension of sixty days beyond [our] regular terms," the company's credit manager asked, "Are we not therefore entitled to payment now? We think you will agree and feeling certain you will no longer delay the payment, we are enclosing a return envelope for your convenience in sending your check or money-order today."[36]

Marshall was broke as he worked on the *Murray* appeal through July. He returned this envelope with a one-line letter: "Gentlemen: A check for the enclosed account will be mailed to you on August 11th, 1936."[37]

A couple months later Houston told him: "I do not advise that you drop everything for N.A.A.C.P. work. Keep a finger on your office whatever you do."[38] Marshall had not yet informed Houston that there was but ephemera left in the office; association work had subsumed his practice. With little choice remaining, he doffed his hat and confessed to Houston: "As it stands things are getting worse and worse and first of all, I fully realize that the Association has no money . . ."[39] That said, he implored Houston to confer with Walter White about any possibility of helping out. He asked for money: just "enough to tide me over, then in return, I could do more on these cases. For example, to prepare briefs and research, etc. on the other cases or any of the legal matters which you would need assistance on." Marshall then listed a few of his bills, to give Houston an idea of his expenses.[40]

Truly it pained him to write such a letter to a man whom he knew believed that, financially, "a thoroughly competent lawyer finds no difficulty in making his way."[41] In Maryland a black lawyer "must depend for the bulk of his patronage on members of his own race. But there the money and the great opportunity for service lie."[42] Marshall was serving valiantly but making no money representing clients pro bono for the NAACP. As a successful private practitioner, Houston had reminded him, "You can get all the publicity from the N.A.A.C.P. work but you have to keep your eye out for cashing in."[43] Marshall understood that, but he "would not give up these cases here in Maryland for anything in the world . . . at the same time there is no opportunity to get down to really hustling for business."[44]

Houston knew that Marshall did not beseech charity; the hard fact was that Marshall spent the lion's share of his time on the association's cases. That this work was ruining him financially was unfortunate but not unpredictable. Houston also knew that "building a law practice is generally slow work."[45] Marshall had not invested the time necessary to build his book of business and now, even with the work Murphy drummed up for him, his time—and professional interests—were wholly invested in the association's legal struggle. Houston sympathized with his former student's predicament and offered encouragement: "I don't know of anybody I would rather have in the office than you or anybody who can do a better job of research and preparation of cases."[46] He promised to try to persuade White to give Marshall a paying job: "an opportunity to come to the national office at $200 per month for six months if that interests you."[47]

Houston's grueling travel schedule provided his best argument for the NAACP's hiring Marshall as his assistant. His success as a self-described "evangelist and stump speaker" increased both faith and membership in the NAACP, but it left the association's law shop unattended for weeks at a time. As its legal campaign gathered steam, Houston argued that the NAACP required at least two attorneys, which "would always put one in the office, except in rare instances when both might be away for a few days in actual trial."[48] Moreover, as *Murray* illustrated, Maryland was ripe ground for civil rights litigation and the Baltimore branch had grown to over 1,600 members; it would prove a wise investment for the NAACP to employ one of Baltimore's native sons in its legal office. Houston urged White to present the proposal to the board of directors, to persuade them to hire Marshall as assistant counsel, a full-time position assisting Houston in all facets of what promised to be a landmark and protracted legal struggle.

White was as persuasive to the board as Houston was with White, and the NAACP offered Marshall the exact deal floated in Houston's letter. For two hundred dollars per month plus expenses, Thurgood Marshall in October 1936 became assistant special counsel to the NAACP.

He was still working as a clerk in the Bureau of Communicable Diseases and immediately asked his boss "for a leave of absence not to exceed six months beginning October 20, 1936."[49] Marshall then excitedly wrote to Walter White, "I will be indebted to you and Charlie for a long time to come for many reasons, one of which is that I have an opportunity now to do what I have always dreamed of doing!"[50] His six-month stint with the NAACP would last twenty-five years.

ALL THE WHILE Thurgood Marshall's case to desegregate Baltimore County's schools was grinding through Maryland's judicial machinery. By now the county had made clear its intention to fight the NAACP on the merits of its case. Marshall's belief that filing a lawsuit demanding integration, in *Murray*'s wake, would jolt county officials into building a high school for the county's black students was proved wrong. *Murray* or no *Murray*, county lawyers liked their odds; if Marshall wanted to argue that the Constitution required black and white teenagers to sit together in class, that was an argument they welcomed. Recognizing the challenge before them, Houston provided Marshall with a detailed outline of how to proceed at trial.

Adding to the pressure, African Americans nationwide followed even the case's mundane procedural developments with devotion. Four states away, the *Atlanta Daily World*'s report on Judge Frank Duncan's overruling a routine state motion recited the stakes for its readers; in the county there were "11 public high schools for white children and not one for colored children. For years colored children have been sent into Baltimore City to attend the colored school there. However, the county has appropriated only so much money for tuition for the Negro students and for many years over half the colored children eligible to go to high school have been prevented from doing so because the county did not furnish enough money for their tuition."[51] The *Daily World*'s story, like the reports in other black-owned newspapers covering the case, failed to note that the lawsuit was asking the court to admit the black plaintiffs to the county's all-white public high school. Instead the article informed only that the lawsuit "seeks to end the condition" resulting in the county's black children having no high school to attend.[52] Perhaps black Americans least of all thought public school integration possible in 1936.

The case came to trial in September. In court the county's lawyers treated Marshall rudely. Rather than present an anti-integration argument, they hurled Marshall and his team into the weeds of arguing minutiae regarding pass rates for the entrance exam African American students were required to take to attend Baltimore City's Douglass High School. Eager to avoid the segregation question, Judge Duncan declared that he would review only whether thirteen-year-old Margaret Williams had passed the entrance examination.[53] Margaret had failed the entrance exam by 2.5 percentage points and her case was lost. Baltimore County would neither build a high school for its black children nor permit them to attend any of its existing high schools. Marshall and Houston, ever students of judicial vicissitudes, accepted the loss as a lesson. Don't shout too soon. They would return to graduate schools for plaintiffs, leaving for another day the revolution of seating black children and white children in the same classroom.

SPECIAL COUNSEL AND ASSISTANT COUNSEL

U PON HIS OCTOBER ARRIVAL in New York City, Thurgood Marshall threw himself into legal evangelism. Like his boss at the NAACP's home office, the assistant special counsel became both lawyer and stump speaker, farmer and shepherd. Marshall took to the lectern-pulpit naturally, as Houston had expected. To gathered believers he inspired faith. He knew when to depart from prepared remarks for a joke and remembered names as easily as any priest or politician.

Buster moved with him to New York City. She and Thurgood were relieved to escape the crowded Marshall family home that had only grown more tense as Aubrey grew sicker and Willie grew angrier and drunker. The couple rented a small apartment on 149th Street and, cramped though the space was, it was theirs alone.[1] Thurgood's salary was meager but reliable; there would be no fretting over the rent. Perhaps at last they would conceive a child. Hope bounded high in the first home they called their own.

Houston beamed at Marshall's joining the staff at 69 Fifth Avenue. He had convinced the association to hire his former student who was working for free, who cared more for the NAACP's cases than for his ability to make a living. In a recommendation letter to executive secretary Walter White, Houston attested, "You would not be able to find a more faithful person than Thurgood or a more dependable office man. But I am afraid he is just not the type to make a success in private practice . . . He is perhaps too conscientious and painstaking to be a commercial scuffling lawyer."[2]

Marshall so far was proving Houston's word true. In 1936's New York autumn, Houston mused that his new assistant one day would contribute more than he to the fight against injustice.[3]

For now, Houston was simply glad to have a lawyer man the office while he traveled the country, sleeping in guest rooms of NAACP members' houses and speaking to gathered groups large and small. In September of 1936 Houston trekked from Los Angeles to Phoenix to El Paso to Dallas to Little Rock to Memphis to St. Louis to Cincinnati and back to New York City.[4] The special counsel committed himself to speaking wherever "the national office [felt] it would be advantageous to the educational, and anti-lynching—legal defense campaigns."[5] And indeed, by now the legal campaign was assuming shape. Progressive Americans, black and white, flocked to hear Houston discuss the *Murray* victory, ask nonmembers in the audience to join the NAACP, and rally their support for what he promised would be a long and tough slog.

When Marshall arrived at 69 Fifth Avenue the month following, his boss was out West again, this time working his way down the California coast. The lawyer come preacherman, salesman and all-round traveling man greeted sunrise on Thursday, October 1, 1936, in Red Bluff, California, after a good night's sleep at the NAACP branch president's home on Cedar Street. He spent the next night in Sacramento, the following in Oakland, then Vallejo, and, by Wednesday the seventh, he dropped his bags on the Delaware Street doorstep of San Mateo's branch president.[6] From there Houston addressed crowds in a different city every day, finally arriving in San Diego on Sunday, October 25, grateful for the respite of enjoying branch secretary Mrs. Alvessie Hackshaw's home cooking before beginning the long trip back East.[7]

Marshall did not yet travel as widely as his new boss, but he did immediately assume a full schedule promoting the NAACP's still-new national legal campaign. At Saint Augustine's Episcopal Church on the corner of Marcy and Lafayette avenues in Brooklyn, he rallied support for black students' equal educational opportunities and pressured Mayor La Guardia for "a Negro member of the Board of Education, additional playgrounds in Brooklyn and courses for teachers on Negro life and history, as well as inclusion of such courses in the public school system for the children."[8] One week later Marshall spoke at his alma mater in Pennsylvania, where his topic was "Educational Inequalities Among Negroes in the United

States." Nearly the entire student body of Lincoln University came to hear him speak. Marshall recounted *Murray*'s trial, appeal and victory, encouraged his fellow Lincoln men to join the NAACP, and described the deplorable conditions in which black schoolchildren were forced to learn not only in the Deep South "but in many border and semi-northern states including New Jersey, Pennsylvania, Missouri, Illinois and Ohio."[9] A few Sundays later he addressed a group at New York City's Association of Trade and Commerce.[10] Marshall enjoyed stump speaking, rallying the faithful, soliciting memberships and donations. The occasions were welcome relief from trial presentations in which he was confined by rules of civil procedure and courtroom custom. His folksy flourishes played well in New York City.

Even as he thrived in New York, Marshall kept alight his Baltimore campfire. His reluctance to completely close his Baltimore practice was both ironic and understandable. The association had signed him only to a six-month contract; he fully expected to return to Maryland by the summer of 1937. A few of his private practice clients were sticking with him for now, although their loyalty likely was borne by necessity: They were mostly the "freebies" he represented because he knew no one else would.

Many nights thus found Thurgood traveling the East Coast's train corridor. "Between 1936 and 1938," he reminisced, "I commuted practically between Baltimore and New York, and there was considerable practice in that period."[11] He moved out of the office building where he struggled to pay rent. "I was based in New York but I maintained an office in my mother's home in Baltimore, and I would come back to take care of the clients that really needed me until they adjusted over to new lawyers."[12] Though exhilarated by working at NAACP headquarters, Marshall was keeping one foot firmly planted on his home state's soil. Indeed, it was the assistant special counsel's links to the Free State that presented the NAACP with its next legal struggle.

ONE SATURDAY IN LATE NOVEMBER 1936, hundreds of the NAACP's Baltimore branch members bundled themselves against the late autumn's swooping wind, known to locals as "the hawk." Baltimore's gusts dissuaded none from attending the night's meeting, for the executive secretary himself, Walter White, was scheduled to address issues of great import to their state. With their own Thurgood Marshall now working full-time as the association's number-two lawyer and their state having provided the NAACP's clearest legal victory to date, branch members arrived early and eager to hear the secretary's plans for Maryland.

White disappointed no one in the hall. With his minimal frame and matching alto, White's speech was far from Houston's rousing thunder or Marshall's folksy baritone. His manner more befitted a fund-raiser on Manhattan's Upper East Side than a branch meeting on Baltimore's old west side, but his credibility and courage were admired by NAACP members and foes alike. They all knew that, as an assistant field secretary years ago, he had risked being tortured and killed by the white mobs he infiltrated. These days, when he visited the White House, White spoke as strongly for equal rights as he did at branch meetings such as this. To the Baltimore branch he presented numbers unassailable and unacceptable: Were they aware that the state of Maryland, to which they paid taxes with every week's work, paid its Negro teachers $500,000 less each year than it paid its white teachers?[13] Baltimore County, which refused to construct a high school for its colored children even in the face of the association's lawsuit, paid its Negro elementary school teachers $602 per year—while paying its white teachers $1,135 annually.

White knew he was in Baltimore City, though, and lest their residents think their teachers fared any better than those in Baltimore County, he informed them that the average annual salary for colored high school teachers was $1,984; white high school teachers earned $2,361 for performing the same job.[14]

Members murmured in their seats. These were not close cases of race prejudice but instead stark manifestations of segregation's immediate costs. How was the association planning to fight these outrages?

White had not traveled down to Baltimore to tell the members what their NAACP was planning to do; he was there to update them on what the association already had done to fight Maryland's heinous race prejudice. Last week, assistant special counsel Thurgood Marshall, who had cut his lawyer's teeth representing some members seated in the hall tonight, met in Baltimore with the state's board of education. At the meeting Mr. Marshall had attempted to reason with Maryland's board officials, to convince them that shortchanging the state's Negro teachers was to shortchange generations of the state's Negro children. Moreover, the U.S. Constitution forbade such in-equality: Under the Supreme Court's *Plessy v. Ferguson* decision, Maryland could divide its children into separate schools only so long as those schools were equal; no two schools could approximate equality when their teachers' salaries differed so widely based solely on race. Mr. Marshall therefore asked the state board of education to equalize the salaries of all its teachers and to vary them only according to merit and experience instead of race. The board rebuffed him.[15]

Undaunted and prepared, Thurgood Marshall immediately filed with the board a formal request that the state equalize its teacher salaries; this was a formality that had to be done before the association could commence litigation. Maryland's board of education of course denied Mr. Marshall's request and, once the association identified a plaintiff, it would file suit against the state. It would fight this legislated race prejudice and the asso-ciation would prevail—an outcome that only the meek and misinformed could doubt.

From the audience arose a volunteer. The audience cheered and White gleamed. An NAACP plaintiff was assured of financial hardships, so the gathering readily took up a collection.[16]

For nearby Montgomery County, however, the NAACP already had its plaintiff. He had written Marshall a few days before Halloween. As both teacher and principal of Rockville Colored Elementary School, William B. Gibbs, Jr., sought redress for receiving an annual salary less than half that of his white colleagues, $612 to their $1,362.[17]

As was true of every black teacher or principal who agreed to file suit against his or her white employer, Gibbs's courage was exceptional. In 1936 Gibbs placed himself at considerable risk by declaring that he should be paid as much as any white man who did the same job. Many African American residents of Montgomery County's Haitian neighborhood so believed in Gibbs's cause that they signed away their homes as collateral for his lawsuit's prosecution.[18] With Marshall's encouragement, the neighbors organized a Montgomery County chapter of the NAACP at Jerusalem Church.[19]

Marshall then explained to Gibbs that, in order to become a viable plain-tiff, he had to fulfill certain procedural mandates. First, he must file a petition for equal pay with the county's school board; once the board denied him, as it surely would, he must file an appeal with the state's board of education.

Marshall had already procured from the state superintendent a promise to rule quickly on Gibbs's appeal. It was denied in time for him to file suit on New Year's Eve, 1936.[20]

THAT CHARLES HAMILTON HOUSTON's NAACP roadwork so often forced him to be absent from headquarters failed to dim Marshall's admiration for Old Ironshoes. If anything, Marshall began unabashedly imitating Houston's compulsive work habits. As Edward Lovett put it, Houston "work[ed] like hell and way into the night," and Marshall did his best in the same.[21] He hunched his still-lanky tall frame over the unforgiving desk and scratched out words to briefs, thoughts to arguments—soon to be scratched out again, for Houston reviewed nearly everything. To the law office's secretary went scribbled pages for typing so that on the typed pages Marshall could scribble anew, assessing each proposition and argument with the most critical eyes he could muster. As with most attorneys, the more confident he became, the more critical he was of his own arguments, the better he anticipated their counters and the less ink Houston spilled onto his drafts.

Houston insisted on confidence in his lawyers, telling one young student, "Don't have any doubts; you haven't time for such foolishness," and, as they matured, he instilled this confidence by deferring to their judgment: "Handle the matter diplomatically," he advised Marshall regarding one thorny issue in the *Murray* case, "but I think that whatever you decide upon, you should put it in writing so as to have a record."[22]

Ever the pragmatist, Houston sought to make Marshall as indispensable as possible during his six-month stint as the association's assistant special counsel. Only by involving Marshall in nearly every aspect of the legal office, by overworking him as he overworked himself, could Houston argue for his continued employment when the time came.

So he took the younger lawyer back on the road with him, this time in the 1929 Ford Thurgood's Uncle Fearless had helped him buy. Houston rode shotgun, typing away at a secretarial clip that amazed Marshall. "He could type up a storm," Marshall recalled decades later, "faster than any secretary—and not with just two fingers going. I mean he used 'em all."[23] Lest the South's dry counties or a fundamentalist host-household get the best of them, Marshall was careful to stash some bourbon in the trunk.

Late in the night, when work was done and dawn promised another hundred miles, Thurgood and Charlie would nip at the bourbon. The senior lawyer forever was educating his former student, challenging, prodding, pushing him over a whiskey glass as easily as over a professor's lectern. From a man who addressed everyone at 69 Fifth Avenue as Mr., Mrs. or Miss, who was revered by black folks nationwide as a warrior-celebrity whose picture was splashed across *Look!* magazine, sharing stiff drinks was a considered gesture. Thurgood treasured the lessons and laughs, and Charlie, ungiven to effusiveness as a giving man can be, knew by now that Marshall was coming to exceed every standard by which he believed any worthwhile lawyer should be measured.

Although he was the more naturally gifted speaker, Marshall learned much by watching Houston rouse believers. When Houston spoke on the last day of the Second Annual Regional Conference of the NAACP in April 1937, over nine hundred members crowded Atlanta's Big Bethel AME Church in spite of numerous other activities simultaneously taking place.[24] Black people wanted to hear their lawyer speak, to hear him testify from the pulpit to the changes taking place in the United States. He urged them to register to vote and described the association's efforts to amend the Harrison–Black–Fletcher Education Bill "so that colored children may have the same amount of training and type of training as white children."[25] At his conclusion Clark University's Philharmonic Society broke into song and the throng into cheers.

Indeed the times were alive with possibility. Kappa Alpha Psi, an African American fraternity founded a few years after Houston and Marshall's Alpha Phi Alpha, proudly presented a check to the association's legal defense fund. Kappa's national publicity director and its chairman of public relations stood before seated NAACP assistant secretary Roy Wilkins. Behind them stood the association's two attorneys, both tall and tailored, the older stocky and the younger still lean.[26]

A few days later down in Washington, a "literary cocktail party" was thrown at the Mu-So-Lit Club at Thirteenth and R streets NW, a few blocks from Houston's parents' house. Howard University professors Sterling A. Brown, the proud recent recipient of the Guggenheim award in literature, and Alain Locke, whose philosophical writings would be studied by ensuing generations, sponsored the party to benefit the newly organized Negro People's Theatre.[27] Professor Brown charged black playwrights in language remarkably similar to Houston's charge to lawyers. "The Negro playwright," he explained to an interviewer that evening, "has not achieved. He has not interpreted Negro life."[28] Clear was the call rising from Howard University's hill above W Street: Time was nigh for stories of the Race, for the Story of the Race, to be told at last by those who awoke to fight its battle each morning.

As MUCH AS he had vowed that he "was through with the Army and never wanted to see it again," Houston continued to monitor, lobby and fight for change in the armed forces for his entire life.[29] The struggles to end inequality in education and transportation were his most immediate legal fronts—indeed they were the battles that the NAACP hired him to fight—but the effort most dear to him was the fight to end the racist policies in his country's military. To this end his vigilance diminished none through the years.

Houston's army experience afforded him detailed knowledge of how the military organized and ran its units and camps. He was able to recognize as false progress the army's ballyhooed announcements of granting more responsibility to African American officers. About one such proclamation, Houston wrote to Walter White: "Note however that [news of the new assignments] does not cover Negro Reserve officers of the line. These line officers would have actual charge of the camps and actual charge of the work and discipline of the men. [Under the army's announced assignments], the men are still left under white camp commanders for general purposes. I think that the agitation should be kept up to get Negro line officers appointed as camp commanders."[30] He closed by assuring White that he would pass his findings along to the press.[31]

For all it had pained him, Houston considered the army an efficient, mission-oriented body. The NAACP could learn from its linear structure: "If the Association is to function effectively and get the benefit of its numbers," he urged Walter White in a memo more terse than others, "it must be divided and sub-divided into smaller units very much after the fashion of an army."[32] The executive secretary, as he so often did, adopted his counsel's advice.

During the interwar years, the NAACP received many letters from black

servicemen detailing the brute racism they battled in their country's service. Now that Houston was officially on staff as special counsel, the association had a resident expert on such matters and White regularly sent
memoranda and letters with opening lines like "Dear Charlie: Won't you
give me your opinion regarding the questions raised in the enclosed letter
from Sergeant Herman E. Irving."[33] Sergeant Irving was a twenty-one-
year army veteran stationed at West Point and an NAACP member actively
organizing a branch in Highland Falls, New York. "Thus," he informed
White, "I feel that I am justified in writing you."[34] The career soldier continued, "As you doubtless know, legislation is now in progress to increase
the regular army something like 40%."[35] Irving presented White with a
litany of specific questions regarding what the increase would mean for the
army's black soldiers. Among other inquiries, he wondered whether they
would receive "a Batallion of Field Artillery, or [be] allowed to enter the Air
Corps . . . will the 25th and 24th Infantry regiments be given back the
Batallions they lost . . . will the colored soldier share in this increase [of
medical personnel]." Irving made clear that the concerns he expressed were
"on the lips of every serious colored soldier," but the men had "no way of
obtaining the answer." He thus asked the NAACP to "make inquiries directly of the War Department at Washington" to ascertain the army's plans
for its black soldiers.[36]

Houston had already learned of black soldiers' concerns as soon as he
"got wind that the Army appropriation was increased."[37] He agreed that
the NAACP should demand answers from the War Department, but that it
should do so as part of its continuous campaign against racism codified in
the military's regulations. So ardent was Houston's response that his letter
to White was marked with typos rarely found in his missives. "We have got
to strike hard, immediately and repeatedly and without let up at discrimination in the armed forces," he asserted. "We should make it a political issue, for approaching fascism as we are, the Army will dominate the country.
If we're not a part of it, we're aliens, and will be treated like hell." Houston
assured White that he had written both "to Roosevelt and the War Department," and in fact had read his letter to White into the record of the D.C.
Board of Education's meeting "so that the letter would become public
property."[38] The former army lieutenant wanted as many as possible to know
that "an Army man is worse than a Southerner, and a Southern army officer

is worse than Hell or anything else except a Southern marine or naval officer." His coda: "Let's go at them."[39] Houston would continue to go at them for years to come. As his national stature swelled and he became a formal adviser to the president of the United States, his "agitation" would bear fruit.

WEEKS YAWNED TO MONTHS ACROSS 1937 and African American teachers in Maryland's Montgomery County were growing impatient. Plaintiff William Gibbs and they had done all Marshall asked of them, the county board of education had filed its motion to dismiss their suit for equal pay, but the court had yet to schedule a hearing. At their urging, Marshall petitioned the court to schedule oral argument on the board's motion to dismiss, and the judge issued an order calling all to court on July 9.

A motion to dismiss presents the judge with a purely legal argument: Even if every fact alleged by the plaintiff is true and every favorable inference is granted to the plaintiff, a motion to dismiss contends that the plaintiff's case should be dismissed because it cannot prevail under the present state of law. Defendants routinely file motions to dismiss suits against them, but these motions fail more often than not because most plaintiffs do not file suit in the absence of law to support their requested relief. William Gibbs's case against the Montgomery County Board of Education did not seek to assign him to a white school so that he could receive pay equal to white teachers'; Gibbs sought only to be given equal pay for the equal work he performed in a separate school for black children. *Plessy v. Ferguson* and every case since buttressed Gibbs's claim; the law was plainly on his side. Less than two weeks after the court heard Marshall argue against the county's lawyers on the motion to dismiss, it ruled in Gibbs's favor. If Gibbs could prove all he alleged—that he was paid half what he would be paid were he a white man—he would prevail.

Marshall was pleased with the ruling but ecstatic when he received a letter from defendant's counsel: The board of education offered to settle Gibbs's suit on quite favorable terms. Over the next two years, Montgomery County would equalize the salaries of its black and white teachers and principals; two years' lapse was necessary because the county needed to raise revenue sufficient to pay the raises.[40]

Maryland's black teachers in other counties exulted and contacted the

NAACP's legal office, in hope of filing their own equal pay lawsuits. In short time they would; the coming months would find Marshall filing pay equalization cases in counties across his home state. Because it ended in settlement, Gibbs's case against Montgomery County set no legal precedent in Maryland; it did, however, make politically palatable the proposition that black teachers could earn salaries comparable to their white colleagues' without overturning Jim Crow.

Before the foam settled on Montgomery County's revelry, Houston met the man destined to become one of the most mysterious civil action plaintiffs in American history. A decade hence millions would have read and heard of Houston's and Marshall's fraternity brother Lloyd Gaines, a cagey, chain-smoking enigma.

10

On the Cusp in Missouri

S LAVES IN AMERICA'S NORTHERNMOST southern state worked more river-boats than plantations and mastered skills in trades white men reserved for themselves elsewhere in the South. In Missouri, African American masons, carpenters and blacksmiths slaved small farms alongside the men who owned them, white men who typically could afford only one or two slaves at $1,000 to $1,300 each. Jabez F. Smith's 165 slaves in Jackson County were hen's teeth exceptions; Missouri's $44.2 million worth of slaves comprised a lot at once scattered and concentrated, dispersed on the farms across the prairies or clustered on riverbanks of the Missouri and the Mississippi. State law mandated that they be lashed for attending "un-lawful assemblies" and "mutilated" for "attempt[ing] to commit assault upon white women," and after 1847 any white person who taught a black person to read or write was fined at least five hundred dollars and imprisoned for up to six months, but, for all Missouri was, it was not Alabama, Mississippi or unfathomable.[1] History's most famous American slave escaped Missouri having never known the field's toil: For his owner, Dr. John Sandford, Dred Scott was something of a man Friday, performing the errands and small jobs common to Saint Louis's slaves.[2]

In the wake of war made inevitable by Scott's lawsuit against Sandford, Missouri adopted a constitution quietly allowing that "separate schools may be established for the children of African descent." Funds to support public schools for black and white children were to be divided "in proportion to the number of children, without regard to color."[3] By the time the 1920s roared in the East, Missouri led in the South in the educational opportunities, meager as they were, offered to its former slaves' grandchildren.

Jefferson City's Lincoln University was the crown jewel of the state's segregated schools for black citizens. Not to be confused with Thurgood Marshall's alma mater in Pennsylvania, Lincoln was publicly funded and more of an advanced high school than a college. By August of 1935, as Charles Hamilton Houston coached Marshall through defending Maryland's appeal of their trial court victory in *Murray*, he learned from his fellow Harvard Law School alumnus Sidney Redmond that the president of Lincoln University's senior class wanted to enroll in the University of Missouri School of Law.[4]

Redmond was Saint Louis's most prominent African American lawyer. Influential in the politics of both the NAACP and Saint Louis, the Harvard College and Harvard Law graduate touted to Houston the bona fides of a young man impeccably credentialed to become an NAACP plaintiff. Lloyd Gaines was one of eleven children born to a farming husband and wife in Mississippi. He was four when his father died. In the Great Migration his family surged North, but, like so many Deep South survivors, the Gaineses made it only as far as the northernmost state in the old Confederacy. Lloyd's widowed mother found work in Saint Louis and he found a path of academic achievement that promised eventual sanctuary among his new hometown's three dozen black attorneys. Graduating valedictorian of segregated Vashon High School earned him a scholarship to Missouri's Lincoln University; his graduation photograph betrayed a son unsmiling between boy and manhood, tall in cuffed cream pants and thin as his necktie with a face too earnest by years. At Lincoln Lloyd again excelled, was elected president of his class and graduated in three and a half years with a bachelor's degree in history.

Lloyd applied to the University of Missouri School of Law and in response received a letter of interest from the registrar, S. W. Canada, who apparently had no inkling that Lincoln was Missouri's state-funded college for black citizens. Canada requested Gaines's transcript and soon thereafter learned of both Lincoln University and the race of its students. Gaines promptly received a rejection letter advising him either to study law at Lincoln—which had no law school—or to enroll in a university in another state, one whose public law schools admitted black applicants. If he chose the latter, Missouri would pay his tuition.

Sidney Redmond excitedly explained to Houston that Gaines was interested in neither option; the twenty-three-year-old wanted to attend the University of Missouri School of Law and was eager to allow the NAACP to file suit on his behalf.

For reasons never explained, Houston greeted news of his potential plaintiff coolly. He advised Redmond to search for other possible litigants but none proved available, and so, on Gaines's behalf in 1936, the NAACP sued the registrar of the University of Missouri in a case filed as *Missouri ex rel. Gaines v. Canada*. Houston's so captioning the suit emphasized the fight as he saw it: Lloyd Gaines was acting *ex relatione*, on behalf of the state of Missouri, even if Missouri was too obtuse to realize it.

The special counsel was optimistic about victory. For all the fanfare greeting its announcement, *Murray* stood precedent only in Maryland; because the association had won at both trial and appeal, *Murray* was Maryland's case to appeal to the Supreme Court of the United States, and, for whatever reasons political and legal, Maryland folded, granting Houston and Marshall their greatest victory yet but robbing them of federal precedent. On behalf of a Saint Louis striver about whom he remained uneasy, Houston hoped to exceed *Murray*'s reach. "I firmly believe," he wrote to Redmond, "the Missouri case is going to set the pace for Negro professional and graduate education for the next generation."[5] In the summer of 1936 he traveled to Missouri with a hope-burdened faith.

THAT SUMMER HOUSTON came to a painful realization about his personal life. He busied himself with near-incessant NAACP travel, preparing the *Gaines* appeal and maintaining advisory ties with the family law firm, but the weariness that alone greeted him each night only brought into relief the loneliness that daylight, work and worry kept at bay.

On his every trip back to Washington, he visited Mag, but by now their hours together were like a penance. In the other's fallen face each saw thirteen years of memory and distance, a marriage that never failed so much as it slipped away.

IN HOUSTON & HOUSTON's upstairs downtown office, Charlie's father, William, maintained a practice more robust than ever. Charlie later would joke with Thurgood about his keeping the firm's flame lit so that ole Turkey would have a place to work when the NAACP's legal defense coffers at last ran dry. His concern for financial matters pleased his father, whom for years Charlie bemused with his apparent preference for jobs as demanding as they were low-paying.

Like any small law firm's senior partner in 1936, William employed a legal secretary who perhaps in another era would have been his junior partner. Henrietta Williams was a lovely daughter of the District whose keen interest in law and its practice attracted Charlie as much as the infectious smile she shone with easy confidence. The thirty-two-year-old legal secretary was not intimidated by Charlie's formal mien or his imposing intellect. During his visits she would ask after the NAACP's legal work and listen intently to stories of black folks' plight from coast to coast. Far from merely flattering the boss's son, Henrietta was genuinely interested in the work of one of the nation's most famous lawyers. That Charlie so treasured her conversation because he was lonely and, at age forty-two stirred, perhaps for the first time, with the joyous turmoil of falling head over heels in love were privacies she showed no signs of knowing.

Before his friendship with Henrietta could swell past propriety, Charlie approached Mag, asked her for divorce, tried to reconcile her to what they both had known for some time now. Mrs. Houston would not so summarily end their marriage. The woman who two and a half decades earlier had complied with his instruction to write the word *perhaps* twenty-five times because she had spelled it *prehaps* in a letter to him reminded her husband that she was Catholic and there was no divorce in the Church. But rather than decide immediately, she would confer with his parents, who had opened their home to her as a teenager.

Over the next four seasons Mag was persuaded to grant Charlie's request for divorce. In the summer of 1937, the couple divorced in Nevada. He married Henrietta just a few months later and the couple happily settled in Harlem. Mag begrudged him nothing and decades later would remember him fondly in interviews.

HOUSTON ARRIVED IN SAINT LOUIS on July 6, 1936. He and Redmond went straight to work on Gaines's case, sweating and scribbling in Redmond's office long after the evening sun went down.

In Sidney Redmond, Houston had a kindred spirit. The Saint Louis attorney dedicated his unapologetically disciplined manner to both the private and public interest sectors. Like Houston, he had come to believe at Harvard that in legal realism lay black Americans' path to achieving the equal protection guaranteed them by the Constitution. Legal realists like Houston and Redmond understood law as a means to an end, a tool to be sharpened and wielded to craft an America as just as it purported to be. When the University of Missouri rejected Lloyd Gaines because of his race, it rejected every qualified member of his race. That the law school excluded tax-paying black Missourians was injustice reaping tangible misfortune. Even as it bubbled with promising pockets of black business, Saint Louis could boast only thirty or so African American attorneys and most of them were the older provincial type Houston lambasted because they did "not know how to study and [were] too shiftless to learn."[6] These were not lawyers who could uplift the race and they were not the sort of lawyer Lloyd Gaines sought to be.

Houston and Redmond outlined their cross-examinations. Some witnesses proved more sophisticated than most, some were more hostile than others; officials scheduled to testify for the University of Missouri's law school promised to be both. Lightning would not strike twice and the lawyers knew how long were their odds of winning the trial. Missouri was not Maryland. As a threshold matter, the university excluded black applicants as a matter of state law, not administrative edict. The lawyers' task loomed daunting. They retired early on the night of July 9; tomorrow would be the first day of trial and they would rise at four fifteen to drive the 120 miles to Columbia.[7]

FROM RISE TO SET THE SUN scorched all of Missouri during the summer of 1936. Cities baked in stench and parched fields cracked open. In Boone County a drought brought farms and farmers to helplessness. Sweat crept down crevasses in leathered faces held in idle hands. Slowly, steadily, the farmers made their way to the county's seat. In Columbia stood the courthouse and clerks' offices and men in neckties who could help them get relief. Like the hungry animals they no longer could feed, men herded up the steps, into this line and that, stained and unshaven, and waited to tell their stories.

As Charles Houston led his client and trial team past this weathered throng, he wondered why there were not more Negroes among those shuffling into the courtroom. Hadn't the association's local branches publicized the trial date?

Yes, they had, Redmond replied, but the two recent lynchings in Boone County deterred most from attending.

Before nine thirty that morning the courtroom reached nearly one hundred degrees.[8] The curious spectacle of black lawyers in court provided welcome diversion for the ruddy white men corralled into relief lines. Along with more than a hundred University of Missouri law students, the farmers crowded the courtroom to capacity. The few black spectators sat crammed next to their white peers; neither the courthouse nor its restrooms nor its water fountains were segregated.

The NAACP attorneys were surprised to learn that they would sit at the same table as the university's lawyers. Houston, Redmond and Henry Espy exchanged greetings and shook hands with opposing counsel, then all and each sat, inches apart. The seating was so tight that the attorneys "looked down one another's throats."[9] Houston was incredulous: "For private conferences at the table we almost had to go into a football huddle."[10]

The close quarters and airless swelter inclined Judge W. M. Dinwiddie toward leniency. Houston was relieved when, before opening arguments, "the Court and all concerned agreed to remove coats so we had a shirt-sleeve trial."[11]

The judge then invited Gaines's lawyers to proceed with their case and, with hundreds of eyes glaring into his back, Redmond rose to address the court. His opening statement was a dispassionate recitation of the facts plaintiff's counsel would enter into evidence. An intelligent and gifted young man, Lloyd Gaines had graduated first in his high school class and was president of his college class. His professors at Missouri's Lincoln University praised him as "an earnest young man who wants to get somewhere," a "conscientious, painstaking" student who would be "an asset in any community where he happens to work."[12] Mr. Gaines wanted to become a lawyer and, with his college diploma and stellar transcript in hand, applied to the

University of Missouri School of Law. His application was received favorably and it appeared that he would be admitted to the law school—until the university learned his race. As soon as the defendant, university registrar S. W. Canada, learned that Mr. Gaines was a Negro, his application was doomed. The university rejected Mr. Gaines from its law school solely because of his race and, in doing so, violated his rights under Missouri law, Missouri public policy and the Constitution of the United States.[13]

Redmond sat down at the sole counsels' table and Kansas City attorney William Hogsett rose to deliver the university's opening statement. Hogsett was swooping and dramatic; he lauded Gaines's ambition and extolled his academic achievements. Indeed as a Missouri citizen Mr. Gaines had every right to earn a law degree, but he could not earn it at the University of Missouri. As the university's board of curators explained in its rejection letter, "The people of Missouri," through their legislature, had "forbidden the attendance . . . of a colored person at the University of Missouri."[14] This was settled law and it was constitutional law. Hogsett's voice rose and dove with his gestures and the white farmers nudged and nodded to each other in approval of his oratory. Hogsett addressed the press corps' table much as he did the bench, staring down scribblers with unvarnished constitutional truth. If Mr. Gaines refused to accept Missouri's offer to pay his tuition at an out-of-state law school, he should apply to Lincoln University, which might develop a course of legal study upon his expressing interest.

"Call your first witness," Judge Dinwiddie instructed plaintiff's counsel.[15]

Sidney Redmond called Lloyd Gaines to take the witness stand. As Hogsett had addressed the press to stoke public opinion, Gaines's attorneys spoke to the record for the appeal they thought inevitable. Before closing arguments Houston would confide to his office memorandum file, "It is beyond expectation that the court will decide in our favor, so we had just as well get ready for the appeal."[16] After the plaintiff swore on a King James Bible to tell the whole truth and nothing but, his lawyer laid evidentiary foundation by asking about Gaines's academic record. Then, gently as if to accentuate his client's youth, he asked, "Have you made up your mind as to what you wish to do with your life?"

"I wish to practice law."

"To what law schools have you made application?"

"I have made application only to the University of Missouri."[17]

Why didn't he want to accept the state's offer to attend a public law school in another state?

There were several reasons. First, Missouri was "a very good law school" and it was "nearer home" in case he "wanted to make a fast trip home and back." Moreover, it would be less expensive than attending an out-of-state school, "taking into account the facts of transportation and communication." And, better than any other law school could, the University of Missouri would prepare him "to practice law here within the state of Missouri."

If admitted, would he obey the university's rules and regulations?

"Yes, sir."

Redmond had no further questions.

Hogsett's cross-examination sought to paint Gaines into the corner of admitting that he was but an instrument of the NAACP's nationwide legal quest to desegregate America's white universities. Before or after he applied, had Gaines "ever seen a colored student in Missouri University?"[18]

No, he had not.

Did his lawyers persuade him "to bring this suit?"

"No, that is my idea—about this suit."[19]

Why didn't he accept the state's offer to attend law school at the University of Iowa?

Because Iowa promised its students "special attention to the needs of the residents of Iowa, for the practice of law within Iowa."

Like most lawyers worth their fee, Hogsett ended his cross-examination with a question to which he presumed there was but one truthful answer, and like some witnesses worth their case, Gaines replied with an answer that could best be described as inaccurate. "Mr. Gaines, did you believe that Negroes were barred from attending the Law School of the University of Missouri?"

"No sir, I did not."[20]

The plaintiff's next witness was the law school's dean, William Masterson. Houston would examine him as a hostile witness, that is, by asking questions beckoning yes or no answers. Howard's former law school dean enjoyed a reputation as a deft examiner, and Masterson girded himself in the witness box.

A student desirous of practicing law in Missouri would do well to attend the University of Missouri School of Law, wouldn't he?

Not necessarily: A legal education was a legal education regardless of what school a lawyer attended.

But at the university "you pay particular attention to Missouri decisions and Missouri law, do you not?"

"We do not."

The university's law review devoted at least one article per issue to matters of Missouri law, did it not?

Yes, it did.

But the law school did not focus on Missouri law.

No, it did not. Mr. Gaines could get just as good an education in Illinois, Iowa or Kansas as he could in Missouri. The schools used the same books and taught the same laws. In fact, Dean Masterson explained, Mr. Gaines could receive a better education at a new law school for Negroes at Missouri's Lincoln University. He could participate more in substantive discussions "with just two or three students in the class."

If Missouri won, however, Houston's client would be the first and only student sitting in class. "But if you had only one student, wouldn't you lose all that?"

No, because in such a case the student's experience would be even more "time-saving."

Satisfied that Masterson's testimony sufficiently strained credulity, Houston moved to questions regarding the law school's admissions process.

The dean testified that he could not remember any details concerning the admissions process at his law school.

Houston then inquired about the school's budget, but the witness could remember nothing about that either. It was "the most complete lapse of memory" Houston had "ever witnessed." While the university's lawyers performed for the press and the gallery as well as the judge, Houston knew his audience was the woman taking the trial's transcript—the record on which Gaines's attorneys would base their appeal.

After Masterson, Houston called to the stand the named defendant, university registrar Silas Woodson Canada, from whom he wanted evidence that the law school rejected Gaines's application solely because of his race.

Canada easily complied. And Negroes were the only race excluded from the university?

Yes, that was true.

"Did you admit a Chinese student?"

Yes.

"Japanese students?"

Yes, sir.

"Hindu students?"

Yes.

"The only students you bar would be students of African descent, is that right?"

"Other things being equal, I think so, yes, sir."[21]

Houston called a few other witnesses to testify to the law school's impressive budget, the fact that only three Negroes had joined the Missouri bar in the past five years and there were only forty-five Negro lawyers in the whole state, and to rebut university officials' testimony that Missouri's Lincoln University could establish a viable law school when in fact the college was "an embryo university."[22] Plaintiff's counsel rested their case and the court stood in recess.

When trial resumed, the defense laid bare its strategy of calling a few of Missouri's most prominent citizens to testify in the integrated courthouse that the university's excluding black Missourians was just an expression of the state's public policy and way of life. The state's former attorney general opined that segregated education in Missouri was "the settled policy of this state ever since you have known it"; university president and state senator F. M. McDavid testified that state law had required the law school to reject Gaines's application.

"What would be the effect," Hogsett asked his client, "of the admission of Negroes into the University of Missouri?"

"I think it would create a great amount of trouble." Integrating the university would do violence to "the traditions of this city and school, running through nearly a hundred years."

On cross-examination, Houston demanded whether the state's "hundred years tradition" should be allowed to "bind progress forever."[23]

"I don't know what you mean by 'progress.' "[24] Even if it meant creating a law school from scratch at Lincoln, the state of Missouri would fulfill its duty to Mr. Gaines.

"They give Negroes a piece of paper, while the white citizens have an actuality," Houston retorted out of character. *Lose your temper, lose your case* was his mantra at Howard, and never did he lose his temper in Judge Dinwiddie's courtroom. But testimony replete with half truths and obfuscations had drawn his temper taut. He tacked immediately back on course. Was the university's president "familiar with the fact that a Negro boy was granted admission to the School of Law of the University of Maryland?"

"I think so."

"Did you make any investigation, in considering the Gaines case, to find out whether any disciplinary problems had arisen at the University of Maryland?"

No, he had not.

Then what led him to believe that admitting Negroes to the University of Missouri would cause disciplinary problems?

Well, McDavid had "talked with a good many students about this," and they agreed that it would be "a most unfortunate thing—an unhappy thing."

Lloyd Gaines's attending law school in his home state would be "an unhappy thing"?

McDavid met Houston's iron gaze. "I don't think he would be happy and I don't think the other crowd would be happy."[25]

It was all Houston could do to dismiss the witness, complete the trial and return to New York City with sufficient verve to outline the appellate points he knew to be necessary even before Judge Dinwiddie's decision arrived two weeks later ruling in the university's favor. After presiding over a trial that would be reviewed by the supreme courts of Missouri and the United States, the judge did not bother even to write an opinion.

HOUSTON APPEALED to the Missouri Supreme Court and the issues presented were of such significance that the court agreed to hear oral arguments en banc, with all judges on the bench. Sidney Redmond flatly told reporters, "We're all set for a long, hard fight."[26] The months between Gaines's summer trial and winter appeal brought Marshall's October hiring, and having an assistant special counsel allowed Houston more time to

devote to preparing the *Gaines* appellate brief and oral argument. In time
the NAACP special counsel arrived back in Saint Louis, checked into the
Hotel Washington and telephoned Sidney Redmond and Henry Espy to
confirm his safe arrival. The next morning the three lawyers traveled to
the Missouri Supreme Court in Jefferson City.

Two months later the court unanimously affirmed Judge Dinwiddie's
decision.[27] Missouri's law mandating that "all youths, resident of the state
of Missouri, over the age of sixteen years, shall be admitted to . . . the university of the state of Missouri" did not mean, as Houston contended, "all
youths."[28] The fact was that "all youths" did not "include negro as well as
white youths."[29] The court explained that "there are differences in races,
and between individuals of the same race, not created by human laws,
some of which can never be eradicated."[30] Citing *Plessy v. Ferguson* and its
progeny, Missouri's supreme court opined flatly that "the right of a state
to separate the races for the purpose of education is no longer an open
question."[31] Again the state refused to admit to law school the man *Time*
magazine ridiculed as "Blackamoor Gaines."[32]

Charles Hamilton Houston was a lawyer never pleased to lose a case,
but he also was an activist impatient by constitution and harried by his
own restlessness. Had the Missouri Supreme Court ruled for his client, the
precedent would have bound only the University of Missouri law school;
Murray and *Gaines* would have opened doors in but two states. The NAACP
could not litigate state by state like salesmen knocking on doors. The time
had come for federal precedent to change the lives of black and white Americans alike, to demand the possible and insist it necessary. In the Supreme
Court of the United States Houston filed a petition for a writ of certiorari
in which he summarized *Missouri ex rel. Gaines*'s case history, postulated
the legal issues presented and argued why those issues and this case warranted intervention by the Court. If the Supreme Court granted certiorari,
Gaines's fate would be decided by the nation's highest court. If the Court
denied certiorari, the Missouri Supreme Court's ruling would stand. His
request garnered the votes of at least four justices necessary to grant certiorari.

As HIS CASE WOUND ITS WAY through appellate courts, Lloyd Gaines tired
of waiting for lawyers to vindicate his right to a graduate school educa-

tion. He tested into the master's degree program in the University of Michigan's economics department and, with financial help from the NAACP and Alpha Phi Alpha, he enrolled in school in Ann Arbor. Gaines knew by now he was symbol as much as student. At Michigan he again excelled academically and savored fellowship with his fraternity brothers on a campus white but not hostile to their presence.

WORK DROVE MONTHS like wind to rain between the Missouri Supreme Court's *Gaines* decision and November 8, 1938. That day, just one before justices of the Supreme Court of the United States heard oral arguments on *Missouri ex rel. Gaines. v. Canada*, Charles Hamilton Houston read again gavel to gavel the *Gaines* trial transcript. He then placed folders from the *Gaines* file into his briefcase. Then he donned his coat against Washington's autumn chill and trod up to the law school where years ago he had pushed, pulled and turned tide like a moon indifferent to the sea's truculence.

At Howard he presented his oral argument before students and professors alike and took questions from them all as if before the black-robed nine. Houston enjoyed preparing for oral argument like this. Some had never before seen Houston in person and in their awe could find no questions, but others grilled the famed former dean imperiously as any justice. After Houston had answered all questions, he received suggestions from the audience.[33]

THE SUPREME COURT of the United States in 1938 was not the Court that had stood just three years before. President Franklin D. Roosevelt had proven unable to "pack" the Court, but he had made two appointments in the past fifteen months: Hugo Black was a former Ku Klux Klansman who would surprise litigants and lawyers for years to come by standing ardently with oppressed minority groups; Stanley Reed was less reliable a vote but remained a persuadable man.

The same could not be said of the most blatantly bigoted justice to sit on the Supreme Court in the twentieth century, James McReynolds, who was born and raised on a plantation.[34] McReynolds's ears and nose were as pronounced as his accent. The serenity in his gaze deceived; he was a man at war with much of what he saw. The conservative southerner Woodrow Wilson rewarded McReynolds's campaign support by appointing him attorney general, but his irascible disposition and general incompetence limited his cabinet service to just one year. Seeking a dignified way to fire McReynolds, Wilson nominated him to the Supreme Court in 1914 and the Senate consented. McReynolds was fifty-two years old and a confirmed bachelor. When he died thirty-two years later, he was buried near the plantation where he was born.

On the Court, McReynolds remained an unabashed anti-Semite who not only refused to speak to fellow justices Benjamin Cardozo and Louis Brandeis, but would not stand next to either to take the Court's official photograph. When Cardozo died not long before *Gaines*'s oral argument, McReynolds refused to attend his funeral. "As you know," he explained, "I am not always to be found when there is a Hebrew abroad. So my 'inability' to attend must not surprise you."[35]

One afternoon McReynolds strolled downstairs from his office to have his hair cut by the Court's barber. As the African American barber pinned the sheet behind him, McReynolds snorted, "Gates, tell me, where is this nigger university in Washington, D.C?" Gates wordlessly removed the white cloth from across the justice, walked around to face him and, as another justice described, replied in a "very calm and dignified manner, 'Mr. Justice, I am shocked that any Justice would call a Negro a 'nigger.' There is a Negro college in Washington, D.C. Its name is Howard University and we are very proud of it.' McReynolds muttered some kind of an apology and Gates resumed his work in silence."[36]

As he led the NAACP's attorneys into the nation's highest court, Charles Houston knew McReynolds had already decided against his client. He was right: As soon as Houston rose to say "May it please the Court," McReynolds turned his chair around and faced the wall for the duration of Houston's allotted thirty minutes.[37]

Conversely, Houston, Redmond, Espy and Marshall hoped to persuade Chief Justice Charles Evans Hughes that the university had violated Lloyd Gaines's constitutional right to equal protection of the laws. Hughes's vote would prove pivotal because, even aside from his stature as the chief justice, the former two-term New York governor was a proven consensus builder; associate justices respected his opinion and admired his intellect. Hughes, an abolitionist minister's son, was serving his second stint on America's highest court, having resigned in 1916 after six years to run for president against Woodrow Wilson. For President Warren Harding he served as secretary of state. President Herbert Hoover appointed him chief justice in 1930.

During his years as an associate and chief justice, Hughes penned twice as many opinions as his colleagues, always with an eye toward the same realist philosophy upon which Houston was constructing the legal civil rights struggle. "We are under a Constitution," he opined, "but the Constitution is what the judges say it is."[38] When Hughes died in 1948, Walter White would praise his vigilance against lynching and the wholesale deprivation of black Americans' constitutional rights. The Court in 1938 was diverse in ability and ideology, but Houston's team believed that if they could convince the chief, they could sway the Court. Justice Cardozo's seat had not yet been filled after his death, so Houston presented before eight justices, only seven of whom faced him as he spoke.

ON DECEMBER 12, 1938, Chief Justice Hughes announced the Supreme Court's decision in *Missouri ex rel. Gaines v. Canada.* He had written it himself and, true to form, garnered five of his seven fellow justices to concur in the opinion. In *Gaines* Hughes crafted an opinion taut with constitutional clarity. After noting that "the fact remains that instruction in law for Negroes is not now afforded by the State, either at Lincoln or elsewhere within the State," the Court dispensed with the university's argument that legal redress was unavailable to Gaines because he had not applied first to Lincoln.[39] Hughes's majority likewise dismissed Missouri's proffered discussion of the high-quality legal education available to Gaines in Iowa, Indiana and Kansas.

With lucidity befitting finality, *Gaines* declared that the question was "what opportunities Missouri itself furnishes to white students and denies to negroes solely upon the ground of color."[40] The federal Constitution required each state to provide for its black and white citizens equally, if separately, and Missouri could not shift this responsibility to its neighbors; "the State was bound to furnish within its borders facilities for legal education substantially equal to those which the State there afforded for persons of the white race."[41] Because Missouri furnished no separate but equal law school for Gaines to attend and because Gaines's right to a legal education was "a personal one," the state had to admit him to the University of Missouri School of Law.[42]

It is difficult to embellish the significance of the *Gaines* victory. Although based ostensibly on the well-settled doctrine of a state's ability to segregate citizens by race, *Gaines* weakened the holding of *Plessy v. Ferguson* in two crucial respects: First, *Gaines* demonstrated that the Court no longer would defer to southern states' dubious claims of providing equal educations for their black and white citizens; the chief justice's opinion made clear that the judiciary henceforth would closely examine whether a defendant-state actually provided equal education to its residents regardless of race. Second, by declaring Gaines's educational right to be "a personal one," the justices preempted any state's claim that it need not establish a substantially equal school for one or two black students.[43] Gaines's right to equal protection of the laws had been violated and therefore Gaines must be made whole in the only way immediately available: enrolling in the law school. *Gaines* was *Murray* writ large—binding federal precedent and an undeniable victory for Houston's equalization strategy.

NATIONWIDE REACTION to the decision predictably varied by region. The *Iowa City Iowan* quipped, "The surprising thing is not the nature of the decision, but the fact that such a decision actually had to be made affecting a neighboring university."[44] The *New York Times* editorial board declared, "Once more the Supreme Court has spoken out in defense of equality of human rights."[45] South Carolina's *Charleston News and Courier* worried that admitting black applicants would reduce southern higher education "to a lowly estate in public opinion" while the *Fort Worth Star-Telegram* encouraged southern states to expand black citizens' educational opportunities "in the form of annexes to state universities or enlargement of existing Negro colleges."[46]

The University of Missouri's student-run newspaper, the *Missouri Student*, offered perhaps the most sober editorial reaction North or South: "We who are students will have no say as to what will be done about the Negro attending school, but it is we who will go to school with him . . . Our actions in accepting him will define our status as Americans." The student-editors' eloquence rang clear with naked American optimism: "Our pilgrim, continental Gettysburg tradition is freedom and equality for all. It is our cue to pioneer the nation out of this last frontier of racial prejudice and superstition."[47]

In interviews Houston expressed confidence that states would accept their responsibilities to open equal schools for black students or admit them into existing universities. Chief Justice Hughes's opinion "completely knocked out as permanent policy" the notion that states could satisfy their constitutional obligations to black citizens by paying their way to out-of-state universities.[48]

From Ann Arbor, Gaines praised the Court's decision with words that soon would prove ironic: "Organized pressure has opened another great gate for our people . . . may we all see that this golden opportunity is never neglected, lost or forgotten."[49]

AFTER THE SUPREME COURT announced the decision bearing his name, Lloyd Gaines returned from Michigan to Saint Louis, arriving just in time for 1938's New Year's Eve celebrations. Amid drinks and cigarette-smoke plumes, he told friends he planned to remain in his hometown until September, when he planned to leave for law school. A week and a half later, he spoke with members of the local NAACP branch and assured them that he was "ready, willing and able to enroll in the law department of the university and had the fullest intention of doing so."[50] Gaines took a job as a gas station attendant and the blustery winter weeks blew by.

After learning his employer was selling low-quality fuel at premium fuel prices, Gaines quit the gas station. At the request of Kansas City's NAACP branch, he left Saint Louis to speak at the Centennial Methodist Church and stayed over a few days looking for work and finding none. Just as elsewhere in America, Kansas City's black folks had followed his case closely and admired his courage and scholastic ability; although work was slow in their town, surely in Chicago he could find a good job. Lloyd boarded a Chicago-bound train.

Days later he mailed a letter to his mother from the Stock Yards Station. In it Gaines laid bare his desolation and disillusionment. He sought "to make [his] own way" and hoped "by this letter to make very clear to [her] the reasons" he came to Chicago.[51] He had found "no possible opening for work" in Kansas City so he traveled to Chicago and stayed with a family friend "before getting a room at the 'Y,'" where he was paid up for the next three nights. In Chicago he had not "been able to dig up a single job prospect, but [was] still trying."[52]

> As for publicity relative to the university case, I have found that my race still likes to applaud, shake hands, pat me on the back and say how great and noble is the idea, how historical and socially significant the case but—and there it ends. Off and out of the confines of publicity columns, I am just a man—not one who has fought and sacrificed to make the case possible, one who is still fighting and sacrificing—almost the "supreme sacrifice" to see that it is a complete and lasting success for thirteen million Negroes—no!—just another man. Sometimes I wish I were a plain, ordinary man whose name no one recognized.[53]

Morning rose on Gaines's fourth day at the YMCA and he had no money for a fifth. His fraternity brothers in Chicago asked him to stay with them at their chapter's house. A short while later he wrote his mother a terse, cryptic postcard that read entirely: "Goodbye, if you don't hear from me anymore, you'll know I'll be all right." Postcard in hand, he donned his overcoat, said he was going "to get some stamps" and stepped out into Chicago's cold night rain.[54] No one who knew him ever again saw Lloyd Gaines.

THE *NEW YORK TIMES* editorial board was wrong as a three-dollar bill when it doubted "that the critics who so often denounce the Supreme Court for 'obstructing the will of the people as expressed through their Legislatures' will object strongly to [the *Gaines*] decision. They will recognize in this case that the Court was acting in accordance with the provision of the Constitution."[55]

Led by self-proclaimed "unreconstructed rebel" John D. Taylor, Missouri's legislature overwhelmingly passed a law to "establish whatever graduate and professional schools [were] necessary to make Lincoln University the equivalent of the University of Missouri."[56] The law was decried nationwide as a cheap skirt around the Supreme Court's opinion, but Missouri vowed to open a law school for Lloyd Gaines at Lincoln University by September 1939. It rented a building and hired four professors and a dean and, on September 21, opened with thirty students.

The Colored Clerks Circle, "an organization of clerks in various stores," picketed the ad hoc law school at Lincoln University, their signs decrying the "Jim Crow law school" and Missouri's "subterfuge."[57] While school officials claimed that enrollment held steady at thirty students, reports indicated that the meager student body had decreased to eighteen since the picketing began.[58]

Missouri's supreme court called a hearing to determine whether Lincoln's new law school complied with the U.S. Supreme Court's ruling. In advance of the hearing, both sides sought to depose witnesses for testimony to enter into evidence at the hearing. In October Houston returned to Saint Louis to represent Lloyd Gaines during his deposition but no one could find the famous plaintiff. The *New York Amsterdam News* exclaimed, "Lloyd Gaines has disappeared!"[59]

Soon after he first filed suit against the university, Gaines had begun receiving death threats. The nationwide search for him was fraught with unspoken fear. Newspapers published his picture daily and asked anyone with information to please contact the NAACP at 69 Fifth Avenue in New York City. As the *Chicago Defender* reported, "At almost every gathering place, one [ran] into persons with 'inside information.' "[60] Indeed rumors roiled upstream and down: Gaines had been murdered and buried by segregationists; he was teaching in upstate New York; he had been bribed by wealthy southerners who demanded he expatriate to Mexico; despondent and destitute, he had killed himself. His lawyers had not heard from him in over six months; his mother was said to be frantic.[61]

By March 1940, Houston surrendered his client to the wind. "The N.A.A.C.P. has exhausted all means of looking for him," he told an interviewer.[62] Missouri's supreme court canceled its hearing to determine whether Lincoln University's makeshift law school, which would close in a few years for lack of students, satisfied the federal Supreme Court's *Gaines* mandate. Houston returned to Washington, Redmond and Espy to private practice.

Whatever happened to Lloyd Gaines has never been discovered. His remains remain unfound decades after his face disappeared among too many or none like it at all. Gaines never studied at the University of Missouri's law school but today his portrait peers down at students of all races: He wears a three-piece suit, his cheeks are plumper than they should be, his slight smile wider than it would be. That the law school would stall for twelve years after his Supreme Court victory before admitting an African American student would have saddened him immensely; perhaps, somewhere, it did.

An Outside Man

THE *GAINES* YEARS left to Marshall the "evangelizing" and stump speaking that had been Houston's bailiwick. He logged thousands of miles speaking at membership-drive rallies and meeting with African American schoolteachers and students to report their oppressive scholastic conditions back to 69 Fifth Avenue. Houston remained the unvarnished voice of the association's legal campaign, but to its burgeoning rank and file Marshall was fast becoming its face. Quick with a joke or a flicked flame to light a member's cigarette, the dapper dandy relished visits to NAACP branches.

Executive secretary Walter White recognized Marshall's easy rapport with folks lofty and low and, even before hiring him as assistant special counsel, enlisted him in the association's lobbying efforts. As early as 1934 White asked for Marshall's help "in the fight against lynching in the next Congress, which will be a bitter and difficult struggle."[1]

Under White the fight to end lynching had become the NAACP's signature effort. Democratic senators Edward Costigan and Robert Wagner drafted a bill that would make lynching a federal offense and would grant federal criminal jurisdiction over local law enforcement officers who abetted or permitted the lynching of suspects in their custody. In no small part due to relentless pressure from association members, a majority of America's senators supported the Costigan-Wagner Bill. Southern senators, however, employed the Senate's rules of order to prevent the bill from coming to a vote. Running for reelection, President Franklin Roosevelt refused to utter a word in favor of the bill for fear of losing southern votes.

Upon Congress's return from Christmas break in early 1935, Marshall wrote to his home state's Great War hero–senator. Millard Tydings was a University of Maryland Law School alumnus and certainly recognized Thurgood Marshall's name from newspapers and conversation. "This morning while talking to the Executive Secretary of the National Association for the Advancement of Colored People," Marshall began, "I was informed that you had not taken a stand on the Costigan-Wagner Bill. This was indeed as much of a shock to me as I am sure it will be to many of your constituents when they become aware of the fact."[2] He assured Tydings that the senator had "always been considered by us as a champion of fair-play and justice"; he "trust[ed] this will continue."[3] Notably, Marshall asked neither if Tydings supported the bill nor if he would consider supporting the bill. Rather: "I trust . . . that when I am called upon I can say that you are one hundred per-cent behind this bill which is aimed at the most disgraceful blemish upon the good-name of this country. We all look to you."[4]

Testament to Marshall's rising stature was Senator Tyding's forthright two-page reply in which he admitted to "hav[ing] had a great deal of difficulty in coming to a decision on this bill."[5] As Tydings saw it, the root problems were "the failure of the courts to function properly and the long delay in bringing the accused to trial." He "believe[d] had trials been had speedily and quickly, most if not all of the lynchings would have been avoided."[6]

Tydings's logic galled Marshall. "I respectfully submit that in view of the facts as they actually exist to-day your reasons are unsound."[7] He dismissed Tydings's concerns for local authority by charging southern states with "open treason and rebellion."[8] Tydings replied that Marshall wrote "as though [Tydings] had expressed [him]self as opposed to the pending anti-lynching legislation" when he had merely expressed his concerns regarding the bill.[9]

When time came due for his committee to vote on the Costigan-Wagner Bill, Senator Tydings departed on a suddenly urgent trip to the Virgin Islands. The bill was "bitterly opposed on Eastern Shore, Maryland, [while] simultaneously advocated for by colored voters in Maryland,"[10] White wrote to Marshall. About Tydings's hastily arranged trip, White quipped, "Looks like he is trying to get out from under."[11]

Marshall's NAACP practice all but subsumed his days during 1936, and his lobbying for federal antilynching legislation gained intensity. He assumed a more pragmatic tone as he sought to persuade congressional representatives. "The States, from the lynching records," he explained, "show themselves unable to cope with the situation. We, therefore, are calling upon our representatives to take steps toward the passage of a Federal Anti-lynching Bill."[12] He reminded them that the antilynching bills enjoyed considerable white support: "From the standpoint of the good-thinking white citizenry, it appears from the testimony before the Senate Committees of the hearings of the past anti-lynching bills that they feel concerned over the fact that lynching tends to create open rebellion and disregard for law enforcement agencies."[13] No longer were the states committing "treason and open rebellion"; it was the mob members.

White thought letters such as these were "swell" and advised Marshall to "keep up the pressure and the publicity."[14] He then asked him to write to House Speaker Joseph W. Byrns and to President Roosevelt.

By 1936's ninth lynching in as many months, a flag hung from association headquarters in Manhattan, white block letters on black: A MAN WAS LYNCHED YESTERDAY.[15] Not three weeks after Franklin Roosevelt's triumphant reelection that year, White wired him a telegram in which, after congratulating Roosevelt on his sweeping victory, he assured the president: [YOUR REELECTION'S] OVERWHELMING NATURE FREES YOU FROM OBLIGATION TO ANY SECTIONAL INTERESTS AND WILL UNDOUBTEDLY ENABLE YOU DURING THE NEXT FOUR YEARS TO TAKE DECISIVE ACTION AGAINST LYNCHING AND RACIAL DISCRIMINATION.[16] Nineteen thirty-six witnessed thirteen lynchings, less than half the twenty-eight such murders during the previous year, and the association attributed the decline to its "vigorous and continuous agitation for enactment of a federal anti-lynching law."[17]

As 1937 dawned, White vowed anew to persuade Congress to enact federal antilynching legislation. He asked the new assistant special counsel to travel to Washington. An antilynching bill was winding its tortured way through the House of Representatives by the time Marshall bounced aboard a D.C.-bound train and settled in for a few weeks' stay in the nation's capital. Over coffee, bourbon and cigarettes, he cajoled congressmen both racist and sympathetic. The House Judiciary Committee chairman was an irascible Texan who vowed to crush in his committee any anti-lynching bill. Marshall recognized that in the House, unlike the Senate, a single member could not block legislation, so he lobbied around the congressman. The NAACP-supported bill survived the Judiciary Committee and was reported to the House floor, where it passed.

As a lawyer who seriously had recently considered running for Congress, Marshall was ecstatic at having negotiated the Byzantine legislative process. The NAACP's thirtieth year was drawing near and America had awakened to it's formidability; the association had enemies in the House of Representatives and Marshall's toil had defeated them.

In the Senate, however, the antilynching bill remained smothered beneath southern obduracy. African American newspapers continuously blasted congress for "twiddling its thumbs over a federal anti-lynching law" as "ghastly mob murders [went] unchecked by the states," but because few black citizens in the South could vote, southern senators disregarded their black constituents' concerns as easily as they disregarded last week's weather.[18] Marshall returned to New York City without the law he had sought.

Houston swelled nonetheless with pride at his former student's maturation. Thurgood was shy of thirty years old, and in his performance on school inequality fact-finding missions, popularity-inducing travels, and proven lobbying skills, Houston saw the traits and skills that would be needed in whoever would succeed him at the helm of the NAACP's law office. By now he had even grown to envy his protégé's relish for the grind. While strolling along a city's sidewalk he remarked to Thurgood, "You know how much money you're making. And you can imagine how much money I make. And I still say you have more goddamn fun than I do."

Marshall chuckled. "Ain't no question about that."[19]

For his part, Houston was engaged in a lobbying campaign against Idaho senator William Borah's proposed resolution that effectively would repeal the Fourteenth Amendment to the U.S. Constitution. The resolution was cleverly worded, Houston explained to his Hill connections and to the press, but it "eliminated all the clauses which put teeth and protection into the amendment." Even in the same Senate that repeatedly buried antilynching legislation, Borah's resolution stood little chance of passing.

Nevertheless, under Houston's guidance the NAACP would "follow actively all developments on the Borah resolution and . . . oppose it vigorously."[20] Lobbying allowed Houston to nurture his contacts in federal Washington. It drew him more often back to his hometown, where, Houston realized, he was pining to return.

At around the time Marshall returned to New York City from Washington, Houston traveled with Mag to Reno, where they would obtain a divorce sadly overdue. When he had arrived in New York City a couple years earlier, Houston needed nothing more than respite from his hometown. Walter White's suggestion that he move to the city to devise and implement a legal battle plan to end segregation proved irresistible. During Houston's tenure as special counsel, the association kept its commitment to his work and vision. The board of directors, in the wake of the *Gaines* defeats at trial and in Missouri's supreme court, affirmed its commitment to the legal slog by declaring the campaign so "vital" that it be continued "at all costs."[21] By the time he departed for Nevada with his wife, Houston was considering whether he could continue the campaign better, if not necessarily lead it anymore, from his hometown.

He married Henrietta Williams shortly after returning East. Ten years Charlie's junior, Henrietta was a stunning woman of auburn curls and lit-lamp eyes.

The black press reported news of Houston's divorce and rapid remarrying with paparazzi's relish. After noting that on grounds of cruelty he divorced his first wife, "a well-known teacher in the public schools in Washington" and "a foster daughter of Mr. Houston's parents," the *New York Amsterdam News* informed readers that Houston "immediately" married Henrietta, leaving his ex-wife "to reside still with Mr. and Mrs. William H. Houston at 1744 S Street N.W. in Washington."[22] Although sudden, the divorce surprised few because "of many rumors concerning marital difficulties between Dr. Houston and his first wife," who, again, was "his parents' adopted daughter." Over time "gossip about him and the first Mrs. Houston became 'thick as flies'" and a trip to "America's divorce capital" was all but inevitable.[23]

Pressed for comment, Houston told reporters, "All parties made an agreement not to give any information and I would consider it ungentlemanly to do so. You can say, however, that I have introduced Henrietta as

Mrs. Houston."[24] About a week later, Mary McLeod Bethune, who then was the director of Negro affairs at the National Youth Administration, told Houston, "When I picked up a paper and saw an account of your marriage it did surprise me but the surprise was pleasant and I hope you are happy."[25]

By all accounts Charlie was happy. Henrietta was confident and convivial enough to live happily with him, to thrive in his demanding company. Supportive and interested as ever in his legal work, she agreed to accompany him back up to New York City, leaving behind the segregated District of their families and childhoods. The Houstons moved into an apartment on 149th Street and were welcomed by Walter and Gladys White, Thurgood and Buster, Roy and Minnie Wilkins and other couples and families in the vast social web woven around the NAACP's chieftains.

For all the association's swirling demands, the needs of the extended Houston family were bubbling to Charlie's attention as he and Henrietta settled into married life. In 1937 President Roosevelt nominated Houston's cousin William Hastie to the federal bench in the Virgin Islands. After typical delay and rancor the Senate consented to Hastie's nomination and he departed for the Caribbean, where news of the first black federal judge's impending arrival was greeted blissfully by residents as weary of all-white governance as their mainland brethren. Hastie would remain in the Virgin Islands for two years before returning to Washington to serve as dean of Howard Law School, and after another world war engulfed the nation, he was named special assistant to Secretary of War Henry Stimson, a position he resigned two years later to protest the military's continued segregation. Three years before Marshall led lawyers to *Brown*, Hastie was appointed and confirmed to the U.S. Court of Appeals for the Third Circuit, where he would rise to chief judge.

Hastie's leaving the District for the Virgin Islands removed another partner from the law firm that had become Houston, Houston, Hastie & Waddy. Charlie's father, William, had been asked to serve as the U.S. attorney general's special assistant. While the appointment allowed William to remain in Washington, he was a Department of Justice attorney and he no longer could perform even mundane legal work for the law firm he founded. From New York City Charlie shared his father's concern that without senior partner leadership, their family's firm might close.

Perhaps after learning from William that Charlie was entertaining notions of returning to the District, Howard University president Mordecai Johnson offered the former law school dean his old job back at a 50 percent raise over his NAACP salary. Approved by the board of trustees, the offer was welcome evidence that the labor-wounds of Houston's revolutionary tenure had healed. The university was offering him $6,000 a year and his father's back channels indicated that the university would negotiate up to $7,500.[26]

Having labored for two years beneath Walter White's imperious gaze, however, Houston felt no inspiration to toil again under Howard's apparent president-for-life Mordecai Johnson. Neither White nor Johnson had ever tried to steer him—White lacked the intellect and Johnson any reason to do so—but each exerted the influence permitted him as his organization's leader.

Houston sought professional freedom. He wanted to fight the fight as he saw fit and necessary, free from review by a president or board of directors. He had come to understand black Americans' quest for constitutional rights as a fight inextricably bound with economic struggle. When he had testified to the Senate Judiciary Committee that lynching was, for all its shameful sadism, most often a crime of economic oppression, he was suggesting the struggle's depth as he saw it: America's poor were oppressed, and those poor and black were oppressed twice over.

As early as 1934 Houston had railed against race-based wage and hour differences in speeches that sparked worried murmurs among audience members, who, like many progressives of that era, were wary of advocating workers' rights for fear of being branded socialists or communists. Habitually he challenged leftists to awaken to an economic reality which, if left unchanged, would mock their years of political effort. Throughout the South, African Americans fell victim to "the economic wage slavery and social suppression" on which those states' economies remained dependent.[27] To the Senate Finance Committee he declared on behalf of black laborers, "If we have not paid more taxes, it is because we have been denied more work." Then forcefully into the microphone: "What we want now is equal work opportunity."[28] For a man regularly chided by his father for caring little about earning a good living, Houston closely concerned himself with the lower-income black American's ability to eat decently and live with dignity.

Houston also believed the time was nigh for him to report less to the executive secretary. His tubercular condition flared beneath the strain of managing the association's every legal interest. His body racked in fits that rattled his two-hundred-pound frame. With Henrietta's consent, Charlie decided to return to Washington.

To his father he explained, "I have had the feeling all along that I am much more of an outside man than an inside man; that I usually break down under too much routine. Certainly for the present, I will grow much faster and be of much more service if I keep free to hit and fight wherever circumstances call for action." As he wrote on the eve of 1938's Internal Revenue Service deadline, finances also concerned him: "I will come home with debts practically closed out, more insurance and no money saved." He added, "But I would not give anything for the experience that I have had."[29]

"Mr. Houston began his work with the N.A.A.C.P. long before he joined the staff in New York," Walter White began in a statement so effusive one never would surmise that he scarcely would mention its honoree in his autobiography. "He gave us invaluable counsel and assistance, without remuneration. Since joining the staff, he has laid before the country and the courts in brilliant fashion the inequalities suffered by the Negro and has fought uncompromisingly for redress." Without specifying, White "regret[ted] greatly that circumstances dictate his return to Washington, but we will not be wholly deprived of his services, as he will still be available for consultation and aid, with some field work in nearby territory, as his time will permit."[30]

Charles Hamilton Houston's return to Washington was a considerable event. He was the architect of the legal campaign and thus far had overseen the movement's construction; with the latticework laid, he now was leaving the office to a man not yet thirty in whom he believed perhaps more than the young man yet believed in himself. Slightly over a year from now, eight African American students would apply to southern all-white public graduate schools. In Tennessee, Missouri and Maryland three applied to law school and one each to schools of biology, education, sociology, chemistry and journalism. Houston would represent the impeccably qualified journalism school applicant and her fight would call him again to Missouri. But by then the association's legal department would be unmistakably under Thurgood Marshall's command.

Houston retained his title of special counsel, and Marshall would solicit his advice even more frequently after becoming responsible for the NAACP's legal affairs. The coming years would find Charles Houston loyal and tireless in the fight but he henceforth would labor as an outside man.

HOPE LOOMS

O N THE SATURDAY NIGHT before Joe Louis thrashed the German boxer Max Schmeling, Walter White hosted a "formal cocktail party" at his and Gladys's well-appointed home on Harlem's Edgecomb Avenue.[1] Charlie and Henrietta and Thurgood and Buster reveled with notables like Judge Charles Toney, one of the first African Americans elected to New York State's bench. Langston Hughes laughed with them over the drinks that poured easily at 409 Edgecomb while Frederic Morrow, an attorney taller than Thurgood who would chop trail in corporate America before becoming an uneasy assistant to President Dwight D. Eisenhower, talked politics with North Carolina native Hubert Delaney, a younger African American Republican who already served as an assistant U.S. attorney in New York and who, along with Marshall, would live to see 1990.

Cigarette smoke floated on laughter as White's guests of honor arrived: Joe Louis's trainer and his wife cut a confident pose in the Whites' parlor. Joe Louis was the heavyweight champion of the world but refused full accolades until he avenged his loss to Schmeling, who was supported by the Nazi Party and one day would be wounded as a Third Reich soldier. After President Roosevelt told the champ days earlier, "Joe, we need muscles like yours to beat Germany," Louis understood the stakes: "I knew I had to get Schmeling good. I had my own personal reasons and the whole damned country was depending on me."[2] Schmeling's corner would throw his towel into the ring after 124 seconds of fighting; like Jesse Owens two years earlier, the Brown Bomber paradoxically exposed white supremacy as fallacy while bringing symbolic victory to his own white supremacist nation. There was no way the Whites' guests could have known the swiftness with which Louis would punish Schmeling, but, like the millions of Louis fans in slums, shanties and shacks worlds and blocks away, they were a buoyant and hopeful lot.

Thurgood Marshall was an engine-guest at any party he attended. His stories and jokes could be as low-down as his hoot was high-pitched, and both reduced listeners to laughter. Marshall's old law school dean, for all his tailored and pressed formalism, enjoyed a bourbon and savored his former student's conversation-performances as more than lively fellowship: They provided collective proof of his protégé's gift for cajoling and persuading friends and acquaintances as easily as juries. Courtroom and parlor were theater just the same and Marshall loved the parties. He remained, as his Lincoln classmate Langston Hughes described, "good-natured, rough, ready and uncouth."[3] An avid Louis fan, he often quoted the Brown Bomber's grammatically mangled, incisive quips, his favorite being "I glad I winned." At Walter and Gladys White's party, the talk was boxing and, as one newspaper reported, "The party menu consisted of an abundance and variety of cocktails, hors d'oeuvres, cheeses, crackers and coffee."[4] Marshall enjoyed a grand time that night even as he began to worry about taking charge of the legal campaign after Charlie Houston left New York City.

BUSTER MARSHALL WAS PROUD of her husband's promotion, but, what with all the parties and engagements, their life in New York City was more expensive than back in Baltimore, where they had lived with his family and pooled groceries and joy and ache in that bursting home on Druid Hill Avenue. Up North life and struggle were theirs alone. The man who had brought them to the city, about whom Thurgood had spoken so highly for years before she ever met him, was now returning with his fashionable wife to their hometown, and Buster could not help but be a bit jealous. Henrietta had her Charlie back; no longer would she endure his four-month train and road trips to northern California and back through the South. Houston's travels from now on would be efficient affairs—witness preparation, depositions, trials and appeals—while Thurgood would be traveling even more.

He did, however, receive a raise in annual pay from $2,400 to $2,600.

"How much is that a week?" Buster asked.[5]

It wasn't much. He persuaded her to join a Harlem co-op food market, where her work could reduce their weekly food bill. Forever fond of her wavy-haired man, Buster agreed.

MARSHALL WAS SUDDENLY alone in the office he used to share with Houston. He returned to fighting the teachers' salary equalization battles. From the border states to Florida he represented and rallied black teachers who wanted to sue their employers for pay commensurate with that of their white colleagues. Their cases would trudge through courts for years, but Marshall's frequent visits assured them that theirs were battles important not just to the local branch but to the home office of the NAACP.

Houston recognized the importance of the teacher salary cases; their success tangibly benefited the bedrock profession of the African American middle class. Before returning to Washington, he wrote Marshall from Reno, Nevada, to ask about any developments in these cases: "I still believe it is unconstitutional for a state to have two scales of pay for the same work and the same grade, based on color; and that to rely on the fact a Negro signs a contract when it is the only thing he can get is not an estoppel to assert his constitutional rights." Houston anticipated southern states' defending the unequal salaries by arguing that African American teachers, by signing employment contracts, had forfeited their right to file a lawsuit claiming those contracts violated the Constitution. This would be an issue the lawyers would have to research further, but he wanted Marshall to be aware of it.

With business out of the way, he extolled the virtues of Nevada. His cryptically ribald language revealed the closeness of their friendship; few were those to whom Houston ever would remark that in Nevada the "men are men and the women double-breasted."[6]

ON ANY GIVEN NIGHT, Thurgood Marshall found himself alone in his office undisturbed by telephone or visitor. More easily than Houston, he had swum into Manhattan's swells. New York City became him and accordingly taxed from him its wearying due. Evenings in the office now recalled his long nights in Howard's law library as he delved into the lamplit pages.

On his desk beside the case law sat letters, telegrams and newspaper articles replete with entreaties each more desperate than the last. Correspondence flooded his office. Indictments, inquiries, the death threats were yet to come, and in the night he read them all into the silence. As Houston had learned before him, this was a job at once crowded and isolating; for every fund-raising soireé there was a solitary night of work. He was just one man, one lawyer working for so little that he sometimes delivered groceries for money to meet the month's expenses. With Houston back in Washington, the association's legal office again was a lonely operation.

Unlike Houston, Marshall refused to spend three or four straight months traveling from the East Coast to the Gulf Coast to California and back again. Among his most difficult tasks was deciding which of the letters, news stories and cases warranted his involvement, necessitated the association's heft. Eugene Burnam's was one such case.

IN THE LUSHLANDS OF FAYETTE COUNTY, Kentucky, in 1939, twenty-year-old Hazel Perkins reported rape. To authorities she described the attack and her attacker, and they, armed with a description vague enough for action, tore through the crooked-lain fens where black folks scraped by. Eight county officers pummeled into Burnam's bedroom and arrested him as he squinted into their lights. He was fifteen years old.

At headquarters police questioned him for hours. Two interrogating officers would receive two weeks of vacation as reward "for meritorious action."[7] Through the ordeal the boy maintained his innocence. Local newspapers in the days following called Burnam "a sex degenerate" who had violated "a beautiful brunette."[8] Prosecutors drew an all-white jury. African Americans were excluded as a matter of custom. Burnam's county-provided counsel hardly investigated and agreed to an imminent trial date. There was little left to be resolved, and all concerned white men in neckties understood this.

Lest a juror run rogue, the prosecution offered into evidence a photograph. Their intent, they explained, was to illustrate that the defendant was capable of the crime with which he was charged.

Burnam's lawyer objected. That the defendant was physically capable of this heinous act was a matter of no dispute. Admitting the proffered evidence would serve only to inflame the jury.

The judge overruled the defense's objection and admitted the exhibit, a photograph of the fifteen-year-old defendant standing naked. It took the jury twenty-eight minutes to return a guilty verdict and recommend that Burnam die by electrocution; the judge accepted the jurors' recommendation and Eugene Burnam was sentenced to death.

Upon the boy's condemnation, the Lexington physician H. A. Merchant organized other black professionals to hire counsel to appeal the verdict and sentence. Burnam's new lawyers wrote to Thurgood Marshall, who packed his bags.

May in Lexington, Kentucky, was like August in Manhattan. Beneath outmatched ceiling fans, Marshall huddled with Charles Anderson, Jr., an African American member of the Kentucky legislature, and Eubanks Tucker—the attorneys hired and committed to save the teenage death row inmate. Anderson and Tucker appreciated Marshall's coming out there to grant such personal attention to this gravely serious matter.[9]

Marshall explained that Burnam's case coincided on four corners with one of the association's legal priorities: ending the exclusion of eligible black citizens from states' grand juries and trial juries. The *Crawford* case a few years ago had declared war on the practice. Fayette County had not seated a black juror in fifty years.[10] In the legal realist tradition he had learned from Houston at both Howard and the NAACP, Marshall contended that this half-century drought, in light of the all-white grand and petit juries that indicted and condemned Burnam, comprised an unconstitutional denial of Burnam's right to equal protection of the laws. Because it likely inflamed the jury, the trial judge's having allowed the nude photograph also warranted a new trial.

Burnam's lawyers agreed and filed a motion for a new trial. In brief and at oral argument in June they contended that a new trial was necessitated by black citizens' systemic and unconstitutional exclusion from Fayette County's juries and by the trial judge's allowing into evidence a nude picture of the defendant.

Circuit Judge King Swope ruled that the trial court's admitting the photograph sufficed for reversible error and remanded the case for retrial.

The lawyers' strategy worked wonderfully. By arguing for a new trial based on the nude photograph's admission into evidence as well as on black citizens' unconstitutional exclusion from Burnam's jury, Anderson and Tucker were providing Judge Swope with an easy choice, indeed a choice commanded by American legal principles: He could grant a new trial based on the photograph's admission and could leave untouched the constitutional issue. If he denied a new trial, his opinion would have to address and reject both arguments and would be subject to appeal. Expediency met justice in Swope's ruling.

After its lawyers lost that appeal, Fayette County budged: The grand jury that indicted Burnam for a second time included two African Americans.

Marshall was and would remain hundreds of miles away from the case's courtroom, even as Eugene Burnam was tried again, convicted again, successful again on appeal and tried again. He advised defense counsel but never assumed an official role in the case. This freedom allowed him to participate at once in dozens of similar cases across the country. After four trials, the Commonwealth of Kentucky executed Eugene Burnam in 1942.

DOWN IN THE DISTRICT, Houston was enveloped by the *Gaines* case, all but dividing his time between D.C. and Missouri. He remained convinced that *Gaines* would be the association's breakthrough case, that it could garner the education campaign's first Supreme Court victory. Because he believed so fervently in the possibility at hand, Houston immersed himself in the case.

The quandary was that he no longer drew an NAACP salary. As a private practitioner on contract, Houston did "not want to make any money out of the Association, [but neither could he] afford to lose anything at this stage."[11] He explained to Walter White that he had assumed responsibility for "the expenses of the office, including secretarial hire, purchase of books, and general overhead."[12] With his father on a leave of absence from the firm while serving in the Department of Justice, Houston's fifteen-dollar-per-day fee no longer covered his costs. To meet his goal of breaking even on NAACP work, he was "obliged to charge twenty-five dollars ($25.00) per day."[13]

Though the text might have appeared to mirror Marshall's letter of a few years back, it differed where difference mattered: If rebuffed, Houston could walk away from association work and live comfortably—more so even without twenty-five-dollar days. White knew that Houston would never forsake the NAACP's legal campaign, and he likewise knew that no attorney in Houston's league would even think of doing so much for so little for so long.

For *Gaines*, Houston "did not keep any time sheets; I worked on the case in all the spare moments I had and immediately before the trial I dropped everything and worked on the case for about a week. The strain of the case was so great that it took me almost a week to hit my stride in the office again."[14] Surely the association's members and donors received their money's worth for his efforts.

Even as Houston secured monumental victories and national renown, his father felt little affection for what he called Charlie's "Abe Lincoln and John Brown stunts."[15] As much as he chided his son for so selflessly devoting himself "to the saving of the 'brother,'" the man Marshall affectionately called "Boss" would have been proud to know how his son insisted that the NAACP ensure that he break even on its endeavors.[16] Fair was not too much to ask for a lawyer called "Don Quixote" by his own father and Houston received his new rate.

GAINES WAS HOUSTON's second victory in the Supreme Court of the United States. Months earlier had come *Hale v. Kentucky.*

Joe Hale lived a black man's quiet smoldering life in Paducah, Kentucky, until the day he was accused of killing a white man. The murder victim had been threatening black women about town, and the prosecutor in McCracken County, buried deep in Kentucky's western pocket, swiftly assembled a grand jury that swiftly indicted nineteen-year-old Hale for murder in the first degree. His lawyers from the local law firm Copeland and Copeland filed a motion to quash the indictment because, consistent with long-standing practice, the county had excluded qualified black residents from Hale's grand jury.[17] County lawyers admitted that no black person had served on a jury in fifty years. The judge denied Hale's motion to quash and empaneled a jury from a pool that likewise excluded black residents. The drawn twelve convicted Hale and sentenced him to death. His lawyers promptly appealed.

The state court of appeals' decision flabbergasted black Kentuckians for the fact underlying its reasoning: Because the trial clerk had omitted from the trial record Hale's motion to quash, the court of appeals declared that it could not consider the issue on appeal.[18] The Paducah Colored Civic League wrote to Houston, who had not yet left New York for Washington. Southern states' wholesale exclusion of African Americans from jury service was the very issue he had raised to national prominence just a few years ago. Would he appeal Joe Hale's case to the Supreme Court of the United States?

Houston assembled his best—Leon "Andy" Ransom, Edward P. Lovett, and the only other lawyer on staff at the NAACP, Thurgood Marshall— and they drafted a petition for certiorari and filed it on January 7, 1938. Twenty-four days later the Court agreed to review the case and scheduled oral argument for February's last day.[19]

The brief they filed on Hale's behalf sparkled with simplicity. Seeking a plainspoken decision in their favor, they filed a plainspoken brief. Houston's brevity tacitly contended that the issues were not complicated. His briefs always spared words for argument, and *Hale* in this respect offered perfection. Houston's brief addressed two points: First, when the state excluded eligible black citizens from its juries on account of race, it prejudiced the black defendant as a matter of law. Second, the trial court clerk's failure to forward Hale's motion to quash his indictment to the Kentucky Court of Appeals "cannot prejudice Hale's rights."[20] From its questions presented flowed a brief so assured that case law buttressed its every curt assertion: "When prejudice is claimed as to an individual juror, prejudice must be proved in fact; but where prejudice is claimed as to an entire class of eligible jurors, prejudice is presumed as a matter of law."[21] On Hale's first point of appeal to America's highest court Houston offered three terse paragraphs. On petitioner's second point, he trusted that the Court brooked no purposeful incompetence: "The failure of the Court of Appeals to complete the record in a capital case such as this, and then [to decide] the case on [an incomplete] record was not an exercise of discretion, but an arbitrary abuse of discretion and a miscarriage of justice which this Court will not endure."[22]

Houston and Ransom argued before the Court a month after initially scheduled. Washington had thawed by March 30 but their presentation remained crisp as frost. McCracken County boasted 40,000 white residents and 8,000 black residents. The county assessor's ledger listed 6,000 white and 700 black citizens eligible and able to serve on juries, but no residents "of African descent" had been called in generations.[23]

The Court's opinion mirrored the brevity of Houston's brief. With little discussion the justices ruled that the record "sufficed to show a systematic and arbitrary exclusion of Negroes from the jury lists solely because of their race or color, constituting a denial of the equal protection of the laws."[24] Joe Hale's murder conviction was overturned and the Supreme Court's unequivocal language left no room for obfuscation: The Constitution did not allow courts to exclude eligible citizens from jury service on account of race.

"LILY-WHITE" JURY TRIALS LOSE AGAIN, trumpeted the *Chicago Defender's* headline above an article proudly noting that the NAACP had won nine of ten cases before the Supreme Court.[25] Walter White congratulated Houston on the victory and Houston's father telegraphed, HEARTY CONGRATULATIONS ON SUPREME COURT DECISION GREAT VICTORY FOR YOU.[26] Optimism crept into African Americans' national discourse: Though the antilynching bill seemed doomed in Congress and the president surprisingly indifferent to their plight, the Supreme Court granted them a fair hearing. One newspaper headline captured the mood: HOPE LOOMS.[27]

The lawyers knew that, clear though the law now was, the fight against race-based jury exclusion would continue. As Houston had written years ago in the *Crisis*, "Nobody needs to explain to a Negro the difference between the law in books and the law in action."[28] *Hale v. Kentucky* received relatively scant if enthusiastic coverage in the African American press; the ruling was all but ignored by white media outlets. Like George Crawford years ago, Joe Hale was not an inspiring plaintiff; black Americans remained agnostic about his innocence. With the legal victory in hand, the association now sought to stir African Americans across the South to insist on their jury rights. To do this, the lawyers needed a better story than Joe Hale's. Months later in Texas they would find one.

THE FIGHT PRESENTED itself in Dallas, Texas, where summer's heat had lingered into September of 1938 like an overstaying guest. A local man had filed suit against Coca-Cola for $2,600—Thurgood Marshall's annual salary after his recent $200 raise—and twenty-eight potential jurors milled about the jury room waiting to be notified whether they would serve. Sitting with the twenty-seven whites was one black man in his best suit: sixty-five-year-old Dr. George F. Porter, the president of a local junior college.[29] He twice before had been dismissed from jury service along with all other black veniremen, and today he refused to be rejected on account of his race. Hours earlier when the deputy sheriff ordered all black potential jurors to leave, Porter had refused, confounding the lawmen.

"We don't know what to do with you," the deputy told him. "You know you cannot serve on the jury with those white men."

"I don't know that," Porter retorted. "Negroes have served on juries in worse states than Texas."[30]

Judge Paine L. Bush took the bench and informed Porter that he was dismissed. He could file an appeal but for now he had to exit.

The bald and slight dark-skinned man replied that he had anticipated the court's decision and filed his appeal days ago when he received his jury notice.[31] Porter returned to the jury room, where he now sat uneasily among his twenty-seven fellow veniremen.

Two white men suddenly seized Porter by his collar's scruff, dragged him struggling through the courthouse's hallways and, as one newspaper reported, he was "thrown headfirst down the front steps of the county building."[32] Bailiffs stood indifferently aside other spectators.

Porter raised to a knee, his palms scraped bloody, best suit shorn and his tongue grit-spittled. To his feet he rose. Watchers' eyes narrowed as he peered up the steps down which he had been hurled. He began to trudge back up as if no other choice availed.

Several more than the first two white men blocked the courthouse door. Porter shoved his way through and they chased him down the hallway. He made it back into Judge Bush's courtroom and stood huffing just past the doorway. The men stamped outside the courtroom like horses.

Again the judge dismissed him. His appeal was duly noted, but for now he had to leave the courthouse. Eyeing the hallway men, Judge Bush ordered Sheriff Smott Schmidt and three of his deputies to escort George Porter to safety.

Porter's being assaulted on courthouse steps shamed many white Dallas residents, with the *Dallas Morning News* devoting a column to condemning the attack. The incident infuriated black Americans nationwide. The

Associated Negro Press presented stories daily to bolster support for Porter's "firm stand."[33] Newspapers reported that the educator was "receiving congratulations from his friends in Dallas and elsewhere where he has worked and is well known for his courageous stand in the face of the imminence of bodily harm."[34] Black Americans of all classes extolled what the black press called his "courage in the face of a brutal assault at the hands of white hoodlums."[35] For his part, Porter vowed to "continue to answer when his name is called and to insist on serving in the regular course of court procedure."[36]

PRESIDENT ROOSEVELT HAD RECENTLY nominated Texas governor James Allred to the federal district bench, and so wanted the governor to become a judge that he had personally handed him the nomination letter when Allred visited the White House in July. Allred's nomination would come to a Senate vote in three months, and congressional elections were less than one month away; the Roosevelt administration wanted the governor to do whatever was necessary to settle the jury trouble brewing in his state. The *Chicago Defender*'s editorial page accurately presented the sentiment held by many observers, black and white, when it opined, "[Allred] is definitely 'on the spot,' and his handling of this dastardly deed will prove whether he is in any sense fit for confirmation by the United States Senate for the high office in the division of justice."[37]

Walter White declared that the NAACP would "watch carefully" how Governor Allred handled the matter.[38] "We have already sent a vigorous protest to Governor Allred of Texas over the brutal treatment meted out to Mr. Porter," White continued, "and we intend to follow this case through because it involves much more than appears on the surface."[39] As he did with most issues brought to his attention, the executive secretary sought to tie Porter's plight with the need for federal antilynching legislation: "This is a striking revelation of why we need an anti-lynching bill. It is obvious in this case that if no action is taken to bring these mobbists to justice, even when they go into a courthouse and drag out a legally summoned prospective juror, then an incentive is open to others to take the law into their own hands and inflict their degenerate prejudice upon other innocent victims purely because those victims happen to be citizens with black skin."[40]

Houston and Marshall read the newspaper accounts of the courthouse attack on Porter and realized the incident should be seized as much more than another opportunity to reiterate the need for a federal antilynching law. Indeed, Porter's being assaulted was but an insult; the ongoing injury was the apparent fact that Texas systematically excluded its black citizens from juries. Citizens were summoned to service without regard to race, but once assembled at the courthouse, African Americans were dismissed en masse.

The thrust of Thurgood Marshall's burgeoning brilliance lay in his blending Houston's unwavering thirst for legal victory with White's unabashed love for the dramatic. Texas was flagrantly violating the U.S. Constitution's mandates as explained by the Supreme Court in Houston's recent *Hale v. Kentucky* victory. That a sixty-five-year-old junior college president was attacked without warning ensured the public's continuing interest. Marshall decided to go to Dallas and investigate.

Word from the Dallas NAACP branch compelled reconsideration. City police chief Robert L. "Bob" Jones explained to his captains and lieutenants that a colored lawyer from New York City was coming to Dallas calling himself an investigator.[41] Chief Jones did not want any of his men to threaten or harm this New York City Negro. "Don't lay a hand on him. Don't touch Thurgood Marshall," Chief Jones commanded. "Because I personally will take him and kick the shit out of him. Personally."[42]

Marshall years later admitted that he considered "not going down there," but his was perilous work in 1938 and the best he ever could hope for were even odds.[43] With White's Rolodex he telephoned Governor Allred. The governor enjoyed a reputation for fairness due in large part to his aggressively insisting that President Roosevelt's New Deal programs reap tangible benefits for Texas's most desperate residents. With Allred's nomination hanging like Damocles' sword above Dallas's courthouse, Marshall told the governor what the city's police chief had said; Allred already knew, and replied, "I give you my word: If you come down here, you will not be injured."[44]

"And sure enough, when I got down there, a Texas Ranger was there," Marshall recalled later. He arrived in Dallas on October 8, 1938. To the press he made clear that he had not come down to investigate the assault on George Porter, but rather "because of the wide implications involved in the denial of fundamental citizenship rights."[45] Governor Allred had assured the association that Texas Rangers, the state's elite law enforcement

unit, were investigating Porter's attack and Marshall would not at all inter-
fere in that matter. A month later newspaper headlines would proclaim:
GOV. ALLRED KEEPS WORD; MAKES ARREST IN JURY ROOM ASSAULT CASE. Texas
Rangers arrested Walter Miller, one of the two men who had assaulted
George Porter.[46]

In Dallas Marshall began probing, interviewing African Americans who
had been summoned to jury duty only to be rejected summarily with
every other black potential juror. As he traveled about town the Ranger
repeatedly addressed him as "boy." Marshall muttered, "This ain't the man
I need," and again called Governor Allred.

"He's the best trained I've got. And if I straighten him out, will that
be okay?"

"Sure." He put the Ranger on the phone. The governor straightened
him out "and, oh, you should have seen his face!"[47] Never again did his
protection call him "boy."

After meeting with jurors dismissed on account of their race, Marshall
met with several judges who had done the dismissing. He gleaned no useful nugget from the jurists, thanked them for their time and left the courthouse. His late afternoon shadow stumbled crooked and lank down the
courthouse steps. At the bottom Marshall strolled to his car, lost as he often was in thoughts of his case.

"Hi, you black sonofabitch!" Dallas police chief Bob Jones shouted
across the parking lot. The Texas lawman was sprinting toward him, gun
drawn. "I've got you now!"

Marshall dashed toward his car, huffing across the blacktop.

As if expecting this and unsurprised by it all, the Ranger appeared atop
the hood of Marshall's car and aimed his gun at Chief Jones. "Fella, just
stay right where you are."

Jones froze, incredulous.

Marshall leaped into the car and slammed the door shut. The Ranger
slid into the driver's seat, started the car and rolled out of the parking lot
with his gun still trained on the police chief seething on the asphalt.[48]

As Marshall continued his investigation, another African American city
resident was called for jury duty. A forty-six-year-old shoe repairman
identified only as W. L. Dickson asked Sheriff Schmidt for protection and
stepped into the courthouse's hostile stares and jeers with a police escort.

The officer quickly tired of the noise and silenced the hallway. Dickson explained to the press after the first day of voir dire, during which he was not dismissed, that he wanted "to serve on a jury and see how courts work."[49] Asked to comment on the potential juror's requiring a police escort to enter the county courthouse, Marshall replied only that his investigation was proceeding well.[50] Dickson would be seated on a jury in Judge Bush's courtroom.

Thurgood Marshall returned to New York City on October 19, 1938. He would file no case in Texas but did draft a letter from Walter White to U.S. Attorney General Homer S. Cummings.[51] Marshall never would adopt White's zeal for law as protest-theater, but in Dallas perhaps for the first time he had struck the necessary balance. Faster than any lawsuit could have, Marshall's publicized investigation effected a quiet revolution in courthouses across Texas. African American jurors began to appear in jury boxes like flowers in desert sand.

MARSHALL AT THE HELM

WHILE THURGOOD MARSHALL INVESTIGATED DALLAS, Charles Houston argued *Missouri ex rel. Gaines v. Canada* before the Supreme Court. Marshall had contributed a good deal of research to the appeal, and both anxiously awaited the Court's ruling. In the meantime, they returned their attention to the fight to make black teachers' pay equal to white teachers'.

Their success in Montgomery County, Maryland, inspired southern black teachers and principals. Along with Hastie, Ransom, Lovett and Oliver Hill, Houston and Marshall coordinated litigation across the South, working with attorneys who had taken the fight to their home states. Working with distant lawyers proved cumbersome but necessary: Most local attorneys were novices at civil rights litigation. They were motivated by Houston's and Marshall's victories and regarded Houston as a remote mentor, asking his advice on their careers and cases. But by now litigating county by county was straining the association's scant legal resources; the office needed a teachers' salary case to stand precedent nationwide.

ALINE BLACK TAUGHT CHEMISTRY at the only black high school in Norfolk, Virginia. Like other African American teachers at Booker T. Washington High, she earned two thirds the salary of a white teacher. Washington High's white janitor made more money than the black teachers, and Black decided to do something about this.

A week after Marshall returned from Dallas, Aline Black, who had twelve years of teaching experience, filed a petition with the Norfolk School Board asking that her salary be made equal to similarly qualified white teachers'. When the board members denied her claim she decided to sue them. The Norfolk Teachers' Association, an African American union to which Black belonged, contacted the NAACP. Marshall traveled to Norfolk and met with several local attorneys, including J. Thomas Hewin, Jr., a talented if unreliable lawyer with a tendency to disappear for days before trial only to resurface bewildered by his cocounsel's exasperation. With Marshall's approval, the local lawyers filed Black's case in state court in March of 1939.[1]

The trial team lost before a hostile bench and zealous defense. Judge Allan Hanckel ruled that he possessed no authority to interfere with either the school board's personnel decisions or a legally executed contract. Black's attorneys promptly appealed to the Supreme Court of Virginia but before the court held arguments the Norfolk School Board terminated Aline Black in June of 1939. Because she no longer was employed by the school district, her case became moot; she was not in a position to collect relief—pay equal to white teachers'—and therefore could not serve as a plaintiff.

Thurgood Marshall was incensed. In a rare act of extrajudicial protest, he persuaded Walter White to join him in Norfolk to rally and march with the city's black folks. Hundreds of schoolchildren would march with their parents, teachers and principals, their signs condemning the Norfolk School Board's firing Aline Black. It was the sort of scene irresistible to White, who promptly packed his bags. The march culminated at St. John African Methodist Episcopal Church. From the pulpit Marshall preached a fight. June's twenty-fifth day shone hot and humid in the church but none in the pews were languid. Children cheered alongside their teachers as Marshall promised that he personally would continue Black's push to equalize black and white teachers' salaries. *Murray, Gaines* and Montgomery County had secured his reputation as a lawyer who delivered. The days when the rural black folks of backwaters and shared crops whispered furtive as any of their forebears, *Thurgood's comin'* still lay years away, but seeds of those whispers were planted in Norfolk, where the sweating congregation fanned themselves with wood-and-paper Jesus fans.

WASHINGTON HIGH SCHOOL'S COMMERCE teacher Melvin O. Alston served as president of the Norfolk Teachers' Association, and on his behalf Marshall filed suit in federal court on September 28, 1939. Alston convinced his fellow NTA members to permit the organization to serve as a coplaintiff. Marshall, Ransom, Hastie and Oliver Hill drafted a petition explaining that their client earned $921 per year while similarly qualified white teachers performing the same duties received $1,200 per year. At Norfolk's elementary schools, white teachers received $850 annually and black teachers $611; in high schools newly hired black women earned $699 and newly hired white women received $970.[2] The attorneys asked the court to void this biased pay schedule. Norfolk filed a motion to dismiss the case.

Federal district court Judge Luther B. Way scheduled the hearing for Abraham Lincoln's birthday. Marshall pointed out that court would be closed that day on account of the federal holiday.

"Well, you follow Lincoln's Birthday up your way," Judge Way huffed, "down here, we follow Jeff Davis day."[3] He rescheduled the hearing on defendant's motion and, upon hearing arguments, dismissed the case. Judge Way accepted Norfolk attorney Alfred Anderson's argument that Alston waived his right to sue when he signed the contract stipulating his unequal pay.[4] Had he refused to sign the contract, he could have sued, but having signed it he was precluded from arguing it violated his constitutional rights. Judge Way's decision ignored a primary tenet of America's legal system: Had Alston refused to sign a contract, he would have had no standing to sue the school board; he had to sign his contract in order to have standing but, under Way's ruling, his having signed the contract enjoined him from filing suit against his employer.

Marshall had anticipated this Wonderland dismissal and announced the association's intent to appeal before Judge Way signed his opinion.[5] With Ransom, Hastie and Hill, he donned his overcoat and fedora, strolled out of the courthouse and lit a cigarette. A *Journal and Guide* photographer snapped a picture of the four appearing none too chagrined. Their course of action was set and the judge had played his part; federal appellate precedent was the prize. Marshall returned to New York City; Ransom and Hastie returned to the District, where the former taught law at Howard and the latter had assumed his cousin's old job as dean of the law school;

and Hill drove the short way back to Richmond, where he shortly thereafter filed their appeal with the Fourth Circuit Court of Appeals.[6]

THURGOOD MARSHALL HAD NEVER ARGUED in a federal appellate court. In
the wake of Maryland's favorable settlements involving teachers' salaries
and Houston's back-to-back Supreme Court wins, black folks' expectations
bubbled high for *Alston* in the Fourth Circuit Court of Appeals. African
American newspaper headlines declared, DECISION IS EXPECTED TO BE FAR-
REACHING, and noted Marshall's observing that "this marks the first effort
of the Association to get a ruling from a high federal court on the question of equalizing the salaries of white and colored public school teachers."[7] The court of appeals heightened tension in April when it ordered
the Norfolk School Board to refrain from sending teachers their contracts
for the upcoming school year.[8] Bill Hastie, who already had served as a
federal judge, would join Marshall in presenting oral argument. As always,
they practiced in moot courts at Howard Law School. When the date at
last arrived, dozens of Norfolk's black residents poured from cars into the
federal appellate courthouse.[9] The three judges maintained custom at oral
arguments' conclusion and stepped down from the bench to shake hands
with each side's attorneys; African American spectators later spread word
across the South that the judges were so impressed with Hastie and Marshall's presentation that they felt compelled to come down from the bench
to shake their hands.[10]

Just a few days later, the court of appeals unanimously ruled in Alston's
favor. The teacher had not waived his right to redress by signing the contract, and that contract in fact did violate the Constitution because it imposed on him a teacher's salary lowered solely because of his race.[11]
Norfolk appealed to the Supreme Court, but in October 1940 the justices
refused to review the case. The Norfolk School Board equalized its teachers'
salaries. Even through thick news of an imminent presidential election and
the looming threat of war, the association's victory impressed black and white
Americans alike.

Houston and Hastie were names by now familiar nationwide, but as late
as spring of 1940, the *Chicago Defender* was still misspelling "Thorogood's"
name.[12] This would change in the coming decade as Marshall embarked
on well-publicized trips into the deepest recesses of segregated America.

This heightened publicity increased the danger of the lawyers' work. Southern conservatives in the 1940s came to view Houston, Marshall, and the other NAACP attorneys as genuine threats to the southern way of life, even as the association's legal victories grew sparse and the horizon bleaker. Segregationists vowed to defeat the lawyers in court and, if necessary, fight wherever they might find them. It was in this perilous environment that the lawyers began to consider how to wage a direct legal attack on segregation. By 1940 all flank battles had been fought. Frontal assault alone remained and, as in any fight, some would fall.

A FEW MONTHS BEFORE *Alston*'s appellate victory, Marshall proudly revisited *Murray*. The recent Oberlin College graduate George B. Murphy, "Mister Carl's" nephew, enrolled in the University of Maryland Law School. On the occasion of the law school's receiving its third African American student, Marshall declared, "We have succeeded in keeping the doors of the University of Maryland open to Negro students."[13] His words intimated that the struggle to integrate the law school had not ended with *Murray*. Indeed, Donald Murray had since graduated and passed Maryland's bar examination, but Marshall personally had to pledge to sue the law school anew before university president Curly Byrd acceded to Murphy's enrollment.

Despite the Supreme Court's handing the school naked defeat in *Gaines*, the University of Missouri refused to admit into the journalism school the managing editor of the *Kansas City Call*. Lucile Bluford was eminently qualified for admission to the school, which was America's oldest and most respected journalism school. The Salisbury, North Carolina, native had reported for the school newspaper and graduated first in her class at Kansas City's Lincoln High before enrolling at the University of Kansas, where she graduated in 1932 with high honors. Bluford eagerly accepted a job in Atlanta with the nationally distributed *Daily World* before returning home to the *Kansas City Call*, where she worked her way up from reporter to city editor to managing editor to editor in chief to publisher. University of Missouri registrar S. W. Canada replied to her 1939 application to Missouri's School of Journalism by instructing her to apply to the state's Lincoln University, which did not have a journalism program, much less a graduate school of Missouri's caliber. It was as if *Gaines* never had happened. Lucille Bluford was not one to suffer insult meekly. Half a

Charles Hamilton Houston, age five, posing in his sailor's suit. *(Houston Collection, Moorland-Spingarn Research Center, Howard University)*

Young Charlie Houston with his parents, William and Mary. *(Houston Collection, Moorland-Spingarn Research Center, Howard University)*

Lieutenant Houston of the U.S. Army. The inscription reads: "To my Dad: I promise to do the very best I can. Charlie." *(Houston Collection, Moorland-Spingarn Research Center, Howard University)*

Walter White, John Davis, and Charles Hamilton Houston investigating labor and housing complaints in Hughes, Arkansas, 1934. *(NAACP Collection, Prints & Photographs Division, Library of Congress)*

Thurgood Marshall, Donald Gaines Murray, and Charles Hamilton Houston. *(NAACP Collection, Prints & Photographs Division, Library of Congress)*

Houston at work, November 1939. *(NAACP Collection, Prints & Photographs Division, Library of Congress)*

Charles Hamilton Houston. *(NAACP Collection, Prints & Photographs Division, Library of Congress)*

Houston in court with his wife, Henrietta, supporting him. *(Houston Collection, Moorland-Spingarn Research Center, Howard University)*

Charles Hamilton Houston with his son, Charles, Jr. *(Houston Collection, Moorland-Spingarn Research Center, Howard University)*

William Hastie. *(NAACP Collection, Prints & Photographs Division, Library of Congress)*

Heman Sweatt (center) with Roy Wilkins (left) and Bob Carter during a press interview in New York City in 1950. *(World-Telegram photo/NAACP Collection, Prints & Photographs Division, Library of Congress)*

George McLaurin and two fellow students. *(NAACP Collection, Prints & Photographs Division, Library of Congress)*

Mr. and Mrs. Heman Sweatt. *(NAACP Collection, Prints & Photographs Division, Library of Congress)*

Walter White, circa 1950. *(NAACP Collection, Prints & Photographs Division, Library of Congress)*

Spottswood Robinson III (left) and Oliver Hill in court with their clients, listening to Virginia's attorney examine a witness in a school desegregation case in 1953. *(NAACP Collection, Prints & Photographs Division, Library of Congress)*

Thurgood Marshall at a press conference in New York City, 1955. *(World-Telegram photo/NAACP Collection, Prints & Photographs Division, Library of Congress)*

century hence, when the nation's first major black candidate for president of the United States kept seven thousand Kansas City residents waiting for two hours to hear him speak, she reprimanded Reverend Jesse Jackson so sternly he could only reply, "Yes ma'am, Miss Bluford."[14]

One would not know by her telegram to the university's president that she was a black woman and he a white man in America in 1939: I WAS DE-NIED ADMITTANCE TO MISSOURI UNIVERSITY SCHOOL OF JOURNALISM TODAY AND REFERRED TO LINCOLN UNIVERSITY. I CAME TO JEFFERSON CITY AND FOUND LINCOLN HAS NO JOURNALISM COURSES. PLEASE REQUEST MR. CANADA TO ADMIT ME TO MISSOURI U. JOURNALISM SCHOOL AT ONCE. PLEASE WIRE ANSWER TODAY.[15]

Weeks passed without a response. Houston and Sidney Redmond, re-united in *Gaines*'s encore, filed suit again against the University of Missouri in both federal and state court. Both petitions were dismissed because Blu-ford had not first applied to Lincoln University as Canada ordered.[16] Be-fore seeking entry into Missouri's journalism school, the courts opined, she should have petitioned Lincoln to establish a journalism school. That a hastily launched graduate school could not at all compete with the nation's best journalism program was of no moment to the court.

Missouri's legislature quickly appropriated sixty thousand dollars to es-tablish a journalism program at Lincoln. Frustrated two years later by the war's draft and Houston's insistence that the new program was manifestly unequal and therefore unconstitutional, in 1942 the legislature shut down both the Lincoln program and the University of Missouri School of Jour-nalism.[17] Bluford ended her legal crusade against the university and returned to the *Kansas City Call*.

Forty-two years later, the since-reopened University of Missouri School of Journalism presented Lucile Bluford with its Medal for Distinguished Service in Journalism. She accepted the medal and, at ceremony's end, asked her student host to drive her to the home of S. W. Canada; he still lived on campus, she knew, and she knocked on his door. The man even older than she lived by himself and knew from newspaper accounts that she was on campus. He opened the door in the slow and eager way peculiar to the elderly and children.

"You remember me?" she asked.

"Yeah, I remember you."[18]

They both laughed at it all in one moment, and S. W. invited her to come inside and sit for a spell. Bluford accepted and together they sat. She asked him why he had rejected her application, and he replied that if he had not he would have lost his job. She had figured as much.[19]

WHILE HOUSTON PREPARED Lucile Bluford's case in Missouri and Marshall secured admission for the University of Maryland's third African American law student, Leon Ransom traveled from Washington to Knoxville, Tennessee, to gain admission for six applicants to the University of Tennessee. Tennessee's lawyers figured that if the university never acted on their applications, the students would forever lack the standing necessary to file suit.[20] With local counsel, Ransom reviewed the university's records and interviewed the applicants. The fact was that until Tennessee rejected their applications, the students had no legal redress.

Ransom sought to negotiate. On a breezy afternoon in late September, he met with university president James Hoskins and other officials. They soon reached an impasse; Hoskins offered no negotiation and asked Ransom to withdraw the applications "in order not to impair good race relations."[21] The short meeting ended when Ransom refused. After conferring with local counsel and with Houston in Washington, Ransom announced, "We are preparing to file a petition for mandamus to force the school to open its doors."[22]

The university's dean shrugged off an explanation: "It is unlawful for white and colored people to attend school together in Tennessee. If my memory serves me correctly there is a fine of $50 and a jail sentence of from 30 days to six months for each separate offense for violation of this law."[23] As he saw it, his hands were bound by state law.

A Tennessee court took eight months to dismiss the applicants' petition on a technicality. Association lawyers rectified their petition but the court stalled the case for over a year, by which time the state legislature began appropriating funds to build separate graduate schools for black applicants.

The Supreme Court of the United States would not hear another school segregation case until 1948. Missouri's decision to close its highly regarded school of journalism rather than admit a single black applicant evidenced how rabid the resistance was and would be. State legislators recognized that not simply law, but the customs and society built on those laws were at stake. Houston's admonition that "law suits mean little unless supported by public opinion" proved truer now than when he wrote it.[24]

IN MAY 1939, Houston persuaded White to promote Thurgood Marshall to special counsel. As Marshall began to replace him as the voice and face of the legal campaign, it behooved the association to designate him special counsel so that senators, volunteer branch office lawyers, judges and opposing counsel knew that when they dealt with Marshall, they were not dealing with the association's "assistant" attorney, but instead were negotiating with one whose word could bind. Last and most important, however, Marshall had proven himself to Houston. In the muted fashion in which he offered praise, Houston explained, "Thurgood has been doing all the work and I have felt comfortable."[25]

After Marshall and Hastie's commanding performance before the Fourth Circuit Court of Appeals, Houston asked to be returned to his "original place on the National Legal Committee." He resigned his commission as special counsel.[26] Hastie was performing deftly as dean of Howard Law School and Marshall had quickly become dexterous in the many facets of serving as special counsel. By no means was Houston retiring, but he felt satisfied that his shoes were being filled by such gifted and gracious advocates.

Houston was especially proud of Marshall. Hastie was his cousin and had studied at Harvard, Leon Ransom was a peer, having graduated first in his class at Ohio State's law school before teaching and practicing alongside him in Washington—but Thurgood Marshall had learned the law, classroom to courtroom, from Houston. "Even if we were both [still] in the office," he wrote to White, "I would endorse Thurgood's being special counsel because we were on a parity at the end."[27] From Old Ironshoes it was high commendation.

And now Marshall was as much "evangelist and stump speaker" as Houston ever had been. One historian accurately noted that "conducting litigation and arguing cases in the Supreme Court, the activities for which Marshall became famous, were only a small part of his work."[28] As it had been for his mentor, the actual practice of law was Marshall's welcome respite from incessantly rallying members, traveling the country, lobbying congressmen, advising Walter White and coordinating with local lawyers across North and South to manage the spawned cases. With Marshall at the helm, the NAACP continued the strategy Houston had devised, fighting on several fronts at once.[29]

A New Jersey mechanic named Ira Collins, who scored high on the state's civil service examination but was not hired as motor vehicle inspector, filed suit against the motor vehicle commissioner, Arthur McGhee. Marshall advised local lawyers in Trenton and rallied contributions for Collins's court costs.[30] Parishioners at the Harlem Unitarian Church packed Sunday service to hear the latest in his talk titled "Our Educational Campaign in the South."[31] He tried to broker a deal with New York City's Housing Authority to funnel more business to black-owned moving companies.[32] In April 1940 he stood alongside Bronx borough president James Lyons to announce the opening of the Bronx NAACP branch, congratulating each of the branch's fifty-five charter members.[33] He embarked on a nationwide speaking tour of NAACP branches. Black press headlines proudly referred to him as the "Famed Thurgood Marshall" who had "gained prominence in the Lloyd Gaines case and was a potent force in the NAACP's fight for equal salaries for colored teachers."[34] His "convincing" talks were designed to update association members on the nationwide fight for legal equality and to inspire the unaffiliated to become association members.[35]

With Walter White, Marshall now publicly led the lobbying effort for federal antilynching legislation. In Washington White and Marshall personally lobbied congressmen the week before the House of Representative's 1940 vote. "We are looking at two things when we look at present-day lynching statistics," White replied to assertions that the number of lynchings had declined dramatically in recent years. "First, while lynchings have decreased in number they have increased in barbarism. Secondly, the statistics which we have on the number of lynchings today do not tell all of the story by any means: What is not brought out is the fact that mob leaders have adopted the technique of spiriting their victims away quietly and doing their dirty work without benefit of crowds or attendant publicity."[36]

Facts justified White's fervency: Just a few months earlier in Canton, Mississippi, black lumberman Joe Rodgers's white boss hit him with a shovel. Rodgers tackled his boss, wrenched away the shovel and hurled it to the ground. His boss assembled a mob that found Rodgers after quitting time, bound his hands and feet and, with open-fired irons, branded him countless times. The workingman's flesh crackled beneath his screams before they finally drowned him in Mississippi's crooked Pearl River.[37]

Among the congressmen Marshall worked more quietly than White. His unassuming fashion scored endorsement when Congress's lone African American member, Illinois Democrat Arthur Mitchell, with whom the association enjoyed an imperfect relationship, declared on the House floor, "I represent the group that has furnished the victims for the mobs."[38] Congressman Mitchell hurled truth at his uniformly white colleagues. "There is more in this bill than merely stopping the mobs. The future of a large group of citizens is wrapped up in it." Newspapers reported that his voice "trembled with emotion" as he challenged his fellow congressmen: "I want you to think with seriousness on what is being perpetrated on 15 million loyal citizens in this democracy."[39] The House chamber and visitors' gallery burst into sustained applause and the bill passed the lower chamber 251–132.

Prospects in the Senate were billed as "better than even."[40] At the Democratic National Convention, Senate majority leader Alben Barkley assured African American delegates that he would bring to a vote the latest anti-lynching bill; after Congress reconvened, Senator Barkley denied making the statement and refused to say whether he would bring the bill to a vote. Marshall's staid reply belied his anger and framed the issue in the war-themed parlance of the day: "The NAACP regards the 'Anti-Lynching Bill' as being just as important as the National Defense Program."[41] But the bill would remain stalled in the Senate.

BECAUSE THE NAACP lobbied Congress, donations to the association were not tax deductible. The legal office's expenses were growing substantially and Marshall realized the office could attract larger donations if they were tax deductible, so, with association support, he established the NAACP Legal Defense and Education Fund. The Legal Defense Fund, or LDF, did not lobby government. In later years the LDF would become an organization entirely separate from the NAACP, but for the first years after its founding it operated as the association's legal arm.

After Marshall was promoted to special counsel and became director-counsel of the newly created LDF, he had to concern himself closely with the legal office's finances. He already had proven himself an effective fund-raiser, but as the legal campaign's needs expanded with its caseload, ensuring that the association and LDF possessed enough money to litigate the cases became one of the chores that consumed much of his time.

Leon Ransom's case to desegregate the University of Tennessee presented the typical scenario. Ransom, like Houston after he resigned as special counsel, was a member of the NAACP National Legal Committee. On the university case he worked with two talented African American lawyers from Tennessee, Carl Cowan and Alexander Looby, who were the only lawyers in the state Houston trusted to handle such a difficult case.[42] The lawyers all but volunteered their services; they accepted nominal fees and enough to cover expenses like travel, filing fees and deposition transcripts. Over the weeks and months required to conduct interviews, review documents, research applicable law, and draft and file a petition, these expenses grew to a considerable sum.

The Knoxville NAACP branch contributed as handsomely as possible to the case, and Marshall turned to the Memphis branch members: "I am sure you have all been watching with interest the developments in the University of Tennessee cases," he wrote. "We are in for a long fight and must have a sufficient defense fund to complete these cases."[43] After describing the attorneys' efforts and expenses thus far, he concluded, "Will you, therefore, please let me know just as soon as possible how much your branch will be responsible for within the next six months on this case."[44]

University desegregation cases were critically important to the association's education campaign—indeed they were the first landmark in Houston's road map to desegregating public schools—but they were not cases on which Marshall could depend to raise money. Even when brought to successful conclusions, their practical effects were often nebulous; in *Gaines* the plaintiff disappeared and the University of Missouri remained segregated, and in *Murray* Maryland's law school had admitted only two African Americans after Marshall threatened to sue the school again. Donations for such cases barely covered the costs of litigating them.

Moreover, with reptilian efficiency, southern politicians were adapting to the NAACP's success. Missouri's legislature, threatened by Houston's *Bluford* case, closed its famed graduate school of journalism rather than admit Lucile Bluford; Tennessee's elected politicians were spending money like they printed it in an effort to construct a legitimate college for black students before Ransom could persuade a lethargic court to rule on his clients' mandamus petition.

In the future, university cases would rise again to prominence. They would inspire confidence and donations sufficient to fund their appeals, largely because their rulings again excited African Americans across the country. Marshall continued to direct education cases nationwide, but as he read the hundreds of entreaties mailed to his office each month, he kept an eye open for the cases where the NAACP not only could correct injustice but also could maintain donors' interest in the legal campaign. Proud though they were of association lawyers' battles in their states, the fact was that most southern black Americans were in no position to apply to graduate school. Attending an integrated school of journalism was an ambition foreign to those scraping by in the rural Deep South. In the pine-whispering badlands, a man stood a better chance of being falsely accused of capital crime than integrating a state graduate school. Consistent with Houston's plan to attack first in the border states where they stood a fighting chance, the association had not yet even filed integration cases in the Deep South. Down there, Marshall's and his local attorneys' tasks were more plain and just as difficult: Save the lives of men condemned by circumstance and jury.

BACK IN MARCH 1938 outside Montgomery, Alabama, Eunice Ward and her sister were picking spring flowers near a Masonic hall when a would-be robber attacked them. Ward and her sister, both of whom were white, were beaten horribly and hurled into a prickly thicket. The robber fled. Neither woman was sexually assaulted, but Eunice, a nurse just like her sister, died from head wounds.[45] The governor offered a one-thousand-dollar reward for finding the killer, and Montgomery's police officers swarmed through the city's black neighborhood interrogating residents and arresting men. One officer informed a self-described "fortune teller" about the award money and she experienced a "remembering" that a restaurant worker named Dave Canty had confided to her that "he was in trouble" and was fleeing to Mobile.[46] Police officers down in Mobile swiftly arrested the twenty-eight-year-old Canty, whisked him to the police station and began beating him with their nightsticks. Why had he killed that woman? Did he ravage her first? He didn't know what they were talking about, so they ferried him back to Montgomery to refresh his memory.

Officers locked him in an "underground dungeon" beneath the city's Kilby Prison.[47] For a week they whipped him and starved him and promised all could end if he would just confess to what he had done. He didn't know what they were talking about. After a week they loaded him into a backseat and drove to Montgomery police headquarters. Officers dragged to the basement the bloodied heap Canty had become. They whipped him until at last he agreed that he had done what they said he had done.[48] He agreed to the method and motive they described to him. He agreed with all they said, and signed the paper shoved his way, and was dragged to a cell on the main floor where he collapsed. Ten years earlier he would have been beaten, burned and hung from a tree; this was progress.

At trial in June of 1938 Canty professed innocence. He had confessed because it was the only way to stop the officers from beating him. He knew nothing about the attack on Eunice Ward and her sister.

The jury convicted him and recommended that he be executed by electrocution.[49] That it took the twelve white men an hour and thirty-five minutes to do so suggests that at least one of them believed Canty.[50] The judge accepted the verdict and recommendation and ordered the sentence to be carried out in one month, on July 15, a date automatically stayed when Canty's lawyers filed his notice of appeal.[51] Alabama's supreme court reviewed Canty's case and his appellate arguments, but on June 22, 1939, it affirmed the trial court's ruling.[52] Another execution date was set, then postponed—three times.

Canty's lawyers wrote to Marshall. Would he review Canty's case file and, if he deemed appropriate, file a petition for certiorari to the Supreme Court of the United States? On January 11, 1940, Marshall, Ransom and Hastie filed a brief and certiorari petition they had prepared with Canty's Montgomery, Alabama, lawyer Alex Birch.[53] Two months later and without hearing oral argument, the Court reversed the now thirty-year-old Canty's murder conviction and remanded his case for retrial.[54] Because it was beaten out of him, his confession was inadmissible evidence and his conviction invalid. It was the NAACP's fourteenth victory in fifteen cases before the Supreme Court and, as many black folks noted with pride,

Thurgood didn't even have to travel to Washington to convince the justices that he was right.

Back in Montgomery, Dave Canty was tried again. A few days before Christmas 1940, a second Alabama jury found him guilty of murdering Eunice Ward even without his illegally obtained confession. The jurors would not, however, sentence him to death. Instead they recommended that Canty spend the rest of his life in Alabama's state prison, where he died, years later, proclaiming innocence.[55]

Canty's case was the sort that convinced Marshall that juries and judges could not be trusted to decide whether a defendant lived or died. Courthouse flaws and misdeeds abounded. Marshall did not enter an appearance in Canty's case until the final appeal, however, and *Canty* alone did not scar his legal faith. There were two cases to come, one in Connecticut's wealthiest enclave and the other in one of Oklahoma's poorest hamlets, and each case swept through the press like brushfire and compelled Thurgood Marshall to action as soon as he learned of the fur coat and the bones.

14

Greenwich Railroad Bones

As 1941 GREW NEAR, John and Eleanor "Ellie" Strubing were still thought to be new to Greenwich, Connecticut, and the couple knew that they would be new for years to come in the wealthy hamlet. John's success in advertising demanded his frequent travel, and on the warmer than seasonal night of December 10, 1940, he was asleep in a Cincinnati hotel room when the Strubings' chauffeur, a sleepy-eyed black man named Joseph Spell, knocked on the bedroom door in their home to ask John's wife if he could borrow a few dollars until payday.[1]

"I've got $6.50," the thirty-two-year-old told him. "You can have anything I've got. You've been very nice." She slowly placed the money in his hand.

"Thank you very much." He smiled. "You've been very nice yourself."

She returned his smile and repeated, "You can have anything I've got."

Spell had come to figure as much. "I thought that all the time," he confessed. "I'd like to be with you."

"It will be all right if you'll promise me you'll never say anything about it."

He nodded, but the promise had to flow both ways. "I won't say anything—what about you?"

"I can't afford to." She led him into the bedroom and pulled back the sheets as he undressed.[2]

As Spell and Strubing lay down together in bed, her pet schnauzer began barking. She worried the dog would awaken Spell's wife, who worked as the Strubings' maid and lived with Spell in quarters above the home. So they dressed, went downstairs and reclined on the settee. Strubing slipped off her girdle and, as Spell described, "we started to do what we intended to do."[3]

Again Ellie Strubing became nervous, fearing now that someone would spy them through the transom. He suggested they go to the car, where they sat talking for nearly forty minutes before resuming intimacies. Before long she whispered pregnancy worries and the sex ended. Spell "had a discharge into my pocket handkerchief."[4]

When they both had dressed he offered to take her on a drive. He was, after all, the chauffeur; no one could question their lone nighttime togetherness in the car. She agreed, retrieved her fur coat and they drove into headlamp–lit darkness.

DAWN STOLE OVER the horizon just a few hours later. Two white truck drivers pulled to the side of a New York State highway, where Ellie Strubing was waving frantically, bleeding and stumbling in the lightening night. When the police arrived she repeated the story she told the truck drivers. Her account held the officers in rapt horror: Hours earlier Mrs. Strubing had been repeatedly raped by her "Negro chauffeur-butler," who then bound her, gagged her and hurled her into her husband's car.[5] Desperate to dispose of her, he drove to Kensico Reservoir in Westchester County, New York, threw her out of the car, pushed her off a bridge and heaved rocks at her until she slipped beneath the surface. She fought her way out of the water and back up to the highway, leaving her fur coat and one shoe submerged in the depths where the rapist had tried to drown her.[6]

Joseph Spell was arrested before the sun rose high. Greenwich police interrogated him for sixteen hours before announcing that he had confessed to the multiple rapes and attempted murder. Spell was not tortured like black defendants in the Deep South but, nine months after Richard Wright's *Native Son* was published, he instantly became proof of the southern Fear gone North. New York newspapers condemned the suspect.

Reading the reports in his office less than two hours south of Greenwich, Marshall knew Spell's case beckoned. The Legal Defense Fund needed Spell almost as much as he needed it. Criminal cases raised membership and money; they guaranteed press coverage and exposed, more dramatically than the education cases ever could, the unconstitutional injustices to which black Americans were subjected regularly. Two days after Joseph Spell was arrested, Marshall boarded a train for the short jaunt to Greenwich. To assembled press he announced, "[My office] intends to fight this case to the limit not only because we are convinced that Joseph Spell is innocent but because we know that winning freedom for this man means strengthening the security of thousands of Negro domestics, chauffeurs, maids and butlers throughout the country whose jobs are jeopardized by this case."[7]

In just the short time since Spell's arrest, the association had been inundated with calls and claims from African American workers across the North who had been fired by the white families for whom they worked. Because they were violently excluded from union-held jobs, domestic employment comprised an economic pillar in black communities. Thousands of families bore a financial stake in Spell's innocence—and his attorneys' ability to prove it.

The association's legal efforts once again were spellbinding front-page news. Marshall promptly wrote to the NAACP National Legal Committee's William Hastie and asked for a significant budget increase. "We will have to spend more money on regular [criminal] defense cases," he explained, "because these teachers' salaries cases and university cases will not continue to keep our name going."[8]

As Walter White took to publicizing the association's commitment to Spell, Marshall met with the bowtied Jewish lawyer hired by the Bridgeport NAACP branch to serve as his defense cocounsel. Samuel Friedman was slightly older than Marshall and, upon reading sensational reports of "the Strubing quadruple rape case," did not think his client was innocent.[9] But before Friedman could comment, Marshall huffed that he did not believe one word of the Strubing woman's "fantastic and unconvincing" story.[10] Together they traveled to the Bridgeport jail to visit their client.

Spell's handsome face belied his muddled life. He was born in Lafayette, Louisiana, in 1909, married at seventeen, left his wife three months later and joined the army without ever bothering with divorce. Six years of service were nullified when he got drunk, stole an officer's car and crashed it; Spell was dishonorably discharged. His most recent arrest, just a few months ago, was for threatening his former employer unless she loaned him money. He was now thirty-one years old and lived in the Strubings' attic with a childhood friend whom he called his current wife. Just across the New York State line he also kept a girlfriend who could not move to Connecticut on account of her still being in high school.[11]

Joseph Spell insisted that the prosecutor was lying; he had not admitted to raping Mrs. Strubing and certainly had not signed any confession. Their relations had been consensual. He relayed to them his version of events.

How did she end up on the side of the highway in the middle of the night?

As he drove, Spell explained, she became increasingly agitated, worried that someone had seen them or would see them and think the worst. He tied to calm her but finally she commanded him to stop the car so that she could get out. She hopped the guardrail and skittered down the reservoir's rocky embankment. Spell drove away to a friend's house in White Plains, New York, where he played blackjack for hours until returning during the same dawn hour in which Ellie Strubing was flagging down two weary truck drivers. He was asleep in the laundry room when police came clanging and cursing and arrested him.[12]

Marshall and Friedman knew that the last part of Spell's alibi skipped a note. Even if he were telling them the morning's truth, his leaving a distraught woman on a desolate patch of road in winter's night would concern jurors. Combined with his assertion that Strubing had propositioned him in her marital bedroom, the facts were sufficient for condemnation from an all-white jury of Connecticut Yankees. Marshall remained nonetheless convinced of Spell's innocence, and Friedman too was persuaded. With their client's consent they rejected prosecutor Lorin Willis's offered plea bargain.

Joseph Spell's superior-court trial commenced in January 1941 in Bridgeport, a city whose restaurants uniformly defied state law by refusing to serve African Americans. For two days the prosecution appealed to the basest hates and fears. State's witnesses proffered testimony laden with America's ugliest stereotypes; Walter White called it the sort of inflaming drivel he "expected in Mississippi, but not in Connecticut."[13] Ellie Strubing's own hysterical testimony concluded, "I'm sure he raped me four times. But I can't remember now." The courtroom murmured. "On a stone floor—or something. It's so confused."[14]

Marshall and Friedman compared Strubing's inconsistency-riddled version of the alleged attack with Spell's unwavering alibi of brief consensual intercourse. She claimed he had written a ransom note, but one was never found; she claimed he hurled her out of the car and into the reservoir with her hands still tied, but she somehow managed to take off her coat in the water; she claimed that Mr. Spell raped her four times at four different locales, but no one heard her scream once. Strubing had sobbed and snapped on Friedman's cross-examination.

On direct examination, Spell told his version of events to a jury and courtroom at once riveted and repulsed. As he described Strubing's bedroom invitation, Friedman asked if she had resisted in any way. "No," Spell replied. "She didn't have no reason to."[15] He testified that he called after Strubing when she stepped out of the car, " 'What's wrong? Come back.' But she said, 'I'm all right. Go on.' She stepped into the water. I thought if I went back to the car she'd come back to her senses and come back. I was scared of what she'd do, maybe she'd hurt herself. She kept saying she was all right and for me to go on."[16]

The all-white jury of six men and six women split across gender lines on their first ballot: six guilty votes to six not-guilty. A few hours and votes later the vote was 11–1 for acquittal. At five minutes to midnight, the jury reached a unanimous not-guilty verdict. Throughout deliberations the jurors were led by Elizabeth Richmond, who was born and raised in the Deep South; she was convinced of Spell's innocence and was the most vocal of the original six not-guilty votes.[17]

When the judge read the verdict in court the next day, Spell exclaimed, "What a relief!" The prosecutor sat "obviously dazed by the verdict" while Friedman addressed the press corps. "The proper thing has been done," he told the microphones. "I couldn't be happier if it was I who had been acquitted."[18] Friedman beamed alone on the courthouse steps, however, because his cocounsel had returned to rural Oklahoma to defend another accused man claiming innocence.

HOUSTON SETTLED EASILY back into private practice. His five years as special counsel and years before that at Howard Law School accorded him prominence in both federal and local Washington. He protested against racial injustices ranging from the Daughters of the American Revolution's

refusal to permit Marian Anderson to perform in Constitution Hall to taxi-
cabs' collectively rejecting African American passengers at Union Station. In
contrast to Marshall, who disfavored public demonstrations, Houston organized and walked picket lines across his hometown, refusing to confine con-
frontation to courtrooms and legal briefs. Comfortably perched in the family
firm's F Street redoubt, he relished his regained independence; no longer
was he obligated to consult Walter White or association board members before accepting a new client or cause. In fact, with his father sheltered away in
the Department of Justice, Houston needed not overly concern himself with
whether a potential client could pay. His professional freedom found pur
pose the afternoon two black trainmen arrived in his office, excited to meet
the famous lawyer on whom they had already decided to depend because
they had heard they could.

FROM THE LATE nineteenth century through the 1940s, much of America's
most difficult, dangerous and important work was done along its railroads.
Generations before the birth of Eisenhower's interstate highway system,
locomotives labored across rivers and plains ferrying people and their goods
home and away. The tons-heavy black engines inspired romantic awe, and
men who commanded them commanded respect. Theirs was a fraternity
fraught with threat of disfiguring injury and death, and yet boys still aspired
to join it. Their glamour was the arduous sort.

From his and his father's work as railroad porters, Thurgood Marshall
had seen firemen and brakemen wager their lives for steam. To Houston
these enginemen lived lives unfamiliar; what little he knew, he had read.
Nonetheless, in 1939 Samuel Clark, president of the Association of Colored Railway Trainmen and Locomotive Firemen, day-journeyed from
Roanoke to Houston's downtown Washington office with J. A. Reynolds,
a fellow union man who also was an active NAACP member. Clark and
Reynolds wanted Houston to "find out what [they] should do to protect
their rights."[19] Before Houston could ask them how their rights were being violated, the railmen stacked a mountain range of papers onto his desk
and began describing their plight.

When they had finished, Houston explained that he knew little about
labor law. Surely Clark and Reynolds understood that they were suggesting
complex litigation on untested grounds. He regarded the papers perched

between him and the two men and answered them as they hoped he would: He promised to "study [the papers] and . . . come down to Roanoke to discuss them" with the black rail operators.[20]

Relief buoyed Clark's and Reynold's excitement. They thanked him for his time and consideration and assured him that they looked forward to his response.

In the coming days Charles Houston devoured the papers and history of America's black railmen with such abandon that their fight would soon become his fight as though it always had been.

BLACK MEN HAD WORKED trains ever since tracks were laid. Antebellum railroad companies owned slaves who fed the engines' blazing fires. A fireman, black or white, earned half an engineer's paycheck for work that was twice as hard. So it wasn't surprising that most firemen aspired to become engineers. But because slaves could never command a train, white firemen did not have to worry about competing with slave firemen for a promotion.

The 1880s saw freemen and white Yankees joining southern railroads, and the latter quickly learned that in the reconstructing South they earned a fraction of their northern paychecks, and this aboard southern trains older and meaner than the ones they had left behind in Pennsylvania and Ohio. Along the rails in the old Confederacy, members of the "Big Four" railmen's unions worked without the safety, wage and tenure protections they enjoyed up North. Southern engines' mechanic regulators could be fickle, making steam explosions common enough to concern any railman on a southern line. Moreover, southern firemen, particularly African Americans, performed most of the menial labor required in the engine. Management freely disregarded seniority, and wages stagnated despite soaring Reconstruction profits.

Union leaders decided to organize in the South as swiftly as possible; their bargaining power was strongest so long as the Reconstruction railway boom continued. Up North the Big Four—the Brotherhood of Locomotive Firemen and Enginemen, the Brotherhood of Railroad Trainmen, the Brotherhood of Locomotive Engineers and the Order of Railway Conductors—were all-white organizations as a matter of course. There simply were not many African American enginemen in the North. As union leaders began organizing southern enginemen, they discovered that in the

South there were enough black trainmen to warrant their mass inclusion in the unions. If excluded from union membership and permitted to work on the railroads, black enginemen could drive down wages by agreeing to work for a nominal increase over their present wages. The unions' choice was plain: Either they could dramatically increase their numbers by integrating and accepting African American trainmen—their charters included no race restrictions—or they could amend their constitutions to declare that only whites were eligible for membership and seek to purge nonunion black enginemen from the railroads.[21]

In 1884 all of the Big Four chose the latter and launched a brutal campaign to rid America's railroads of black enginemen. They intimidated their fellow railmen with violence and their employers with strike-threats. The Norfolk & Western, the Baltimore & Ohio—one by one the nation's largest carriers agreed not to hire African Americans in operating jobs as menial as baggage handler.[22] Reconstruction gave way to the Great War, but the brotherhoods yielded no ground. Despite wartime's manpower droughts, the unions refused to admit black men and vowed to strike against any carrier who hired them. Through the Great Depression and looming shadow of another world war, the brotherhoods, as one leading historian recounted, "practice[ed] what amounted to industrial genocide."[23] By the time Samuel Clark and J. A. Reynolds made their way to Charles Hamilton Houston's F Street office, no rail carrier had hired an African American fireman, brakeman, switchman, flagman or yardman since 1928. In twenty years the number of black trainmen had dropped from nearly fifteen thousand to just over five thousand.[24]

Houston understood after reading their documents that his meeting with Clark and Reynolds was a conference with two of what would be the last generation of black enginemen unless he took their fight for his and won. Nothing in Houston's constitution would allow him to reject them as clients. Asa Philip Randolph, who had organized the railroads' African American porters, maids and dining car workers into a union, later remarked that Houston "was racially oriented . . . he wasn't ashamed to fight for black people."[25] With his law firm partner Joseph Waddy, Houston made arrangements to visit Roanoke to meet some of Clark's and Reynold's brethren and to determine how together they could begin to end the end of black men working on the railroads.

The meeting, in a brakeman's Roanoke home, moved Houston as deeply as any he ever attended. The railworkers were proud and furious, and believed the traditions of their labor were being stolen from their grandchildren. Waddy recalled that, with what money their Colored Railway Trainmen's union had, it wanted the lawyers "to save these jobs for their children and grandchildren, so there would be other generations of black men on the railroads."[26] One of them, Waddy remembered, turned to Houston and "used this phrase that filled Charlie up emotionally."[27] Not only were white unions destroying opportunities for future black generations, they were ruining the livelihoods of the men gathered in that living room. Houston's potential clients were growing old, yes, but their railroad jobs allowed them to grow old with dignity. They were proud workingmen who now needed help in a bad way. The oldest among them told Houston and Waddy that they had to "protect these old heads blooming for the grave." The old man's words struck Houston hard and he agreed to represent them. He rose from his seat and promised them: "You don't have any laws to protect you, but I'm going to make some laws that will protect you. I'm going to make them."[28]

Although their union could afford to pay his firm barely more than nominal fees, Houston immersed himself in their fight for years. He visited train piers, climbing all over the equipment, asking copious questions and learning everything he could without actually feeding train fires or braking trains on downhill rain-slicked tracks. When he met with managers they respected his knowledge of their business but uniformly explained that their hands were bound by the white brotherhoods: If they hired even one black engineman, the white unions would cripple their national operations with an immediate strike. Houston soon understood that the problem lay not with management but with the white brotherhoods. "To me a fascist is a fascist," he seethed in the *Crisis*, "whether he wears a black shirt or blue overalls. I think a closed union with a closed shop is a form of fascism and should be prohibited by law."[29] He decided to sue some of the most racist unions his country had ever known.

HOUSTON WORKED SEVERAL CASES for members of the Association of Colored Railway Trainmen and Locomotive Firemen but had yet to litigate a case whose trial record he deemed worthy of appealing to the Supreme

Court of the United States. His quandary was a syllogistic riddle: White unions had intimidated the major carriers into eliminating black enginemen, but if the enginemen filed suit against this racial discrimination, their claim was confined to an arbitration board controlled by the white unions.

The Brotherhood of Locomotive Firemen and Enginemen provided daylight when, in yearlong negotiations culminating on February 18, 1941, it revised its collective bargaining agreement with railroad carriers to add clauses stipulating that African Americans could account for no more than half the firemen in any service district and should be reclassified as "non-promotable" firemen, effectively stripping them of their seniority.[30] The brotherhood did not inform black firemen in these negotiations, and the new contracts were put into effect before the newly classified "nonpro-motable" firemen received word from the railroad companies. Congress, by passing the Railway Labor Act just a few years earlier, had designated the Brotherhood of Locomotive Firemen and Enginemen as the exclusive bar-gaining representative for all members of their craft.

Houston believed that the congressional action imposed upon the brother-hood a fiduciary duty to represent all craft members fairly regardless of race or membership in the brotherhood. Alabaman Bester William Steele had worked the railroads for thirty years when he was fired on April 8, 1941, and he became the plaintiff for whom Houston had been waiting. Another of Houston's fraternity brothers, the only black lawyer practicing civil rights law in Alabama, filed suit in state court.

Arthur Shores was a brown-skinned Birmingham native with a sniper's patience. In the decades to come, his house would be bombed twice and he would be elected to the Birmingham City Council. In 1996 he would die peacefully at home in his hometown, and Theodora, his wife of fifty-eight years, would mourn alongside their two great-grandchildren. But in the winter of 1943, Shores found himself scribbling away on legal pads at counsel's table as Charles Houston rose to argue their client Bester Steele's case before the Alabama Supreme Court, where, as expected, Steele's case had landed.

Houston beseeched the court to enjoin the Louisville and Nashville Rail-road Company and the Brotherhood of Locomotive Firemen and Engine-men from acting under their "secret, fraudulent agreement."[31] He charged that the brotherhood "ha[d] refused to represent the Negro firemen fairly and impartially, ha[d] been persistently disloyal and hostile to them, ha[d] sought to destroy their vested seniority rights and to drive them out of service," and because the brotherhood enjoyed congressionally conferred exclusive bargaining power, these violations comprised breaches of the fiduciary duty the union owed to members and nonmembers alike.[32]

When Alabama's chief justice, Lucien D. Gardner, interrupted Houston to remark that this was the first time in his nearly thirty years on the bench that a Negro had argued before the highest court in the state, Houston and Shores accurately surmised their chances to be slim: The Alabama Supreme Court ruled that the brotherhood "did nothing illegal."[33] Houston announced his intention to appeal to the Supreme Court of the United States.

Steele's case against the railroad and union bore implications that rippled through American industry like a seismic tremor. Numerous unions excluded African Americans and squeezed management into hiring only their members; although Congress had not declared them exclusive bargaining agents, they knew that a Supreme Court ruling for Steele would provide their employers legal and political cover to negotiate freely with black trade workers. Overqualified domestic laborers followed *Steele* as closely as they did Joseph Spell's criminal trial. If white unions were enjoined from excluding them wholesale from trades, thousands of African American chauffeurs and gardeners could return to work as pipefitters, boilermakers and plumbers.

Union leaders knew this. Their attacks on Houston's labor activism were predictable and persistent. Four years after he argued for firemen at the Supreme Court, a reporter from *Counterattack: The Weekly Newsletter Against Communism* telephoned Walter White to discuss an article he was writing on the lawyer who without compensation chaired the NAACP National Legal Committee. The "long telephone call . . . cause[d White] to believe that [Houston would] shortly be attacked."[34] *Counterattack* would contend that Houston's defending "colored railway trainmen" resulted from "Communist inspiration." White "very bluntly" told the reporter that Houston's "efforts on behalf of Negro trainmen had no connection whatsoever with any Communist activities and that [he] had been hired by them to defend them in courts of law against the vicious discrimination of the railroad brotherhoods and the railroads."[35] Houston appreciated White's notice but knew that such publications reached conclusions irrespective of factual basis.

Houston submitted to the Court petitions for certiorari in *Steele* and *Tunstall v. Brotherhood of Locomotive Firemen and Enginemen* on behalf of the black railroad fireman Tom Tunstall, who held a grievance nearly identical to Steele's. Houston's petition briefs masterfully mixed conventional legal theory with realist advocacy. First he contended that when Congress granted the brotherhood exclusive power to negotiate on behalf of all workers in the trade, it necessarily imposed on it the responsibility to comply with the federal Constitution's Fifth and Thirteenth amendments.[36] Second, Houston reasoned that the brotherhood's goal and method of oppression incited violence on the rails, impeded the needed flow of commerce and thereby hampered the nation's war effort: "The seeds of industrial warfare which will adversely affect the war effort are present. It is paramount in the public interest that the rights and duties of the collective bargaining and grievance representative under the Railway Labor Act be determined peaceably by the Courts."[37] With biblical flair he charged the Court to engineer society: "In short, the Railway Labor Act has entombed the minority worker without hope of resurrection unless judicial relief is available."[38]

The Supreme Court agreed to review *Steele* and *Tunstall* and combined the cases. In his briefs on merits, Houston again struck a realist note by reminding the justices that black railroad workers could "strike as [a] last resort against undemocratic treatment" and this "could paralyze commerce" so the justices were well advised to reach their decision "in the light of all its foreseeable possibilities."[39] America had entered its third year of the Second World War, and further destabilizing the civilian labor force presented a precarious option for a Court that so recently had evaded President Roosevelt's packing scheme.

That the Court faced a momentous decision escaped no one. The Department of Justice, American Civil Liberties Union and the National Labor Relations Board filed amicus briefs in support of the black railworkers. On behalf of the NAACP Thurgood Marshall filed a brief as well. The amici agreed that it was "essential for the preservation of the basic principles of our democracy," as the ACLU brief contended, "that the deprivation of the right to work on account of race, which is at issue in this case, be declared unlawful."[40] The *Chicago Defender* proclaimed, "Unless the Supreme Court intervenes, the ranks of rapidly-diminishing Negro locomotive firemen on Southern railroads face complete annihilation."[41]

On the brisk morning of November 14, 1944, Houston again strode the steps up to the door of the nation's highest court. Prepared, confident and, even after years of delivering such arguments, still feeling the familiar fluttering deep inside, he readied for the *Oyez! Oyez!*

The justices eagerly engaged counsel. When Houston reiterated his client's position that the brotherhood and railroads had reduced black firemen to "economic servitude," Justice Hugo Black asked for clarification. Was Houston stating a racial discrimination claim?[42]

Not at all, he replied. Petitioner's position was based solely on the rights of the minority vis à vis the majority. Because it was responsible for negotiating a contract for all craftsmen, the majority—who were brotherhood members—could not ignore the minority without violating the minority's rights. That the minority in this case comprised black enginemen was immaterial to the substantive legal claim. What mattered was that Congress had granted the union exclusive power to negotiate a contract for those whom it excluded from membership, and if the union could exclude black firemen today, it could well "bar Catholics, Jews or a man six feet tall tomorrow."[43] It now was incumbent upon the Court to compel the union to represent those excluded workers' interests regardless of their membership status.

Houston's old law professor Justice Felix Frankfurter turned to the union's lawyer and asked him directly whether "promotable men" could be black.

"Not on the railroads of the United States," answered Harold Heiss. "That is the policy of the roads. We have nothing to do with it."

Justice Frank Murphy's interest was piqued. "Then the idea of non-promotable men is based on races?"

"That's railroad policy."[44]

On December 18, 1944, the justices unanimously ended that policy by ruling that the brotherhood was "chosen [by Congress] to represent all [firemen], regardless of their union affiliations or want of them."[45] The Court so thoroughly adopted Houston's argument that their words seemed his:

"Unless the labor union representing a craft owes some duty to represent non-union members of the craft . . . the minority would be left with no means of protecting their interests, or, indeed, their right to earn a livelihood by pursuing the occupation in which they are employed."[46] The sweeping decision immediately halted railroads' mass firings of nearly four thousand African American firemen, enginemen and brakemen and made those workers eligible to collect damages and be reinstated to their previous positions.[47]

Acting NAACP secretary Roy Wilkins congratulated Houston on his "thrilling victory" and declared that Houston "deserve[d] the thanks and appreciation not only of the plaintiffs in this particular case and of all the Negro railroad firemen everywhere, but of the entire Negro population because this opinion undoubtedly will affect the economic future of great masses of Negro workers."[48] Wilkins's effusive praise was accurate; the victory was as grand as any won thus far. As Houston explained to the press, the decision "affect[ed] every union that exercise[d] bargaining rights under statutory authority."[49] He cautioned them that the legal fight against the unions had just begun; this victory, while momentous, had merely established the legal basis on which to base future claims against discriminatory unions.[50] Black laborers nationwide nonetheless welcomed dawn's rising on a horizon Charlie Houston had just brought nearer.

A FEW MONTHS BEFORE Houston filed Bester Steele's lawsuit, while national newspapers marveled at a jury's finding Joseph Spell not guilty of raping Ellie Strubing, Thurgood Marshall traveled back down South to meet a man whose suffering he strained to imagine. That he trekked from Connecticut to Oklahoma with hardly a wardrobe change in New York City was not unusual. Letters, mostly from southern states, deluged his office. For each one that described a lawsuit or criminal trial promising legal or social significance, he rode a train hours, even days, to a city where a bus would catch and carry him, in its rear colored seats, to a prospective client. This is how in 1941 he found himself in Hugo, Oklahoma, on January's last Sunday.

All concerned prayed to believe that Elmer Rogers, his wife and one of his children had been shot in the head before their throats were slit, but everyone knew that did not make too much sense. It was a noisy mess, had to have been, or else the killers would not have burned down the Rogerses' house to destroy evidence. Elmer's nine-year-old son Glen hid in a closet and heard the whole grisly ordeal before he ran from his burning home.

The county arrested two white men who promptly confessed to the murders. They had killed the family while on a New Year's Eve furlough from a nearby state prison. The public's incredulous fury rained on Governor Leon C. Phillips, a bespectacled first-term politician who was as bigoted as he was religious and years earlier had studied to become a Methodist minister. That two hard-core felons had murdered a family while on a furlough from prison was bad news for Phillips's reelection prospects. He decided that, despite their confessions, the two convicts had not committed the murders. Phillips ordered that the charges be dropped and then dispatched his "special investigator," a hayseed sadist named Vernon Cheatwood, to find him a murderer in Hugo.[51]

With local police, Cheatwood roused a twenty-year-old black sharecropper from a night's sleep at his mother-in-law's house, hurled him into a police car and drove to a lonely copse, where they dragged him from the car, stripped off his belt and began lashing him with it. He would confess, they told him, to killing that family. His blood drawn in just minutes, W. D. Lyons told them he had no idea what they were talking about. Officers threw him to the ground, kicked him in the head, picked him up and repeatedly rammed his head into a tree. Then they flung him back into the police car and took him to jail.[52]

At the jail more officers were waiting for him in the sheriff's office. They assured him he would confess. "They started beating me with their fists," Lyons testified at his murder trial.[53] "One of the men had a blackjack that looked something like a milk bottle with which he beat me across the table, but I still continued to tell him that I knew nothing about the crime."[54] The county prosecutor arrived and joined in the interrogation.

The officers beat and starved Lyons for eleven days. Each morning, Governor Phillips's special investigator ordered his hotel's porter to fetch him his "nigger beater"—the blackjack with which he bloodied the sharecropper during the day.[55] And each morning, Cheatwood took to bragging to the crowd gathered around him in the hotel lobby how he beat Lyons "from his head to his feet" with the sawed-off leather-handled nightstick.[56]

In the middle of the eleventh night, Cheatwood entered Lyons's blood-ied, soiled cell. He would confess, the lawman promised. Hardly able to move from a cornered heap, Lyons steeled himself for another thrashing. Instead, as he described during his murder trial, "they brought a pan full of [burned] bones they said came from the slain couple and laid them in my lap."[57] Jawbones, teeth and child-sized limb-bones rattled in the stench.[58] The murder victims had been dead for twenty-two days.[59]

"There's the bones of that baby you burned up!" Cheatwood screamed. He tossed aside the pan of bones, flogged Lyons in the cell until at last the young man hollered guilty.[60] Minutes later he signed a confession and the next morning, after officers drove him to visit Oklahoma's death row pen-itentiary, he signed another confession stating that he had not at all been coerced.

Thurgood Marshall arrived in Hugo on January 26, 1941, just the night before W. D. Lyons's trial was scheduled to begin. He met the defendant and his lawyer, a white ACLU attorney named Stanley Belden, and pre-pared in what little time there was for what promised to be a battle for his young client's life.

MORE THAN A THOUSAND Choctaw County citizens, white and black, crushed into the district courthouse. There was the trial to see—Hugo's moment of national fame—and for the first time there sat a colored lawyer in the courtroom. Judge J. R. Childers sat squat on the bench smoking a cigar and welcomed schoolchildren into the crammed courthouse.

Marshall described the jury as "lousy" and, by the end of trial's first day, told Walter White there was "no chance of winning here."[61] He would "keep the record straight for appeal."[62] Belden agreed to help with the trial but leave the crucial confession issue to Marshall. Trial's first day ended without the state's seeking to enter the two confessions into evidence. Disappointed white spectators grumbled, "That nigger lawyer hasn't said anything."[63]

Next morning when the prosecution called the state's penitentiary war-den to testify as to Lyons's second confession, Marshall objected and asked that the jury be excused while the court heard arguments on the confes-sion's admissibility. In the jury's absence Marshall presented testimony that Lyons had confessed because he was tortured. Compelling witnesses, in-

cluding Mrs. Rogers's father and sister-in-law, testified that Cheatwood
had bragged to them about how he beat Lyons with his customized blackjack. Marshall cross-examined Cheatwood and Lyons's other tormentors
with skill and relish whet by the gallery's audible encouragement. "I did
all the cross-examining of the officers," he later told White, "because we
figure[d] they would resent being questioned by a Negro and would get
angry and this would help us out."[64] The tactic worked wonders. "They
all became angry at the idea of a Negro pushing them into tight corners
and making their lies so obvious. Boy, did I like that—and [so] did the Negro[e]s in the Court-room like it."[65]

White spectators began rooting for Lyons's acquittal as well: "After this
particular session many white people stopped us in the halls and on the
streets to tell us they enjoyed the way the case was going and that they
didn't believe Lyons was guilty." Marshall estimated that 90 percent of
white observers "were with Lyons. One thing this trial accomplished—
the good citizens of that area have been given a lesson in Constitutional
Law and the rights of Negro[e]s which they won't forget for some time."
In courthouse hallways several white spectators confronted officers whom
they knew had perjured themselves by maintaining they never had struck
Lyons. Outside, Marshall smoked hard on his cigarette before returning to
the crowded courtroom for the judge's decision on whether the jury
would hear Lyons's confessions.

Cigar-chomping Judge Childers announced that the governor's special
investigator and Choctaw County police had procured a confession through
unconstitutional beatings. He distinguished, however, between the first
and second confessions, and ruled that Lyons's second confession, signed
eighteen hours after his last beating (but, according to Lyons, signed under
the threat of continued torture), was constitutionally permissible.

The jury heard the confession and convicted the now twenty-one-year-
old black sharecropper of slitting the throats of three white people, shoot-
ing them dead and burning their bodies. Then they recommended that
W. D. Lyons be sentenced to life in prison. Marshall believed that the all-
white jury's refusal to sentence Lyons to death illustrated "clearly that they
believed him innocent."[66] He knew that no Oklahoma jury would acquit a
black man accused of such a crime. "I think we are in a perfect position to
appeal."[67] While Marshall prepared Lyons's appellate brief, he heartened

White regarding *Lyons* and *Spell*: "We can raise money on these cases. We have been needing a good criminal case and we have it. Let's raise some real money."[68] In a welcome omen, C. A. Colclasure, the father of Elmer Rogers's murdered wife, joined the NAACP without being asked.[69]

After losing at the first appellate level in Oklahoma, Marshall enlisted Leon Ransom and William Hastie for Lyons's appeal to the Supreme Court of the United States. They alleged that allowing Lyons's second confession to be entered into evidence deprived him of his Fourteenth Amendment due process rights because it was as surely procured by torture as the first confession eighteen hours earlier.[70]

The Supreme Court granted certiorari, heard oral arguments and, in a surprising 6–3 decision, sustained the trial court's decision to admit Lyons's second confession. Officially, "the NAACP expressed shock" at the decision, but Thurgood Marshall was more than shocked. He was devastated by his first Supreme Court defeat.[71] For over a decade to come he would correspond with W. D. Lyons, who faithfully wrote back from the Oklahoma State Penitentiary. Each letter scrawled in the sharecropper's script impressed upon Marshall that mere moral victory was not enough.

WAR AT HOME AND ABROAD

WAVY-HAIRED AND PREOCCUPIED, the Philadelphia-born Harvard Law student strode up Seventh Street's slight hill and turned right at F Street. Behind him Pennsylvania Avenue chortled its traffic and bustle. In Washington winter was yielding to spring, returning sun and breeze like jewels to a lock-picked box, but William T. Coleman, Jr., was not charmed by the city, still segregated in 1943. He had come to visit the man whose framed photograph sixty-five years later would hang in the center of his office wall. "When I volunteered to be an aviation cadet," Coleman recounted, "I went to see Houston to talk to him."[1]

After Houston and Hastie, Coleman would become the third African American to earn a place on the *Harvard Law Review.* By five votes he missed becoming its first black editor in chief, an honor five decades later accorded to a likewise gifted student named Barack Obama. Unlike Houston, Hastie or Obama, Coleman would graduate first in his class at Harvard. But first he had to go to war.

Young Bill Coleman prided himself, as Houston did, on having volunteered for military service. Although angry at the prospect of serving in a segregated military, neither man waited to be drafted. Coleman signed his papers and took a leave of absence from law school. Despite the heroic efforts of black soldiers in World War I, his generation found that the American military remained a brutally racist institution. Black officers were leaders of last resort, and black soldiers, enlisted and commissioned alike, were subjected to indignities spared even the white German prisoners of war. For the second time, African Americans were volunteering to fight a world war to preserve overseas the freedoms denied them at home. Coleman recently had received orders to report for training in Biloxi, Mississippi, and made his way to Houston's downtown office burdened by the question: "How the hell can I go into this segregated army?"[2]

Houston considered the law student, whose mien and temperament, far more than Marshall's, matched his own. Coleman had graduated first in his class from the University of Pennsylvania and favored pocket-squared three-piece suits. In over six decades of legal practice, he, like Houston, would largely eschew the public sector for private practice, and still presidents of the United States would seek his counsel. Presidents Roosevelt and Truman consulted Houston; Presidents Eisenhower, Kennedy, Johnson, Ford and the first president Bush would ask Coleman's advice. The fretting student now in Houston's office one day would serve as secretary of transportation and president of the NAACP Legal Defense Fund and would eulogize Justice Thurgood Marshall at his funeral.

Perhaps because he knew Coleman's potential in a better America, Houston listened to his concerns, nodded commiseration and finally said, "You have to go."[3] Yes, the army was segregated and the navy was worse, but the nation needed gifted young men like him to win this awful war.

Coleman knew then that he would board a Mississippi-bound train. Had the paternal World War I veteran told him to refuse to serve in a segregated military, Coleman would have. "If it weren't for his advice, I would have [refused induction and] gone to jail."[4] Instead, he went to war as Houston had done two decades earlier, as thousands of men were doing each day in 1943.

Charles Houston believed this benefited America's young men. From Birmingham, Alabama, he excitedly described to association lawyers the disciplined black sailors and soldiers with whom he rode the train: "This morning they were lined up at the wash basin taking turns freshening up . . . the lounge was clean, no litter on the floor . . . the toilet was clean, and no waste on the floor."[5] They were cleaner and more orderly than the civilians aboard, and Houston offered this as evidence for his belief that "the longer our boys stay in the service and service habits become a part of their established routine, the more our health level and general appearance will rise."[6]

THURGOOD MARSHALL'S WAR remained in America, where he now was traveling 2,500 miles each month to investigate, litigate, fund-raise and in all ways barnstorm the nation. Buster proudly endured his tireless devotion when he was away and often when he was not, as so many nights found him in his office wading through work that had stacked up while he was on the road. Strong as she struggled, Buster grew jealous of her friends whose husbands worked regular jobs with regular hours, jealous of wives who had become mothers. And jealousy was a wearying emotion.

Thurgood desperately wanted to become a father, believed he and Buster would be wonderful parents, and, in time, they conceived again. Doctors prescribed bed rest for the expectant mother. But this pregnancy ended in another miscarriage, and sorrow settled on their marriage.

Marshall took refuge in the struggle. The association's legal successes in the 1930s had forged believers from the hopeless, and now thousands of these converted belonged to America's armed forces; they barraged his office with letters detailing the bigotry and systemic injustices to which their white commanders subjected them. If he could save the lives of black sharecroppers and butlers, surely he could defend soldiers against dishonorable discharges, demotions and false criminal accusations.

A few months after Coleman sought Houston's advice, Private Rieves Bell took a furlough trip from his base in Massachusetts to visit his parents in Starkville, Mississippi. He stood on a corner talking to two pretty young black women his first night back in town when four white men, all civilians, passed by. One of the men pushed Bell, who shook off the insult and continued bantering with his lady-friends. Another man doubled back around, pushed Bell again and demanded, "Where did you get that uniform?"[7]

Private Bell replied that Uncle Sam had given him his uniform.

"Take off that soldier suit."

Bell refused and the four attacked him.[8] He fought as hard as he could against the locals and held his own until authorities arrived. Starkville police arrested Bell and charged him with assault. The army private was sentenced to three and a half years in a Mississippi prison.[9]

Cases like Bell's proliferated nationwide. Marshall handled some of them but soon was overwhelmed by their number and severity. Black military men were catching hell. Marshall hired the Legal Defense Fund's first three staff attorneys: Milton Konvitz, Edward Dudley and, later, fellow Howard Law alum and Army Air Force veteran Robert Carter.[10] Their work defending black servicemen allowed Marshall to rally continued African American support for the war effort. He stressed that black Americans would fare worse under Axis rule than would white Americans and could gain a great deal by answering again their country's call to arms.

Memories of brutal assaults on their returning World War I veterans, however, scarred many African Americans' thoughts of military service in the Second World War. Last time, they had fought abroad, returned home proud and were slaughtered by the dozens North and South. One African American columnist declared, "Although the Negro is loyal and will stick by the United States government, just as he has always done in the past, he now wants to share in the benefits of the democracy he has been told exists in this country and for which he fought in 1918."[11]

Again black Americans would fight for their country, but this time they concurrently would fight for themselves; they would fight for their liberation at home as hard as for French and British liberation abroad. The association's 1941 annual convention thundered its theme "Defend Democracy at Home" through national media and, while attendees lined up to hear about the infamous W. D. Lyons case, first on the agenda that hot Houston week in June was ensuring equality in both military service and the civilian defense industry.[12] As early as 1937, the association had warned President Roosevelt that if Europe's war should again engulf the nation, black Americans "would not endure the humiliation and insults which were heaped upon them and their soldiers" during the last world war.[13] Soldiers' and civilians' wartime activism proved the admonition no idle threat.

Civilians' ire was equally patriotic and economic. America's wartime economy ended years of Depression. Black workers were determined to contribute to and benefit from the surge, but white labor unions threatened and cajoled the major defense contractors to exclude African Americans from their payrolls. Around the time Houston filed his most significant railroad cases, Asa Philip Randolph, president of the Brotherhood of Sleeping Car Porters, called for a march on Washington to demand an end to federal government contractors' racist hiring policies. Randolph announced the March on Washington movement. He would lead 250,000 black workers through the District's streets.

Panic ensued. A quarter million angry black people marching through the nation's capital was a prospect that alarmed Congress as much as it scared white Washingtonians. President Roosevelt knew he had to avert the march, and on June 25, 1941, he created the Fair Employment Practices Committee. Executive Order 8802 read, "There shall be no discrimination in the employment of workers in defense industries or government because of race, creed, color, or national origin," and empowered the FEPC to investigate discrimination allegations and punish violating companies.[14] The committee comprised three labor representatives, three management representatives and a chairman.

New York City mayor Fiorello La Guardia called the order "a landmark in the progress of American democracy" and told a packed Harlem church, "I believe that the executive order signed and drafted by President Roosevelt will remain one of the most important documents in our history and the man who signed it will take his place among the true champions of liberty and the true champions of democracy."[15] Randolph, who with Walter White had met with La Guardia and Eleanor Roosevelt to negotiate the FEPC's creation, called off the march. Five years later he would revive his threat, and two decades after that, his organization would join others in carrying out a historic march on Washington.

Executive Order 8802 was not the first touch of progress to grace black folks during the war. Symbolic and substantive promotions peppered the time. As defense industry jobs became available, southern black families migrated north as their relatives had done generations ago. The army promoted Colonel Benjamin O. Davis, and the native Washingtonian became America's first black brigadier general.[16]

That same month, President Roosevelt appointed William Hastie to be the secretary of war's civilian aide. The president announced that Hastie, who was serving as dean of Howard Law School, would work on devising and implementing policies to ensure "the fair and effective utilization of Negroes in all branches of military service."[17] By now Hastie had served as a federal district judge and assistant solicitor for the Department of the Interior, and he accepted the appointment only after noting his consistent "opposition to any policy of discrimination or segregation." He vowed to use his post to help integrate the armed forces.[18]

Two years later the War Department had rejected Hastie's resignation no fewer than three times. The military remained relentlessly racist in Washington and on the battlefield. Its commanders and civilian leaders ignored Hastie's recommendations but refused to release him.[19]

FOR ALL THE FANFARE greeting its creation, the Fair Employment Practices Committee launched to inauspicious effect. Through national media outlets the government publicized the method by which citizens were to file their claims, and this campaign worked perhaps too well. The commission created to end discrimination against African American job seekers was "literally swamped with letters of complaint" from "foreign born, Indians, Jews" and even a group of one hundred thousand American-born white New Englanders who claimed to "comprise a minority group being discriminated against since local politicians in those areas g[a]ve jobs to foreign born persons" instead of them.[20] At its first racial discrimination hearing, the FEPC made no decision and instead referred the case to the War Department.[21] The commission two years later agreed to hold hearings on southern railroads' systematically eliminating black firemen—the very issue Houston was litigating in courtrooms across the nation—but abruptly canceled the hearings under pressure from southern congressmen. The *Atlanta Daily World* called the cancellation the "most vicious set-back the Negro people of the United States have received in recent years."[22]

President Harry Truman asked Charles Hamilton Houston to join the Fair Employment Practices Committee in March of 1944. Houston accepted the appointment, replacing a management representative and becoming the second African American committee member. Houston explained to Roy Wilkins that he harbored "no illusions about [the FEPC] but the job appears to be a spot which may be important on account of future implications; and it will put me on the inside of many problems which otherwise I would not reach."[23] The outside man recognized that he sometimes was more valuable "on the inside." He promised to "do my best to protect all minorities."[24]

The same week President Truman announced Houston's appointment, the FEPC reached a settlement with the Chicago & Northwestern Railroad whereby black workers received retroactive promotions and raises.[25] Despite its unpromising initial performance, the FEPC boasted some results by 1944, and expectations rose even higher with President Truman's appointing a man whom black Americans nationwide knew to be one of their truly tireless fighters.

JUST MIDWAY BETWEEN thirty and forty years old, Thurgood Marshall was engaged in a subtle dialogue with the Supreme Court of the United States. The justices knew him, his astute deference and easy insistence, and he had come to understand them, individual intellectuals collectively averse to moral judgment and to drastic reform and to Marshall's best-laid pleas for both. By their questions, asked and unasked, they told him their concerns and advised him where and how they were willing to step next. Particularly in coming years, when the NAACP again focused full bore on its education cases, Marshall's ability to discern the justices' oblique suggestions, to lead them where they were willing to go but could not lead him, proved invaluable. It was more dance than conversation.

Relating to the Court sometimes meant meeting the justices where they were. Thanks to an earlier case in which they unanimously rejected a litigant's constitutional claim, the justices were familiar with the Texas Democratic Party's exclusion of black voters. Democrats refused to let black Texans vote in their primaries, and because Democrats won nearly every election in the state, the party's racist policy had the effect of disenfranchising Texas's black citizens. Southern elections were often decided in Democratic primaries, which meant the Democratic Party had disenfranchised black voters across the South by enacting whites-only rules similar to those of Texas.

In the aforementioned case, the Court had ruled that the party's whites-only primary did not violate black Texans' constitutional right to vote because the party's exclusion was not an act of the state.[26] That ruling, *Grovey v. Townsend,* had been weakened by a subsequent Court decision, and Marshall decided that if he was going to ask the justices to admit that it had reversed itself, he might as well ask them to do it where they had erred in the first place. He traveled to Houston, Texas, where he met with an association member who on account of his race had been deprived a Democratic Party ballot in 1940.

Marshall was no longer the slim, dapper neophyte who with Charles

Houston had won *Murray* and fame. He carried a frame grown heavyset by stress, long hours and end-of-day bourbons. He smoked Winstons all day. Years ago he and Houston stormed the South and lived on brown bag-ripened fruit; in those same southern states Marshall now was greeted at the train or bus station by armed NAACP guards and whisked to a home where someone's wife had been cooking Sunday's best on account of "Thurgood's meeting." In Houston he met Dr. Lonnie Smith, on whose behalf he filed a complaint in Texas state court three weeks before millions of Americans heard for the first time the name of a faraway naval base attack bombed Sunday morning by Japanese fighter pilots.[27]

TEXAS'S STATE COURTS dismissed Smith's case swiftly, as Marshall had expected. As he prepared his petition for certiorari, he was drawn into a squabble that had been simmering since *Murray v. Maryland*. Marshall's beloved fraternity was becoming a bother to his practice. Alpha Phi Alpha's general counsel, the respected Washington litigator Belford V. Lawson, Jr., was, according to Alpha brother and noted attorney Prentice Thomas, "still peeved about the case of *Murray v. University of Maryland . . .* [and] claim[ed] that the Fraternity started the case, largely through his efforts, and in the end the NAACP received all the credit."[28] Thomas, a Kentucky lawyer who like Marshall had blossomed beneath Houston's demanding instruction, explained that Lawson's umbrage mattered because "Brother General Counsel" had "power to withhold the money [allocated] for the Texas Primary case if, in his opinion, the Fraternity [did] not receive some credit."[29] Lawson even threatened to file his own Texas primary lawsuit. Thomas noted that he and Marshall had not paid dues in nearly a decade; while "Charlie, of course, tops both of us" in paying his annual dues. Perhaps the time had come for them to "do a lot more on the inside than on the outside."[30]

Marshall replied on the day he received Thomas's letter that he would "be happy to cooperate in any way possible in seeing to it that the fraternity gets due recognition for what it has done."[31] He had grown impatient with Lawson's imperiousness, however, and if the general counsel refused to believe that Marshall's sole interest was "in getting a job done," then "I, for one, do not care." To Marshall "the question of credit means nothing."[32] The Supreme Court accepted his latest case and he commenced working on the brief and oral argument with Hastie and newly hired assistant special counsel Milton Konvitz.[33]

Their case seeded itself in constitutional pragmatism. Although the Texas Democratic Party's primary was not a government-sponsored activity, the Court had recognized after *Grovey* that "where the state law has made the primary an integral part of the procedure of choice, or where the primary effectively controls the choice, the right of the elector to have his ballot counted at the primary is [constitutionally protected.]"[34]

On January 12, 1944, Marshall and Hastie argued to the justices that *Grovey* no longer was good law, that the Court implicitly had ruled already that race-exclusive primaries violated the Constitution; the NAACP now was asking the justices to make explicit what they already had implied. As Marshall explained: "The right to vote includes three distinct steps: 1) qualifying to vote, 2) selection of candidates, and 3) the actual election. The Supreme Court has held that Negroes cannot be prevented from taking part in steps one and three. We maintain that the selection of candidates by a primary election pursuant to state statutes is just as much a part of the elections machinery of the state as the actual election."[35] He impressed upon the justices that "since 1859, all Democratic nominees have been elected in Texas with two exceptions." The Democratic Party employed "the county clerk and other state officers in these primary elections and follow[ed] the state machinery."[36] The party's elections were, in operation and effect, state actions.

Three months later the Court agreed and explicitly overruled *Grovey*. By excluding black voters, the Texas Democratic Party, "a party entrusted by Texas law," was committing a state action.[37] The Democratic Party no sooner could exclude African American voters than could the state of Texas itself. More than the high-profile criminal cases or the education desegregation cases, *Smith v. Allwright* immediately affected the country.[38] Decades later Marshall would still consider the *Smith* victory "the greatest one."[39]

In 1944 Houston's and Marshall's landmark Supreme Court victories firmly established the NAACP as a legal force. With Bill Hastie, Prentice Thomas, Bob Carter and others, they were fulfilling Houston's twenty-year-old vision of black lawyers successfully wielding the Constitution against oppression. During the year coming, Houston would resign from the Fair Employment Practices Committee in a public protest against President Truman and his tepid enforcement of black workers' rights in Washington. "The failure of the Government to enforce democratic practices and to protect minorities in its own capital," he wrote to the president, "makes its expressed concern for national minorities abroad somewhat specious, and its interference in the domestic affairs of other countries very premature."[40] Walter White proclaimed the letter "magnificent" and "unanswerable," but the president did reply, accepting Houston's resignation "to be effective immediately."[41]

Houston's scathing open letter to the president ensured that he would never be selected for the federal bench as his cousin had been and Marshall would be. Like other official positions and trappings, however, this did not matter to him. To university campuses the fight would return. Only now, when college registrars and presidents received letters on NAACP Legal Defense Fund stationery, they knew they were reading the words of lawyers whom most Supreme Court justices believed were right much more often than not.

SUPREME BROKEN COVENANT

THE EXTENDED HOUSTON FAMILY rejoiced on March 20, 1944, when Henrietta gave birth to seven-pound Charles Hamilton Houston, Jr. Charlie and Henrietta had traveled a long road to parenthood, and during her pregnancy's final weeks, he rushed home from long days working on the railroad cases to pamper her as best he could. Unlike Marshall, who enjoyed cooking recipes he had learned from his grandmother, Houston was bereft of domestic talent. In the weeks surrounding his son's birth, he compensated with earnestness for his inexperience in keeping house. He doted on Henrietta, and after little Charlie, Jr., was born, he doted on him as best he knew how. The beaming new dad held his son so lovingly, adoringly, that his parents and wife could only smile more broadly as he fussed over the baby in the fumbling new-father way.[1] Charlie, Jr., who soon acquired the nickname "Bo," was the brightest light and deepest anchor in his father's life, and he forever would be.

REMNANTS OF AMERICA'S Second World War victory presented a landscape uniquely fertile for Houston, Marshall, Hastie and the lawyers they led to launch, at last, a direct assault on American segregation. The NAACP's well-publicized efforts defending black servicemembers both won their faith and loyalty and exposed white Americans and allies to the brutish racism to which the United States subjected its black soldiers and sailors. As the *Pittsburgh Courier* explained, America's armed forces adhered to "the doctrine of white supremacy and racial separatism with a zeal that [Nazi propagandist] Dr. Joseph Goebbels would regard as commendable."[2]

Although the nation had defeated a German regime of white supremacists, its ingrained domestic white supremacy—its WHITES ONLY southern signs and white Christian restrictive covenants—became a source of international concern and embarrassment. Its racist culture, North and South, "had acquired foreign policy implications" during the war, and the association challenged that "our government, raising its hands in horror at persecution on the other side of the world, might take a moment to glance at its own back yard" where "Hitlerism . . . is directed at citizens who happen not to be white."[3] In speeches across the country Houston reminded audiences that they were members of a minority only in America, "a white country in a colored world."[4]

This militancy combined with demographic shifts to rework the nation into one in which desegregation was possible. During the war years, more than 1.5 million black southerners migrated to the North to work defense industry jobs made available to them in part by the FEPC and Houston's Supreme Court union victories. Once North, they found they could vote, obtain housing and educate their children more easily and better than back down South. They were scratching their way into the middle class. Aspirations long reserved to a privileged class of fair-skinned black Americans at last became the masses' collective hope: Education, health, music, encouragement, sympathy, laughter and other species of self-invested capital flourished.[5] NAACP membership increased nine times over during the war.[6]

THE GRANDSON OF A FREED SLAVE turned successful businessman, Spottswood Robinson III was longer, lankier and a little younger than Marshall and was meticulous to a fault. In a few years, to relieve stress from his exacting legal practice, he would begin constructing a boat. Marian Wilkerson, who married Spottswood when he was twenty and lived with him until he died sixty-two years later, knew that when he stole away to their basement she might not see him for hours. Bow to stern, deck to fenderwale and keel, Robinson cut and bent and willed wood into place. Sanded edges he pressed together for sealing, his thin lips pressed together with the effort. When he at last launched his boat in 1953, Robinson eagerly invited friends to witness the event, and to a man they were amazed: Spottswood had built the entire boat without nail or screw.[7]

Like Thurgood Marshall and his good friend and law firm partner Oliver Hill, Robinson believed in the Houstonian ethos espoused at Howard Law School. The lay of the legal land demanded social engineering, and a lawyer who shirked this responsibility was a parasite on society. Robinson's doggedly meticulous nature lent itself to engineering and demanded the quibbling occupation occasioned by litigation.

The opening of the school year 1938–39 found Robinson determined to research and report on an issue that years later would again unite the two lawyers he admired most. Houston and Marshall during the war prepared separate cases to attack racist restrictive covenants, written agreements between buyers and sellers of real estate by which the former agreed never to sell the property to Jews or blacks or whomever else most neighbors had declared undesirable. As the *Washington Post* described in 1948, racist covenants barred citizens "from large parts of hundreds of American cities and towns. Many State courts and the United States Court of Appeals [for D.C.] have put teeth in them by ordering Negroes and others to move out of homes they bought that were subject to race covenants."[8] As a student Robinson drafted a thesis paper assaulting the covenants' legality. His report impressed Marshall, who in 1944 commissioned him to expand it for use in litigation.[9]

It was not long before Marshall tired of Robinson's habitual delays. That the younger lawyer was a painstaking perfectionist proved inconvenient, and Marshall bristled at his explaining why he could not estimate when his revised report would be complete: "I merely keep at it until I am satisfied that a good job has been done."[10]

Ever the wily pragmatist, Marshall cited Robinson's delayed report as reason for the nearly three dozen attorneys challenging racially restrictive covenants nationwide to postpone action and instead coordinate their cases through the Legal Defense Fund. Because they were not working for the Legal Defense Fund, Marshall could only hope to persuade them to coordinate their efforts behind his lead. Robinson's thorough examination would help them harmonize their arguments. Prominently figured in the report would be data on the actual effects of racist covenants—how they

skewed neighborhoods and cities in the same way as state-sponsored segregation. Marshall believed this evidence indispensable in convincing courts
to enjoin the covenants' enforcement and wanted the lawyers to include
the evidence in their cases.

In this way, the anticovenants campaign was Thurgood Marshall's first
major attempt to organize the nation's civil rights attorneys to play from
the same sheet of music. Their personalities varied as widely as their ac-
cents. Each shared both a conviction that the restrictive covenants were
unconstitutional and the belief that his own particular strategy was the one
most likely to prevail. These were not homespun country-corner lawyers
but rather men with ego and reputation. Indeed, one of the lawyers Marshall had to corral was Charles Hamilton Houston, who was working to
invalidate covenants in Washington.

Realizing his challenge, Marshall convened a Chicago meeting of all
anticovenant lawyers in 1945. Thirty-three lawyers gathered and, to the
special counsel's relief, agreed that sociological evidence delineating how
racist covenants harmed excluded citizens was crucial to their cases. That
Houston provided vocal leadership certainly surprised no one; by relying
expressly on the covenants' real-life effects, the attorneys were launching
the first major test of the legal realist theory in which he so publicly held
faith. Houston was the most prominent lawyer present and, after hearing
him, the gathered lawyers dispersed from Chicago energized to fight their
cases.[11]

TWO YEARS LATER, in 1947, Thurgood Marshall again assembled the attorneys. A few of them by now were preparing certiorari petitions, and this
concerned them all because an adverse Supreme Court decision could end
all their cases for naught. Ever his friend's advocate, Houston agreed to
chair this second meeting. Marshall sought to postpone Supreme Court
review until a case with a record better than those thus far litigated became available.

A month before this January meeting, however, J. D. Shelley's lawyer
filed a petition with the Supreme Court. Shelley and his wife, Ethel, had
worked hard during the war, laboring at construction sites and in a muni-
tions plant in Saint Louis. With their savings the couple bought a home in
which to raise their six children, only to be sued by a white couple, the

Kraemers, living ten blocks away. The complaint alleged that the Shelley's contract to buy their home was void because a restrictive covenant forbade black Americans from buying or owning the house.

Not long after the anticovenant lawyers' second meeting, the Supreme Court agreed to review the Shelleys' case and Houston's case, *Hurd v. Hodge*. Marshall surely was relieved that the Court consolidated the cases because the Shelleys' attorney, George Vaughn, was an NAACP member loath to coordinate strategy with other lawyers. In Houston, Marshall always had an ally, and together they persuaded Vaughn to permit Marshall to present oral argument as well.

Oral argument opened dramatically on January 16, 1948, when Justices Rutledge, Jackson and Reed rose from the bench and, having recused themselves, left the courtroom.[12] They earlier had announced that they would not hear the case because their houses were subject to racially restrictive covenants. "It shows how deep the case cuts," Houston later quipped to reporters, "when one-third of the nation's highest court disqualifies itself."[13] Chief Justice Vinson and Justices Black, Frankfurter, Douglas, Murphy and Burton remained to hear the case, presenting the uncomfortable possibility that four justices could decide the case—a majority of the bare quorum but a minority of the Court.

Solicitor General Philip Perlman presented first and to great effect. The Truman administration's decision to intercede on behalf of the African American appellants was a lobbying victory for the NAACP. In the wake of the administration's 1947 report, *To Secure These Rights*, Perlman, the federal government's designated Supreme Court lawyer, delivered his argument with as much authority as any "tenth justice" ever has. Racist restrictive covenants, he told the justices, "should be relegated to the limbo of other things as dead as slavery."[14] As he spoke, Perlman could feel on his back the eyes of so many black Washingtonians who had arrived early and packed the courtroom. "They have been told time and again by this Court that this is a government of laws and not of men and that all men are equal before the law. They wait—millions of them—outside this courtroom door, to learn whether these great maxims really apply to them."[15] Perlman later told a friend that arguing for black Americans' rights in their presence was a professional revelation.

To help prepare his case, Houston had recruited Spottswood Robinson III, who hardly could believe that first Thurgood Marshall and now Charles Hamilton Houston had hired him.[16] Even the perfectionist Robinson was floored by Houston's relentless revising and disregard for fatigue. Hunched at his desk beneath his familiar green visor, Houston scribbled to shreds Robinson's draft brief and handed over the remnants at four A.M. He asked the young man to please rewrite. In fifty years Robinson would preside as chief judge of the Court of Appeals for the D.C. Circuit, often referred to as America's second-highest court for its deciding so many federal government appeals. He would remember long hours working the covenant cases with Houston and recount that "thoroughness was Charlie."[17]

In addition to constitutional argument, Houston and Robinson's brief contended that judicial enforcement of racially restrictive covenants violated public policy. Marshall thought little of this argument—Houston's clients had purchased a house in the District, where segregation was public law and policy. He tried in vain to persuade Houston to excise his public policy argument.

Houston should have heeded Marshall's counsel. Opposing counsel James Crooks, whom the *Washington Post* described as "the anchor man of the covenanters' squad of lawyers," pressed upon the justices Marshall's precise argument. There was a public policy in the District of Columbia and "it was a policy of race segregation."[18] After reminding the Court that judges cannot divine public policy from their own personal morals but must find it in the laws and mores of society, Crooks recalled that D.C. law provided for segregated schools, segregated public housing and certainly most Washingtonians lived segregated lives. For the Court to rule that judicial enforcement of racially restrictive covenants violated public policy, it would have to vitiate the definition of the term.

Of course public policy was but one aspect of Houston's argument, the remainder of which he presented unassailably. As a longtime D.C. litigator, he understood that presenting constitutional argument to invalidate District of Columbia law was a dicey proposition: The Fourteenth Amendment, on which the NAACP typically relied, applied only to states; Washington, D.C., as something of a federal colony, was subject only to the Fifth Amendment, which the framers drafted to protect citizens' right to "due process of law" as opposed to "equal protection of the laws." When Houston presented the social science data as further evidence that the covenants should be banned, his old professor Justice Frankfurter perked up: "This all goes to the inequities of the case."[19] That the justices extensively questioned both him and Marshall on the sociological evidence intimated its worth in their decision making.

In contrast to the "intellectual strength and moral force" of Houston's presentation, George Vaughn's argument was unlike any other in recent Court memory.[20] The Saint Louis attorney was intent on arguing that racially restrictive covenants violated the Thirteenth Amendment, which outlawed slavery. Marshall, Houston and other attorneys tried to dissuade him but Vaughn, whom Marshall decades later described as a "blunderbuss," was intent on arguing that the racist covenants held black people in bondage.[21] The association's lawyers held their breath as Vaughn rose to address the court.

After dispensing with the "May it please the court" formalities, Vaughn launched into an impassioned harangue sweeping across ancient Jewish enslavement to Jim Crow segregation. His voice boomed as he cried, "And Moses looked out across the River Jordan and across the Mississippi River and said, 'Let my people Goooooooooo!'" In every row of the packed gallery eyes widened and jaws dropped. The justices dared not ask him a question.[22] Vaughn roiled to climax, his gestures grand as his theme: "As the Negro knocks at America's door, he cries: 'Let me come sit by the fire! I helped build the house!'"[23]

In the ensuing silence Houston and Marshall sat staring straight ahead. Next was Marshall's turn to address the Court, and he knew that he would receive all the questions the justices were afraid to ask Vaughn, whose Thirteenth Amendment claims would go unaddressed in the Court's opinion.

Marshall presented his argument in what one of the chief justice's law clerks called his "typically elegant and articulate way."[24] He handled the justices' questions with an ease illuminating his extensive preparation. In response to a question posed by Chief Justice Fred Vinson, Marshall contended that state action commenced when buyers and sellers entered into a contract because the force of their agreement depended on judicial enforcement of the contract.[25]

The covenanters' lawyers were equally prepared and at day's end none could surmise with any certainty how the Court would rule. The *Washington Post* reported that, based on the justices' questions and apparent concerns, "there were several ways the cases might go"; a decision was not expected "for months."[26]

CHARLES HOUSTON IN 1947 was a man in manifold demand. Churches, congressional committees, unions and labor groups and presidential commissions invited him to speak and sought his counsel. Government committees summoned his testimony not just for his erudite forthrightness but also because his testimony never lacked for intellectual honesty. Before President Truman's Committee on Civil Rights he declared, "I am a states rights man as distinguished from a federal rights man, because I can conceive of the Federal Government being a juggernaut which can roll over minority rights, as well as protect them, and the present performance of the Federal government in the witch hunt against Communists, and its fight against labor, gives me no belief that the Federal Government either is the repository of all wisdom or should be entrusted with all the police power of the United States of America." The committee could best fulfill its duty, "speaking so far as the Negro is concerned, if you will make it so that the population can help itself."[27] This rather conservative line surely surprised some committee members, but it was wholly consistent with Houston's deep-seated belief in self-reliance and self-determination. He truly had become "free to hit and fight" on fronts as diverse as his interests; still, he remained chairman of the NAACP National Legal Committee.

Up in New York City, Marshall's staff at the association's Legal Defense Fund had grown to four attorneys. Even having achieved lawyer's fame himself, Thurgood Marshall was loath to make major legal or strategy decisions without first consulting Houston. He sometimes disagreed with his advice—as when Houston insisted on arguing public policy in the restrictive covenant cases—but Marshall preferred knowing Houston's thoughts on matters of import. Realizing that many organizations were competing for Houston's time, Marshall punctuated his meeting invitations with lines like "It is really urgent that you give us as much time as you can possibly spare on both these matters;" and then, as if to soften the letter's typed demand, he would scribble beneath his signature, "Charlie, please try and make it."[28]

At the NAACP's 1948 annual convention, Marshall planned to convene the National Legal Committee's members to strategize "the handling of education, voting and transportation cases" and to devise a plan to facilitate better communication among the Legal Defense Fund lawyers, National Legal Committee members and the branch office attorneys. "I think that if it is at all possible," Marshall wrote Houston, "you should be present and it would be most helpful if you would preside during the meeting. At any rate, your suggestions as to the meeting itself will be most helpful."[29]

"While I should like much to be with you June 21," Houston replied, "I do not believe I can make it." He was scheduled to address the convention on June 25 but would be unable to arrive before then.[30] With his happy marriage and three-year-old son at home, gone were the days when Houston gleefully traveled whenever to wherever he was needed. He knew that Marshall was logging thousands of miles each month and responded with pragmatic advice on how best to conduct the meeting.

IN MAY 1948, the Court issued its restrictive covenants decision on the day when the justices read several decisions from the bench. While other decisions were being read, as Walter White recalled, "Chief Justice Vinson sat relaxed in his leather chair stroking the side of his nose with a finger in characteristic fashion and chatting occasionally with [Justice] Hugo Black." The chief justice sparked to life when it came time to read the covenants decision. With "his face and voice filled with deep feeling, [he] leaned forward to read the unanimous decision."[31]

"We hold," the chief justice read in a baritone befitting the moment, "that in granting judicial enforcement of the restrictive covenants in these cases, the States have denied petitioners the equal protection of the laws and that, therefore, the action of the state courts cannot stand . . . Because of the race or color of these petitioners they have been denied rights of ownership or occupancy enjoyed as a matter of course by other citizens of different race or color." The Fourteenth Amendment to the Constitution forbid just this discrimination.[32]

In Washington, D.C., where the Fourteenth Amendment did not apply, the Court ruled that the Civil Rights Act of 1866, drafted in close conjunction with the Fourteenth Amendment, enjoined racially restrictive covenants. "That statute by its terms," Chief Justice Vinson explained, "requires that all citizens of the United States shall have the same right 'as is enjoyed by white citizens to inherit, purchase, lease, sell, hold and convey real and personal property.' "[33] Moreover, in vindication of Houston's public policy argument, the justices held that because *Shelley* had just invalidated racist covenants in the states, federal public policy demanded that they be abolished in Washington, D.C., as well.[34] The NAACP lawyers' victory was unanimous.

IN RESPONSE TO THE NAACP's earlier success and continued litigation to desegregate southern graduate schools, fourteen southern states entered into a pact to provide regional education facilities for their African American graduate students. Specifically, the states would assume control of Tennessee's Meharry Medical College and send all their black medical school applicants to the blacks-only school. Regional graduate schools for law, journalism and other disciplines could be established "if found necessary."[35]

The Senate Judiciary Committee summoned Marshall to testify regarding the legality of segregated regional schools, and the special counsel plainly explained the association's position: "It is clear from decisions of the United States Supreme Court that the States covered by the proposed compact cannot escape their responsibilities under the Fourteenth Amendment by sending their Negro students to Meharry and paying their tuition and expenses in lieu of admitting them to their State medical schools." The regional schools compact was "merely an effort to circumvent the effect of these decisions."[36]

Wisconsin Republican senator Alexander Wiley reminded Marshall that segregated schools were perfectly legal, to which the witness replied that the law demanded equality and "the truth is that in order to increase educational opportunities for its citizens, the South must give up segregation. The Southern States can neither jointly nor severally provide equality in a segregated setup."[37]

This bold pronouncement was one of the first official indicators that the Legal Defense Fund attorneys had shifted their stated aim. University desegregation was now their express cause; no longer were they content with the legal fig leaf of beseeching separate equality. Desegregation was becoming both the means and the end of black Americans' fight for equality.

PEACE OF MIND

B Y 1949, HOUSTON at last acknowledged that in his chest brewed a familiar fatigue that had gained strength. Tuberculosis, hernia and years of travel and strain coalesced in his chest to form an unseen palm that pressed against his breath just hard enough to remind him that it kept time. Weakness hurt proud men most, so Houston wrote to Marshall's deputy, Bob Carter, instead of to Thurgood: "These education cases are now tight sufficiently so that anyone familiar with the course of their decisions should be able to guide the cases through." He imposed finality. "You and Thurgood can proceed without any fear of crossing any plans I might have."[1] So lightly was the baton passed that Marshall and Carter might have missed its delivery, mistaken certainty for courtesy. But Houston soon suffered a heart attack.

ALMOST EXACTLY FOUR YEARS EARLIER, Marshall had drafted for Houston a lengthy memorandum describing his meeting with an attractive recent graduate of Oklahoma's Langston University. Ada Lois Sipuel was a southern beauty with a midwestern heart. Marshall met her in a branch member's office just after the University of Oklahoma Law School issued her race-based rejection. She was their second-choice plaintiff; her brother decided to attend Howard Law School, which Professors James Nabrit, Leon Ransom, Houston and Dean Hastie had by now developed into a three-year boot camp producing civil rights lawyers. As its most famous alumnus,

Marshall hardly could fault Sipuel's brother for choosing Howard and instead asked her why she "would not attend Howard, where all the finest civil rights lawyers go."[2]

Sipuel firmly replied that she wanted an Oklahoma legal education based on Oklahoma law and sought the Oklahoma connections she knew necessary for successful legal practice. More personally, her widowed father was not well and she wanted to remain near him. The proud preacher and his homemaking wife had moved their children from Tulsa after the Great War's horrific riots when white mobs burned down their house and state militiamen imprisoned their father. Marshall told Houston that Ada Lois Sipuel's "determination to attend an all-white law school" was but the "product of her family's commitment."[3]

That afternoon was the second time she had ever seen Marshall; the first was back when she was a Depression-time elementary schoolgirl in Chickasha, Oklahoma. Black folks in Chickasha who wanted to see the picture show paid full fare at the box office and then climbed up the fire escape and slid through the window to balcony seats.[4] Marshall spoke at her school while on a tour of local NAACP branches and segregated schools, and, she later recalled, "[He was the] most handsome, articulate, brilliant and charismatic man I had ever seen."[5] To ease his client's nerves at meeting the famous lawyer who had flown in an airplane from New York City to Oklahoma to meet her, Marshall eschewed her offered hand to swallow her in one of his belly-bursting bear hugs.[6] They laughed and she relaxed in the presence of this "warm and gregarious man."[7]

Tension relieved, Marshall set about learning facts, his ear cocked to questions Houston was sure to ask upon reading of this too-good-to-be-true client. With Roscoe Dunjee, publisher of Oklahoma's only black newspaper and president of Oklahoma's NAACP, Sipuel had hand-delivered her application to the law school's dean of admissions, who explained that she certainly was qualified for admission but that Oklahoma law levied a five-hundred-dollar misdemeanor fine on anyone who taught blacks and whites in the same classroom.

Dunjee took Sipuel to the university president's office perhaps knowing that, for all George Lynn Cross resembled bespectacled President Woodrow Wilson, he was not a man void of empathy. "I'll put anything in this letter you feel will get you into court," Cross told Dunjee.[8] He "was sympathetic" to her cause and "wanted to cooperate."[9] Cross accordingly wrote that Sipuel would have been admitted but for her race. This admission would do.

Marshall assured Houston that Sipuel was "willing to endure the years of hardship which this case will entail." Perhaps recalling Houston's reservations about Lloyd Gaines, he continued, "Miss Sipuel's goals are very much those of the NAACP. She wants to attend Oklahoma State University [*sic*]; we want her to go there, too." She possessed "the character and commitment" to see a case through the end.[10]

The special counsel then turned to legal strategy. "The government of Oklahoma is implacably racist" but "we should bite the bullet and file in state court." Due to a doctrine recently issued by the Supreme Court in *Railroad Commission of Texas v. Pullman Co.*, a federal judge would likely decline to hear the case. Under the equal protection clause of the Fourteenth Amendment, Marshall planned to ask "the court to admit that, in Oklahoma, as well as in the rest of the country, a system which forcibly separates Negroes and whites cannot promote equality.

"In other words, we want the court to overrule *Plessy v. Ferguson*. 163 U.S. 537 (1896)."[11] As if seeing Houston's eyes widen beneath his green visor, Marshall swore that he did "not suggest this lightly . . . Several factors favor a charge at *Plessy*, with a view to presenting our case to the Supreme Court during the 1948 term.

"First, this is the best bench we will get for some time." Among Justices Reed, Black, Douglas, Murphy and Rutledge and President Truman's handpicked new chief justice, Fred Vinson, the attorneys "could hope for a 6–3 vote in favor of overturning *Plessy*." Second, "Harry Truman is a genuine anti-segregationist." In a point unwittingly prescient of the violent resistance that would greet *Brown v. Board of Education*, Marshall noted that the NAACP could rely on Truman's executive branch to enforce the Court's decision. Last, if the Court refused to overturn *Plessy*, "the worst case scenario is that we settle for a repeat of *Gaines*."[12]

On this last point Marshall's claim was less than earnest. The worst case scenario was that the Court could expressly affirm *Plessy*. It could firmly state that the Constitution allowed for race-based separate but equal accommodations and thereby vitiate African Americans' struggle for equal rights. The worst case scenario's effects both immediate and long term would be cataclysmic.

In 1946, Oklahoma's supreme court judges affirmed the trial court's decision that Oklahoma need neither admit Sipuel nor construct a law school for African Americans absent evidence that enough black students would attend. Marshall appealed the case, *Sipuel v. Oklahoma State Board of Regents*, to the Supreme Court of the United States. In his brief he contended with Houston's blessing that segregated public education was "designed and intended to perpetuate the slave tradition." Even two schools with comparable facilities could not be equal because "there can be no separate equality."[13]

The *Washington Post* reported that at oral argument "counsel for the State of Oklahoma took a severe hazing from the Supreme Court." As if peeved they had been called to address an issue they thought settled, "the justices asked sharply—again and again—why did Ada Lois Sipuel, a Negro girl, have to come clear to the Supreme Court to get into the State law school, which is open to students of other races."[14]

Oklahoma assistant attorney general Fred Hansen explained that the state was bound to provide equal education to all its citizens, but that it could do so in segregated schools. The state could not help it if Sipuel was the only student at the school for black students.

"A law school for just one student wouldn't be equal," Justice Jackson declared. "It wouldn't be much of a law school, would it?"

Oklahoma was one of seventeen states with a policy of segregation and she must abide—

"Why should she abide by it more than a white person? Why should she waive her constitutional rights?"[15] Justice Jackson's angry incredulity foreshadowed the Court's ruling.

On January 12, 1948, just four days after oral argument, the Court issued a unanimous unsigned per curiam decision ordering Oklahoma to offer Sipuel a legal education "in conformity with the equal protection clause of the Fourteenth Amendment and provide it as soon as it does for applicants of any other group."[16] *Sipuel* was an enigmatic decision that cited *Gaines* but went no further. The Court all but ignored Marshall's impassioned brief and argument that segregation itself violated the Constitution because under segregation equality could not exist.

The Oklahoma Board of Regents promptly memorialized the Court's apparent ambivalence by concocting a blacks-only law school composed of a roped-off section of the state capitol and three part-time teachers. Sipuel refused to participate in the sham. The University of Oklahoma's law students were embarrassed and angered by the ordeal; a survey found that 83 percent of them wanted Sipuel admitted.[17] Oklahoma law professor Henry Foster decried the purported law school for black students as "a fake, a fraud and a deception."[18]

Thurgood Marshall returned to the justices; surely Oklahoma's roped-off section defied Court mandate and constitutional demand. Again he argued that segregation itself—and not merely Oklahoma's manifestly unequal segregated law schools—was at issue. Seven of nine justices disagreed with him; segregation's constitutionality was not the issue *Sipuel* presented, they ruled, and, try as he might, Marshall could not compel them to rule on a question not presented by the facts and record in the case. Oklahoma's slapdash law school for black students satisfied their earlier ruling, and they had no further instruction about Sipuel's case.

The Court's insouciance was a scathing surprise. Marshall fumed. Not yet forty years old, he was smoking two packs a day. There were so many other cases to be worked, interviews to conduct, witnesses to depose, briefs to revise, lawyers to supervise. The Court had spoken with finality on Ada Lois Sipuel's case but, by declining to affirm *Plessy* expressly, had left him to fight another day.

Sipuel still refused to attend Oklahoma's concocted law school. The next year, university president George Cross ordered her admitted to the University of Oklahoma Law School provided that, pursuant to a new state law, she sat in a part of the classroom that was roped off and designated by a sign: COLORED STUDENTS SECTION. She faced the humiliating marker with optimistic stoicism. "Somebody had to be first," she told a *Daily Oklahoman* reporter. "It will be hard, but maybe soon there'll be other Negroes with me."[19] Indeed there were other black students enrolling in the state's graduate and professional schools suddenly available to them, but none could sit next to their white classmates; they were cordoned off on the side or back of the classroom. To remedy this problem Marshall would take Oklahoma back to court. With these facts—admitted students segregated within classrooms—the justices could not evade answering whether segregation violated the Constitution.

IN THE MARSHALL-RUN Legal Defense and Education Fund office, Charles Houston wielded considerable and quiet power. His heart attack seemed only to intensify his work habits. Briefs, memoranda and proposed strategies crossed his desk weekly at 615 F Street NW. His replied assessments could be just one line but they were prompt and heeded; one response read entirely, "The memorandum on 'Housing' February 1, 1949, is very good."[20] That year Marshall postponed the National Legal Committee's meeting "because [Houston] had not sent in [his] recommendations" for whom to reappoint to the committee.[21] In a letter offering his recommendations, Houston, as was his wont, suggested an assignment to his former student: "You have no representation in Kansas City," he wrote. "The bar out there is none too strong, and I am not advised about any work done there for the N.A.A.C.P." Moreover, Marshall "might want to give some consideration to giving St. Louis some representation," and Houston explained how he should accomplish this.[22]

Houston's chairing the NAACP's National Legal Committee justified close involvement with LDF planning and strategy, but Marshall's reliance on his mentor caused some association power brokers to whisper about whether it was Houston or Marshall who commanded the association's legal campaign. Tension boiled over at a regional NAACP meeting when the Baltimore branch's longtime president, Lillie Jackson, declared that Charlie Houston was "the daddy of the NAACP lawyers." She demanded to know if Houston was in fact controlling the association's legal campaign.[23]

"Well, in the first place," Marshall retorted, "I think Charlie will resent being called the 'daddy' of the lawyers . . . in that all of these lawyers are too old to be his sons and some of them are older than he is." Second, "Charlie started this NAACP legal work" and, with Governor Hastie, was one of the best lawyers in the country. Finally, "Charlie and I [have] never had any serious misunderstanding about legal cases or any other NAACP matters; we usually thought alike and where there was doubt, I believe that

I have always given in to my respect for Charlie's ability."[24] In defending himself Marshall appeared to prove Lillie Jackson's very point: If he and Houston disagreed on a legal issue, Marshall deferred to Houston and did so unapologetically.

"Frankly, I believe Mrs. Jackson is trying to drive a wedge between Charlie and me," he told the *Afro-American*'s publisher, Carl Murphy. "People have tried to do that before and have been unsuccessful in their efforts. Charlie and I have worked together too long and too hard to let anyone use one of us against the other."[25] To Houston he promised, "[Lillie Jackson] is not going to drive me into a position of picking a squabble with you, especially when there are no grounds for a squabble."[26]

"I do not know what all this is about," Houston reassured. "There is no conflict between you and me."[27] Down in Washington Houston was consumed with private practice, the civil rights course he agreed to teach at Howard Law School, advising and advocating for over a dozen organizations and maintaining some semblance of family life. He lacked time and temperament for the association's internecine personality conflicts. As afternoon in autumn he could feel his days growing short.

MARSHALL BELIEVED a Texas mailman's lawsuit against the University of Texas School of Law stood a better chance of prodding the justices to rule on the issue left avoidable by the *Sipuel* opinion. By the end of World War II Heman Marion Sweatt had wearied of delivering mail door to door day to day. He had fought for his country. He held a bachelor's degree in biology but could find work only in the postal service. In 1945 his supervisor declined to promote him to a desk job and Sweatt decided to become a lawyer so he could sue the postal service. Despite his unaccredited undergraduate degree, Sweatt promised to be a superior plaintiff. The slight, bespectacled postman explained why he sought to study law: "As a basis for political interpretation, and knowledge of writing as a weapon of expressive leadership. And God granting me life, the hope which I see in incessant struggle as the basis of social enlightenment will find me forever reaching toward those goals."[28] To a reporter's hackneyed suggestion that his integrating the law school would abet interracial marriage, Sweatt retorted, "I am already happily married—and there are laws against bigamy in this country."[29] In time Sweatt's marriage would yield to his case's burden; his wife would leave him and his health would fail him. But before any of this, and perhaps like any sane man in his shoes, Sweatt bitterly recognized that "Jim Crow America has so warped my life."[30] On February 26, 1946, he applied to the University of Texas School of Law.

Dean Charles McCormick promptly wrote to Texas's attorney general "respectfully request[ing]" his "official opinion" on the dilemma posed by Sweatt's application. "This applicant is a citizen of Texas and duly qualified for admission into the Law School at The University of Texas," he flatly wrote, "save and except for the fact that he is a negro." It was clear to McCormick that "this [was] to be a test case on the question of the admission of negro students in the higher educational institutions of the State." The Supreme Court already had held that black students "were entitled to the same facilities and advantages as white students in respect to higher education," and now the dean believed they soon would seek entry into schools of "medicine, law, pharmacy, dentistry, journalism and other similar professional subjects."[31]

Attorney General Grover Sellers replied that Texas's "wise and long-continued policy of segregation of races in educational institutions" had "prevailed since the abolition of slavery" and "ha[d] been repeatedly sustained" by the Supreme Court of the United States. The question of whether Heman Sweatt could sit in class with white students was settled—so long as he was offered "equal educational advantages" in Texas. If the state could not or would not establish a law school for its black citizens equal to the one set aside for its whites, then, the attorney general declared, "he must be admitted to The University of Texas."[32] But even though there was no other law school in Texas that black students could attend, the university rejected Sweatt's application and he filed suit on May 16, 1946.[33]

Ada Lois Sipuel's case had been filed in Oklahoma but one month earlier. Unlike the judges in the Sooner courts to the north, however, Judge Roy C. Archer of Texas was determined to adhere to the separate but equal mandate set forth in *Murray* and *Gaines*. If the Lone Star State offered substantially similar legal education to its white and black citizens, then, as state attorney general Grover Sellers had explained to Dean McCormick, it could do so in separate schools under the Constitution. Judge Archer ruled that Texas had violated the Constitution by providing no law school for its black citizens while simultaneously excluding them from the

University of Texas. He gave the state six months to open a law school for black Texans.

State officials scrambled to erect a law school for this aggrieved mailman and the possible handful of other black Texans who would seek an in-state legal education. "Let us build for the Negro youth of this state a university worthy of the name Texas," Governor Beauford H. Jester challenged the state legislature.[34] One influential state legislator urged his colleagues to look past the proposed university's staggering price tag. "We are now to the point of passing this bill or permitting the destruction of segregation laws in all schools," he prodded. "We can't take a chance that our own courts might hold Sweatt can go to the University of Texas."[35] After some false starts, the state appropriated $3 million in 1947 to create the Texas State University for Negroes. Undergraduate courses were slow in coming, but the law school opened immediately in temporary basement quarters with three University of Texas law professors assigned to the staff. As testament to black Texans' growing faith in the NAACP's legal efforts, not a student enrolled in the assembled law school. Yet just one day before the start of the school year, University of Texas Law School dean Charles McCormick had claimed, "We shall have at least one student in the Law School for Negroes." He had arranged to "have a custodian present to see that the building is open and in condition to be used at that time" and for a bursar's official to be present to accept tuition payment.[36]

Again Marshall filed suit, determined to construct a more perfect record. "It is easier to prove that a law school is unequal than it is to prove a primary school is unequal."[37] Having attended Howard Law during Houston's Harvardization revolution, Marshall well understood what separated excellent law schools from mediocre ones. He assembled professors and deans from some of the nation's most prestigious law schools to testify, including the only person known to hold doctorate degrees in both anthropology and law.

The trial was scheduled to take five days. Before the opening gavel, newspapers reported that the case known as *Sweatt v. Painter* likely would "be fought all the way through the court of civil appeals, state supreme court, on to the U.S. Supreme Court."[38] Texans knew that the stakes exceeded the University of Texas Law School. "I am unable to see how segregation could be constitutionally maintained below the college level," the university's professor of educational administration declared, "if it is abolished at or above the college level." Having apparently divined the NAACP's precise strategy, he averred that "the effect of abandoning segregation on the lower level would definitely set back public education in Texas."[39]

Thurgood Marshall was shocked that so many white Texans thought this strategy some kind of secret. Addressing "a huge non-segregated audience" in Austin on a warm April night before trial, he proclaimed the NAACP's express aim of "completely eliminating segregation from American life." This had never been secret. "Quite the contrary," Marshall continued, his steady southern accent bent low to the crowd, "this is the job to which we're all dedicated."[40]

After the special counsel's rousing speech, a University of Texas law student named Marion Ludwig stepped onstage to close the rally. The Associated Negro Press described the young man as "speaking in a firm voice, vibrant with sincere determination" when he proclaimed it to be "a tragic denial of the democratic principles in which Americans profess belief, that the University of Texas refuses to admit a student because his skin is not white." A fellow Texas Law student joined Ludwig onstage to announce that as of that night there was "a new vigorous American organization on the campus." He paused for sufficient effect. "I should now like to say that a college chapter of the National Association for the Advancement of Colored People has been established at the University of Texas!" The integrated audience members leaped to their feet in cheers and applause so raucous that no one heard anything else the student said.[41] By trial's start the college's NAACP chapter was engaged in a spirited membership drive, recruiting members with the peppered ferocity peculiar to student activists.[42]

Texas appointed a racist man named Price Daniel to defend its segregated law schools. (Daniel later would serve his state as U.S. senator and governor and through the years would steadily intone on the white supremacist dirge that carried him into office.) From the trial's outset Daniel made clear that he intended to make a name for himself by defeating Thurgood Marshall. He did not so much prepare his witnesses as train them to resist Marshall's deft cross-examination. When his witnesses weren't evading Marshall's questions, Daniel was objecting to those questions. He objected without regard to established case law. After the judge sustained one too many of these objections, Marshall fumed in the hallway to cocounsel James Nabrit, "I'm gonna tell that judge what I think of him today." The older lawyer urged caution; Marshall brushed him aside. After court adjourned for the day, Nabrit found Marshall pacing and muttering to himself in the hallway and later asked him, "What was that all about?"

"I told you I was gonna tell that judge what I thought of him—and I just did."[43]

Heman Sweatt, whose name necessitated Marshall's repeated spelling to newspapermen, proved plainspoken on the witness stand. Daniel's cross-examination attempted to paint him as an NAACP pawn corralled into seeking an education he hardly wanted from a school he scarcely knew. Texas had allotted $3 million for a black Texans' university, which included a law school; why wouldn't Sweatt enroll there? "A first-class law school is one where a person will have contact with the people with whom he'll come in contact in his profession," Sweatt replied. Given the condition of Texas's other schools for black students, he doubted that "the law training to follow at the Houston University will be the equal of that at Austin."[44] Daniel failed to rattle Sweatt, who repeatedly buttressed his lawyers' contention that "there can be no separate equality."[45]

A month after trial's end Judge Archer surprised no one by ruling in Texas's favor. Over the coming years, as *Sweatt v. Painter* labored its path toward the Supreme Court, Heman Sweatt resigned from the postal service and was hospitalized with stress-induced ulcers, and the Lone Star State's elected and university officials worked hard to make credible their newly formed university for black students. The college Charles Houston derisively called "Sweatt University" enrolled 2,300 black students in the years between *Sweatt*'s trial and Supreme Court hearing.[46]

BACK IN WASHINGTON, Henrietta Houston tilted the fired pan left, right, then left again to let the stock lap against the lip and deglaze the pan. No fattening flour or milk added, she drizzled the reduced stock over Charlie's full plate. He posed little danger of becoming a fat man, but Dr. Edward Mazique had recommended a strict diet for his patient growing old faster than time.

As he did most evenings, Charlie had come home for dinner, was upstairs washing up, and would leave after the meal to attend some organization's meeting. City bus drivers, the Council on Inter-American Relations, American Aid for Ethiopia, black women denied entry to a nursing school and the District of Columbia School Board were merely a few of the groups whose members he advised. Charlie's presence guaranteed coverage of their meeting in the black press, and if he spoke, in the white press too. All held out their hands for his time, for energy he fought to muster.

After dinner, Henrietta laid a warm washcloth over his eyes and tried in vain to persuade him to forgo the meeting and stay home for a change.[47] Knowing that her husband believed "the test of character is the amount of strain it can bear,"[48] she wondered why she even bothered having this conversation with him. She understood—better than anyone else—his herculean schedule because she lived with it and knew what it was doing to him, and yet she admired his dedication to the struggle for equal rights. Surely the people attending tonight's meeting would understand his absence this once. He needed rest.

"Rest is what I need," he conceded, "but there is too much to do in such a short time."[49]

They had moved to a redbrick, spacious rowhouse on New Hampshire Avenue NW, north of Georgia Avenue's meridian bustle and just south of Grant Circle. Theirs was a tranquil Washington neighborhood called Petworth, where grass and oak leaves in Grant's and Sherman's namesake circles blushed bright green. Strollers and streetcars trolleyed about, and above summer crickets' cracking roared the integrated crowd's cheering the Negro League baseball game down the hill at Griffith Stadium. Henrietta adored it all and wished her husband would spend more time at home with her and Bo.

THURGOOD MARSHALL's 1948 *Sipuel* victory inspired several African American professionals to apply to the University of Oklahoma's graduate schools. They did not want to become plaintiffs; they believed the Supreme Court had made clear that, unless the university could offer qualified black applicants a separate graduate school of equal caliber, it had to admit them. Incredibly, University of Oklahoma officials refused to admit these eight applicants on racial grounds. Marshall and his staff were still shepherding

Sweatt through appellate courts when he learned that one of the rejected aspirants was a sixty-eight-year-old teacher who long ago had earned a master's degree and now sought a doctorate degree in education. Marshall thought the older George W. McLaurin would make an unassailable plaintiff: "The Dixiecrats and the others said it was horrible. The only thing Negroes were trying to do, they said, was to get social equality. As a matter of fact, there would be intermarriage, they said. The latter theory was the reason we deliberately chose Professor McLaurin. We had eight people who had applied and who were eligible to be plaintiffs, but we deliberately picked Professor McLaurin because he was sixty-eight years old and we didn't think he was going to marry or intermarry."[50]

The NAACP Legal Defense and Education Fund filed *McLaurin v. Oklahoma State Regents for Higher Education,* and because the state so blatantly defied Supreme Court precedent by offering McLaurin neither admission nor a comparable in-state education, a federal district court succinctly ruled in his favor. Unless and until Oklahoma established a graduate school for black students substantially equal to its one for white students, it had to admit qualified black applicants to the University of Oklahoma's graduate education program. Oklahoma's government responded in a fashion shamelessly noxious even for Oklahoma's government: In every one of his classes, George McLaurin was forced to sit by himself just outside the classroom so that segregation could be preserved; in the cafeteria he ate in a grimy back area at an hour separate from all other students; in the library he could sit only at one desk shoved behind a newspaper cart. McLaurin described the treatment as "humiliating."[51]

On McLaurin's behalf Marshall returned to federal district court but this time found no relief. He appealed directly to the Supreme Court of the United States. As personally incensed as he was at his client's treatment, the special counsel could hardly suppress his excitement at the legal issue that treatment forced upon the Court. As he explained in a memorandum to Charles Houston, Oliver Hill, William Hastie and others, "In this instance we have a class of students sitting down studying together, etc. and one student is ostracized from the immediate classroom and forced to study in a position of seclusion for the obvious purpose of humiliation, degrading and what have you." At the district court hearing, McLaurin had testified "that it is impossible for him to do his best work under these conditions and, as a matter of fact, he has threatened to withdraw for this reason."[52] A few months later Marshall invited Houston, George Johnson and James Nabrit to New York City to devise appellate strategy for *Sweatt* and *McLaurin*. Together they would call groups likely to file amicus briefs. He sought to confer with the same group they had assembled for the conference on the restrictive covenants cases.[53] Houston, as always, answered Marshall's call for counsel.

TWO YEARS EARLIER in May of 1947, Charlie's mother had died. Losing his wife nearly felled seventy-six-year-old William Houston, whom grief seized so tightly that he professed to have "little or no interest in life."[54] Charlie felt suddenly responsible for his wife, son and stricken father. From 1947 to 1949 he nursed his father's spirit to health until the old lion, dean of Washington's black attorneys' corps despite his son's fame and nephew's prominence, returned to the law firm he had founded generations ago.

In October 1949 Charles Houston clutched his starched shirt, steadied himself at his desk and awaited pain's abatement. It passed, always, the clenching stab. Breath returned, and after a couple hard blinks so did clear vision, all a despised inconvenience. But this time the pain didn't pass. Right hand still gripping his left chest, he blinked, sought breath, found it and blinked again. He had to get to his car, had to get home.

When at last he did Henrietta called Dr. Mazique, who raced to their New Hampshire Avenue house, conducted preliminary examinations and ordered his longtime patient confined to Freedmen's Hospital, where he was diagnosed with acute myocardial infarction.[55]

As Charlie's hospitalization stretched from days to weeks Henrietta collapsed beneath the strain and worry. Strong though she sought to be and had been, in November she was hospitalized. Five-year-old Bo spent most of 1949's holiday season moving among family friends.

Charles Houston was discharged before Christmas and he and Bo moved in with Dr. Edward Mazique and his wife, Jewell. It pained such a proud man to be reduced to convalescing in a friend's home, too weak to go Christmas shopping for his son, but Houston had little choice. Dr. Mazique, whom Bo called "Uncle Eddie," insisted on Houston's following a regimen of medicine, diet and rest. His wife hospitalized, his body failing him on account of a wartime debt, he struggled to maintain his spirit. Up in New York City Thurgood was preparing his lawyers for their most forceful attack yet on segregation. *Sweatt* and *McLaurin* would be the association's most significant cases since *Gaines*, and Houston was unlikely to attend oral argument even as a spectator. It was a bleak December.

Mostly Houston worried about Bo. He felt himself growing stronger and hoped to return home soon, but Henrietta remained in the hospital and it had been some time since he entertained notions of longevity. Insurance papers were in order; the firm had never wanted for business. His worry was not financial. He asked Mazique for a tape recorder; he wanted to record thoughts and words his son one day would understand. "There's a long history," he said into the microphone in a didactic talk that would reach from discussing the "indivisibility of liberty" to oppressive governments' attempts "to cut off the intellectuals from the masses." Native Americans, black Americans, colonized Africans and Mexican American immigrants found voice in Houston's last recording. His talk of "an expanding economy" in a contracting global market was heartfelt but hardly intimate. In time he would make amends.

THE JUSTICES DECIDED to hear oral arguments on *Sweatt* and *McLaurin* on the same day. In advance of the April 4, 1950, hearing, Texas's lawyers submitted a brief even more strident than their lower court presentations. Price Daniel emphasized that Marshall's brief failed to cite a single case holding that separate but equal education violated the Constitution. This was because no such case existed. Despite *Gaines* and *Sipuel* and any other case that petitioners' counsel saw fit to cite, the Court would have to overrule *Plessy v. Ferguson*—discarding the case on which so many Americans' way of life depended—in order to rule for Heman Sweatt and George McLaurin.

Thurgood Marshall retorted in brief and at argument that this was exactly what he was asking the Court to do. When George McLaurin sat by himself at a desk just outside the classroom, he could hear his professor's every word; he took the same examinations as his white classmates. Because he was separated from his classmates solely on the basis of race, however, McLaurin's education simply could not be equal to that afforded to white students. It had been six months since he and Bob Carter had received

Houston's letter bowing out of the education cases. *Sweatt* and *McLaurin* were their most daring cases yet, and for the first time Marshall faced the justices' questions without first facing Houston's.

In June a unanimous Supreme Court issued its decisions. First, it ordered Heman Sweatt admitted to the University of Texas School of Law because, even though Texas had established a law school for black students that wanted for little by way of facilities, the new law school was far from substantially equal to the University of Texas in "those qualities which are incapable of objective measurement but which make for greatness in a law school. Such qualities, to name but a few, include reputation of the faculty, experience of the administration, position and influence of the alumni, standing in the community, traditions and prestige. It is difficult to believe that one who had a free choice between these [two] law schools would consider the question close."[56]

Second, the Court ordered the University of Oklahoma to end its systemic humiliation of George McLaurin. His sequestration "handicapped [him] in his pursuit of effective graduate instruction . . . [and] impair[ed] and inhibit[ed] his ability to student, to engage in discussions and exchange views with other students, and in general, to learn his profession."[57] Both decisions turned on the intangible facets of education Marshall sought to litigate.

Chief Justice Vinson's opinion pointedly refused, however, to take the leap urged by the Legal Defense Fund. The Court refused to "reach petitioner's contention that *Plessy v. Ferguson* should be re-examined in the light of contemporary knowledge respecting the purposes of the Fourteenth Amendment and the effects of racial segregation."[58] Again the justices eschewed the hard and momentous decision at hand and, again, *Plessy* remained law.

IN THE NEW YEAR 1950 Charles Houston brought his son home to New Hampshire Avenue and Henrietta soon joined them. He returned to his second home at 615 F Street NW, where work offered routine's comfort.

Chest pains flared again but less acutely and more frequently than before. His body was keeping no secrets from him. He asked Henrietta to please travel with Bo down to Louisiana to visit her sister.

She refused. She would not leave him like this. She was well now, stronger. She could take care of him. She would not leave him.

She had to, he argued, because his body was weakening. It was giving him up. He didn't want Bo to watch him wither. The boy was five years old and memories were all he would have of his dad for most of his life. Sure, there would be pictures and news clippings, but those were nothing of what a son needed to remember—what he loved about his dad and how much his dad had loved him. She should take Bo down to Louisiana. Make it a fun visit. And Bo would, Houston hoped, "remember his father as vigorous, impressive and strong."[59]

Henrietta relented, packed and told Bo about their surprise trip to Louisiana. He was excited to go but disappointed that his dad wasn't coming too. The date and time of their train's departure arrived and Henrietta Houston kissed Charlie good-bye.

WEEKS LATER the fifty-four-year-old was back in the hospital, where he suffered a second heart attack. Medicated and weary, Houston set about assigning his pro bono cases to colleagues. Lest they hesitate to accept one of his daunting cases, he cashed in chips. "[Tell] George Hayes and Jim Nabrit [that] they owe me and [to] take your case," he instructed a D.C. public school parents group.[60] If he again made it out of Freedmen's Hospital, he would stop practicing law. Dr. Mazique allowed Houston few visitors. William Houston, Bill Hastie and Joseph Waddy frequented his bedside to chat him awake or asleep.

After distributing his cases, Houston returned to a book given to him by a saved aunt worried for his baptized but unpracticed soul. Joshua Liebman's *Peace of Mind* touched him so much that he asked Aunt Clotill to promise that, should he not again look back at the building he was in, she would give his copy to Bo. She did and she would.

Freshly bathed and shaven on an April's sun-crisped midday, Charlie lay in his hospital bed. He had eaten well at breakfast but now waves of nausea swelled and passed over him. *Peace of Mind* lay still as he at his bedside. On a middle page he had written a note to his son. By now he knew that Aunt Clotill would have to give the book to Bo. For Charlie the tide was lapping low, pulling itself and him away.

"Tell Bo I did not run out on him," he had written in the book, "but went down fighting that he might have better and broader opportunities than I had without prejudice or bias operating against him, and that in any fight, some fall."[61]

At quarter past two that afternoon, Dr. Mazique visited, and the two men after whom institutions one day would be named exchanged greetings. Houston told Mazique of his nausea but assured him, "It'll pass."[62]

Mazique insisted on checking him out just as Joseph Waddy stepped into the hospital room. Charles Houston welcomed his friend, "Hi Joe," took a deep breath and surrendered to the tide's gentle pull.[63]

ROOT AND BRANCH

T HE LEGAL STRUGGLE against segregation pivoted in the weeks after Charles Houston's death. A unanimous Supreme Court delivered *Sweatt*'s and *McLaurin*'s victories, and in those opinions Thurgood Marshall saw pages pocked with road markings.[1] For over a decade now he and the Court had engaged in a civil public dialogue on an issue often demagogued elsewhere. If the Court was not uniformly welcoming, it was never hostile: Unlike Houston, Marshall never argued before a justice who turned to face the wall rather than the African American lawyer before him.

Marshall understood that the NAACP's first steps in *Sweatt*'s and *McLaurin*'s wake would be significant for either their boldness or timidity. Since their Howard days Houston had told him, "When you plan, plan twice."[2] Now that Houston was gone, Marshall was left to plan for an association and a people who looked for a parting of the waters. Fourteen years ago Houston had told them, "Don't shout too soon," but too soon had since passed. For black Americans who were neither qualified nor interested in attending southern graduate schools, Marshall's labor and leadership so far had yielded tangible little.

When the Court ruled that the University of Oklahoma had to grant George McLaurin a seat in its all-white classrooms because it offered no equal program for black students, it necessarily suggested that any separate program for black students was inherently unequal on account of its being reserved for students separated by race: If forcing a student, on account of his race, to sit just outside an all-white class violated the Constitution, how could forcing thousands of students, on account of their race, to sit in buildings separate from all-white schools remain constitutional? *McLaurin* thereby called *Plessy*'s bluff and raised it double. With *McLaurin* and *Sweatt*, Thurgood Marshall and his staff fulfilled Houston's plan of placing segregation at war with itself. But "we wouldn't have been any place," he famously remarked, "if Charlie hadn't laid the groundwork for it."[3]

JUST THREE WEEKS EARLIER William Hastie had eulogized his cousin in Howard University's Andrew Rankin Memorial Chapel. As for every fallen soldier and sailor, the American flag draped Houston's coffin, which was flanked by Howard's ROTC Honor Guard. Supreme Court justices Tom Clark and Hugo Black, numerous judges, civil rights attorneys and activists, and hundreds of regular Washingtonians, black and white, packed the integrated church in the segregated capital.[4] Remembering a man who "stopp[ed] only when his body could no longer keep pace with his will and his spirit," Hastie fought through words thick with sorrow in his throat: "As we grieve, we cannot forget that he believed, perhaps above all else, in strength; strength to do and to bear what lesser men would re-gard as impossible or unbearable." The federal judge surrendered tears to the cousin he so admired. "He counted nothing, no physical weakness and not even death itself as an obstacle to the onward sweep of strong men and women in the accomplishment of worthwhile ends . . . I know he would wish all of us to carry on in that spirit."[5]

In the congregation sat eighty-year-old William Houston, grieved by every awful thought and sorrow harbored by parents burying their chil-dren. The front pew was never a place for fathers—for wives, husbands and ushers, yes, but never for fathers or young sons, and Charles Houston had left behind both.

Service ended and mourners left in their hats and sadness to the sun-drenched day. They drove to Lincoln Memorial Cemetery. The cars of Houston's funeral procession parked beside a dust-tracked cornfield. In sight lay a big house and a barn and hilltop trees bent over by the farm-wind's blow. Lincoln Cemetery was as segregated as any facility Charles

Houston ever had sought to integrate, but here he would be buried.[6] There was no choice and there would be none for some long time.

HOUSTON'S FUNERAL had been difficult for Marshall. He served as pall-bearer and the weight he carried with Oliver Hill, Joseph Waddy, Edward Lovett and others, he would carry for years to come. For advice, consolation and blessed assurance he had relied more on Charlie than anyone save Buster; except for his days at Lincoln he had lived with his parents all his life and held no other prospect until Houston had persuaded the NAACP to call him away to New York City. Charles Houston had recommended Marshall's admission to the New York bar: "His moral character is excellent, likewise his professional reputation; he is industrious and his legal scholarship is sound and he is developing as a trial lawyer."[7] Even as the black press lionized Thurgood Marshall in the first years after *Brown*, reporters referred to Houston as his "idol."[8]

The time following the funeral saw heartfelt public recollections and recognitions for Houston. Mary McLeod Bethune mourned the loss of a "fine young warrior in the prime of his life, who through all his years carried high the flaming torch of informed courage . . . He gave ceaselessly and unstintingly of his mind and substance and energy—and finally, with substance and energy gone, he gave up his life."[9] The NAACP posthumously awarded Houston its thirty-fifth Spingarn Medal for outstanding achievement; Marshall smiled warmly onstage behind Henrietta and six-year-old Bo.[10] The special counsel remained uninterested, however, in publicly speaking of all that was lost in Houston's death. Later in life, he would often expound unprompted on Houston's import and legacy, but for now, he kept private his loss and grief.

NOT THREE WEEKS after laying his friend and mentor to rest, Thurgood Marshall convened the most pivotal NAACP meeting since W. E. B. DuBois called together the few brave dozens to found the organization in New York City forty-one years earlier. Forty-three attorneys from the Legal Defense Fund and the National Legal Committee and fourteen branch and regional presidents gathered at association headquarters in New York City's late-June swelter. They met to construct a consensus on how "to end segregation once and for all."[11] Its stated purpose rendered the meeting revolutionary. Save a smattering of border state graduate schools and the University of Delaware's college body, the lives of America's southern millions remained as segregated as spring from August.

Segregationist politicians closely read the Court's decisions, and by June 1950 many of their most racist lot were spending aberrant sums to renovate their counties' COLORED ONLY libraries and swimming pools. Even before *McLaurin* imposed integration on a graduate school classroom, southern school districts feared the worst and siphoned overdue funds to public schools for black children. Against this backdrop of undeniable progress toward equalization, association lawyers decided that equalization was no longer their goal. They would insist on the integration they believed to be demanded by the Constitution and declare that segregated facilities' inequality was but "evidence of the unconstitutionality of segregation."[12]

After a long meeting during which Marshall mostly sat silent and smoking, the assembled attorneys agreed on their argument: Public schools segregated for black children violated the Fourteenth Amendment because they were unequal to *and* separate from the schools for white children. The lawyers resolved that every school case they henceforth filed would "be aimed at obtaining education on a non-segregated basis and that no relief other than that [would] be acceptable."[13]

THE HARVARD LAW STUDENT whom Charles Houston had told during the war, "You have to go," indeed had gone and returned to graduate magna cum laude from Harvard. Justice Felix Frankfurter then hired William T. Coleman, Jr., as his law clerk, the first African American to clerk for a Supreme Court justice. (One day he would serve as secretary of transportation in Gerald Ford's administration.) On account of racist tradition no law firm in Coleman's hometown of Philadelphia would hire him after his clerkship; he became an associate at New York City's white-shoe law firm Paul, Weiss. After each long billable day, Coleman volunteered for the Legal Defense Fund. Thurgood Marshall held the young lawyer in high regard and closely considered his counsel. So attorneys like Marshall's deputy, Robert Carter, were dismayed when Coleman incredulously stared them down all at once and wondered what the hell these damned dolls had to do with overturning *Plessy v. Ferguson*.

Carter had introduced Marshall to the dolls and their steward, a thirty-seven-year-old social psychologist named Kenneth Clark. Bob Carter's all-substance, no-flash reputation lent immediate credence to what Coleman and Spottswood Robinson III dismissed as a distracting stunt. He argued that they enter the results of Dr. Clark's so-called doll test into evidence in school desegregation trials. As usual, Marshall sat and smoked, listened and said little. His reticence made clear that the doll tests at least intrigued him

Clark and his sociologist wife, Mamie, presented four foot-tall dolls, identical but for their color, to African American children ages three to seven. Two dolls were brown and two were white. "Give me the white doll; give me the colored doll; give me the Negro doll." Three of every four children answered the control questions correctly. The Clarks then instructed each black boy or girl: "Give me the doll you like to play with"; then, "give me the doll that is the nice doll," and "give me the doll that looks bad," and finally, "give me the doll that is a nice color." Most black children, from New England to Arkansas, displayed "an unmistakable preference for the white doll and a rejection of the brown doll."[14] Some children, particularly in northern cities, glared at Kenneth Clark before crumbling to tears at his gently asked questions.

One Arkansan boy wordlessly pointed at a white doll when Clark asked, "Which doll do you like?"

"Which doll don't you like?"

He pointed at the brown doll. Clark wordlessly waited for explanation and the boy blurted, "That's a nigger, I'm a nigger."[15]

Kenneth and Mamie Clark were so "disturbed by [their] findings" that they "sat on them for a number of years." Asking little boys and girls as young as three these questions only to repeatedly receive the same brutal answers "was a traumatic experience" for the psychologists. "What was surprising was the degree to which the children suffered from self-rejection," Kenneth later explained. "I don't think we had quite realized the *extent* of the cruelty of racism and how hard it hit."[16] The Clarks' research revealed segregation's earliest effects on black Americans with children's pithy cruel plainness.

Kenneth Clark's heartbreaking tests touched Marshall in a place where neither William Coleman's nor Spottswood Robinson's arguments could reach. As when he and Charlie years ago watched a Mississippi black boy bite into an orange like an apple, Clark's doll tests reminded Marshall that every law he fought and imagined was obeyed by someone someplace who all his life had known no otherwise.

Like any worthwhile lawyer, however, Marshall did not make decisions of consequence based on his gut alone. The Legal Defense Fund's first school desegregation trial was drawing near—in South Carolina no less—and association lawyers had yet to devise a final strategy; they awaited Marshall's verdict on the doll test. Marshall finally told his staff, "We ha[ve] to try this case like any other one in which you would try to prove damages to your client." Their client, an African American schoolboy in unreconstructed Charleston, South Carolina, undoubtedly had been harmed by the state's forcing him to attend a dilapidated segregated school. "If your car ran over my client," Marshall continued, "you'd have to pay up, and my function as an attorney would be to put experts on the stand to testify to how much damage was done." Clark's dramatic test results indicated how segregated schools had severely damaged their client, and therefore Marshall would seek their admission into the trial record. As he later explained, "We needed exactly that kind of evidence in the school cases. When Bob Carter came to me with Ken Clark's doll test, I thought it was a promising way of showing injury to these segregated youngsters. I wanted this kind of evidence on the record."[17] That decided, Marshall, Carter and Clark caught the overnight train from New York City to Charleston with dolls and briefs in tow. They would have flown, but Dr. Clark in 1951 was not yet convinced that twenty-five thousand feet was a safe distance for man from ground.

ON AN EARLIER TRIP Robert Carter had cleared the way in South Carolina, explaining to potential plaintiffs the rigors and retaliatory dangers they would face. Having lived in Clarendon County all their lives, these twenty parents of elementary school children knew better than Carter what lay ahead. Governor James Byrnes would vow to shut down the state's public schools before integrating them.

In South Carolina, Marshall, Carter and Clark convened with Spottswood Robinson, Birmingham attorney Arthur Shores and local counsel Harold Boulware. In late 1950, they filed *Briggs v. Elliott* in federal district court.

On cue African American maids were fired, mothers refused credit at the few stores accepting their money, sharecroppers denied renewed farmland leases and those with picked cotton could find not one gin. Economic hell was unleashed on black folks of Clarendon County, South Carolina.

Several months later, on May 28, 1951, trial convened before three federal judges. Over five hundred South Carolinians, black and white, jammed Charleston's seventy-five-seat federal courthouse. Women fainted in the claustrophobic heat and violence threatened, and all this before South Carolina's white-suited attorney Robert Figg rose to concede that yes, South Carolina's schools for black children were woefully inferior to those for white children and yes, Your Honor, this state of affairs was unacceptable. The fact was that funding for schools in rural districts had fallen behind that for urban schools and therefore the colored children had suffered. But South Carolina's government had just levied a 3 percent sales tax on all its residents in a bid to raise $75 million for school equalization. In good faith South Carolina was seeking to comply with its constitutional duty to provide equal education to all its children and therefore offered no objection to the Court's issuing an order requiring equalization. All South Carolina asked, Figg posed, was that it be given "a reasonable time to formulate a plan for ending such inequalities and for bringing about equality of educational opportunity."[18]

Figg's gambit stunned Marshall. Association lawyers had prepared numerous witnesses to establish that South Carolina's segregated black schools were manifestly inferior to its schools for white children. While the man lauded in the courthouse's colored section as "Lawyer Marshall" sat jarred by Figg's swift turn, the three-judge panel accepted the state's concession for the record and prepared to adjourn the hearing.

The plaintiff's brief accorded with the Legal Defense Fund's June 1950 mandate, however, and therefore expressly argued that segregation itself, even in the case of two perfectly equal schools, violated the federal Constitution. Charleston's own Judge J. Waties Waring reminded his fellow impaneled judges of this argument and declared, "This court has got to face the issue of segregation, *per se*."[19]

Marshall caught the wind that had been knocked from him and, with the court's permission, called the first in a two-day series of witnesses on whose testimony he would construct a record that would delineate in aching detail how sharply and deeply state-mandated segregation wounded children in ways the Constitution forbade.

Columbia University professor of education Horace McNeely testified, "There is basically implied in the separation . . . that there is some difference in the two groups which does not make it feasible for them to be educated together . . . [f]urthermore, by separating the two groups, there is implied a stigma on at least one of them."[20] Harvard psychologist David Krech opined that "legal segregation hampers the mental, emotional, physical and financial development of colored children and aggravates the very prejudices from which it arises."[21] "Segregation cannot exist without discrimination," declared Howard University professor of education Ellis Knox. "The children in the Negro schools very definitely are not prepared for the same type of American citizenship as the children in the white schools."[22]

This groundwork laid, the plaintiff's star witness took the stand. Since arriving in South Carolina Dr. Kenneth Clark had been threatened by white racists and devastated by the contempt in which so many of Clarendon County's black children held themselves. Based on his doll test Clark testified that in Clarendon County a black child "accepts as early as six, seven or eight the negative stereotypes about his own group." Segregated schools had wreaked their havoc on these young lives. "Children in Clarendon County, like other human beings who are subjected to an obviously inferior status in the society in which they live, have been definitely harmed in the development of their personalities."[23] Marshall followed with a closing argument in which he contended that "in view of these facts, segregation should be abolished now as the only means to equalization. Every day the matter is delayed the constitutional rights of the plaintiffs are being denied."[24]

Less than a month later the court ruled against Marshall's clients. The June 23, 1951, decision refused to hold segregation unconstitutional; what the plaintiff was asking, it said, should be asked of a legislature, not a court. Thurgood Marshall and his legal team in due time would appeal *Briggs v. Elliott* to the Supreme Court of the United States. By then it would be bundled with several other school desegregation cases filed and fought by attorneys who called them *the education cases* or *the desegregation cases* but whose collective outcome would be remembered by history and learned by schoolchildren as *Brown v. Board of Education*.

THE AUTUMN OF 1951 returned Thurgood Marshall to Manhattan at once chastened and emboldened by the task at last before him. In Charles Houston's life they had brought the goal into sight, and now as the last levee it stood, the only one that ever had mattered to any on either side. The fight and its stakes were with him. "He wasn't conservative, but he was cautious," remembered Oliver Hill. "His prevailing sense, I think, was that we just couldn't afford to lose a big one."[25] Many of the Legal Defense Fund's largest donors, according to James Nabrit, thought that "if we lost before the Court on overturning segregation *per se*, we'd be set back a generation."[26] The days therefore found Marshall smoking Winstons in fierce succession, their fallen ashes sprinkled atop his lapels and heavy glasses sliding beneath his sweat-furrowed brow. Nabrit believed that if association lawyers lost on a direct challenge to *Plessy*, "[they] could come back into court the next day arguing [equalization]." Marshall disagreed; he detested the prospect of arguing for *Plessy*'s equalization mandate in the wake of a failed stride to overturn the case. There was but a David's shot against Jim Crow and Marshall held the slingshot close.

IN KANSAS, Robert Carter and Jack Greenberg, a talented recent Columbia Law School graduate who had won the case desegregating the University of Delaware, litigated on behalf of African American parents who were suing Topeka's board of education in the case that would ultimately give its name to the landmark Supreme Court ruling. Marshall had chosen Topeka because its school facilities for black and white students were substantially equal; the harm visited on Topeka's black schoolchildren was inflicted by segregation itself.

Topeka schools were segregated more as a matter of course than of principle, more Missouri than Alabama. Bus and train station passengers waited in integrated lobbies and African Americans were not confined to city buses' rear seats. Kansas's three-judge *Brown* panel veritably joined Marshall's obvious strategy to reach *Plessy* when it wrote that "segregation has a tendency to retard the educational and mental development of Negro children and to deprive them of some of the benefits they would receive in a racially integrated school system."[27] Despite their accepting plaintiffs' argument that segregated schools injured black schoolchildren, the judges explained that *Plessy v. Ferguson* demanded their ruling for Topeka's board of education. Carter and Greenberg returned to New York City knowing that, for appellate purposes, they could hardly have asked for a more direct opinion.

OLIVER HILL AND SPOTTSWOOD ROBINSON tried a stirring case out of firmly segregated Farmville, Virginia. Unlike *Brown v. Board*'s trial, which interested so few Topeka residents that empty courtroom seats abounded, *Dorothy E. Davis et al. v. County School Board of Prince Edward County* garnered fierce interest in central Virginia. Hill and Robinson represented 197 students of Robert Russa Moton High School—teenagers who, just weeks earlier, had walked out of the school on a general strike called by a precociously inspired sixteen-year-old preacher's niece named Barbara Johns.

Moton High was a dreadfully typical Virginian high school for black students: The roof leaked, students wore winter coats against the rickety windows and broken heating system, classes were so overcrowded that overflow classes were held in tar-paper shacks. "Look at the white school just down the road," Johns implored her classmates. "The white students have a real gymnasium, up-to-date science labs and shiny new buses. We have to walk out now and not come back until white leaders have agreed to make improvements." Standing at the auditorium's podium, Johns took off her shoe and banged it against the lectern as Moton's student body poured out the doors.[28]

Johns and her schoolmates wanted the county to invest in their school and two days later telephoned Hill and Robinson, who agreed to meet with them. During their drive to Farmville, the two lawyers agreed to hold no truck with the students' strike and planned to tell them that they would not represent truants. As Hill described the meeting, however, the students "handled themselves so well and their morale was so high that we didn't have the heart to say no."[29] Instead they explained that the NAACP's Legal Defense Fund no longer accepted equalization cases; if Moton's students and parents wanted Hill and Robinson to represent them, they had to sue for desegregation.

Silence ensued. Black people did not vote in Prince Edward County; four years after the Supreme Court's *Brown v. Board* ruling, Prince Edward County's board of supervisors would vote to cease funding public schools rather than integrate, and until 1964, would provide no public education for any of the county's children, black or white. And here in 1951 the two lanky lawyers were telling black children and their parents that they would sue only for integration—that mere equalization was yesterday's fight. As Hill later explained with succinct sincerity, "I went to law school so I could go out and fight segregation."[30]

Nearly two hundred students and their parents agreed to sue for integration. Robinson and Hill filed suit in a federal district court which one week after trial delivered its inevitable ruling. Thurgood Marshall already had appealed the South Carolina and Kansas cases to the Supreme Court of the United States, and the justices, none too pleased to confront *Plessy* so soon after their *Sweatt* and *McLaurin* gambits, received yet another appeal they possibly thought years premature.

Amid and above all this Thurgood Marshall was becoming an American folk hero. For the past two years he had been the face of the NAACP, ever since the ever-wily Walter White tarnished his reputation by leaving his wife of twenty-seven years. He quickly married Poppy Cannon, a white mother of three children by three different husbands.[31]

Not a year after the Court's 1954 *Brown* ruling, after several heart attacks and a month's sojourn in Haiti and Puerto Rico, Walter White would die of coronary thrombosis. He was sixty-one and had lived a life so full that it burst at last from work, love, cigarettes, travel, stress and his new wife's famous "rice and gravy, hominy grits and broiled ham slices."[32] Poppy White sat with him in his bed as he slipped away from her and it all. Thurgood Marshall buried his intramural competitions with the secretary beneath a photograph widely published with notice of White's death; in it Marshall's big right hand rested atop White's double-breasted jacket-shod shoulder as White puffed his pipe at the last NAACP national conference he would attend.[33] White had served on the NAACP staff since he was twenty-five years old, and, as association founder and medal namesake Arthur Spingarn mourned, it was "under [White's] guidance [that] the association was developed from a small society into its present position as the Nation's largest civil rights organization."[34]

But even before White's passing, Marshall had become the NAACP's bulwark and face, its conscience and ambition. In his rasp southern white folks heard a warning bell. Black Americans called him "Mr. Civil Rights" and flocked to pack courtrooms where he was rumored to appear so they might touch or talk to their tireless, fearless warrior who by then was so privately full of worry and weariness.

AFTER THE SUPREME COURT accepted and consolidated the cases, the NAACP's band of lawyers retreated to their scattered sculleries steeled as butchers for the looming months' innumerable tasks. In law libraries and offices, the LDF's staff and volunteer attorneys sharpened their reasoning and dug deeper into research. From sundown to midnight they argued strategy, with Spottswood Robinson and William Coleman favoring a purely legal approach until Marshall, with his feet on the conference table before a cloud of Winston cigarette smoke, announced that they would argue the social science evidence before the Court. It was in the trial records and Marshall believed it important to illustrate to the Court precisely how segregation injured black schoolchildren.

Ever the realist, Marshall knew that even if they persuaded the Court to overturn *Plessy*, *Plessy* would not die; segregation would survive and so would the fight to kill it. The year before *Brown*'s ruling he assured parish elders gathered at the A.M.E. Church on Sixth and Herr in Harrisburg, Pennsylvania, "The fight to end segregation will not stop with the Supreme Court ruling in these cases. We will have to go on fighting until we have broken out of the ghettos and can live where we want to."[35] But those were champions' fights, and for now Marshall and team were challengers. Exhausted and hopeful, they submitted their briefs to the Court, and Chief Justice Fred Vinson ordered oral arguments for Tuesday, December 9, 1952.

Black spectators comprised half the crowds of three hundred in the courtroom and four hundred in the hallways.[36] Thurgood Marshall, Spottswood Robinson, James Nabrit, Robert Carter, Jack Greenberg and the association's other attorneys argued for three days before a Court so fractured that it could not even decide to decide the incendiary case. Six months after hearing oral arguments, the Court ordered a rehearing. *Brown*'s second round of oral argument was scheduled and rescheduled for December 7, 1953. In the meantime sixty-three-year-old Chief Justice Vinson died of a heart attack. Despite having written the *Sweatt* and *McLaurin* decisions, Vinson opposed desegregating the nation's public schools. Justice Felix Frankfurter, after leaving Vinson's Kentucky funeral, quipped to a friend, "This is the first indication I have ever had that there is a God."[37] The recently elected president, Dwight Eisenhower, appointed California's three-term governor to be chief justice; Eisenhower later would lament choosing Earl Warren as his life's "biggest damn fool mistake."[38]

To flg leaf its reason for demanding another round of argument, the Court had posed five questions. Three were questions of law and two concerned how the Court would implement a decision overturning *Plessy*. The Legal Defense Fund attorneys returned warily encouraged to their Manhattan redoubt. In time they would respond to the Court with a 235-page brief that cost forty thousand dollars in research and printing expenses; two dozen attorneys donated their time and association members campaigned for donations. One Baltimore man who had saved five hundred dollars to buy a car, "a lifelong ambition," instead donated the money to the Legal Defense Fund. "Since I've waited this long for a car," he explained, "I can wait a little more and be satisfied that this money will go as a down payment on freedom for my children and grandchildren."[39]

After that first round of oral argument evinced the Court's seriousness in addressing school segregation, Mississippi's state legislators debated abolishing the state's school system if the Court ordered integration. On the House floor in Jackson, Representative Blaine Eaton hollered, "Let a Negro child go into a white school in the next four or five months and he will be tarred and feathered! Is this what they want for that child? The Negroes of Mississippi don't. They want their own schools. Negroes would be persecuted by the death of segregation and they are not in sympathy with Marshall and the New York Negroes."[40]

Marshall dismissed predictions "that blood will flow in the streets" as propaganda. "They said the same thing when we attacked the white primary in South Carolina. Eighty thousand Negroes voted in South Carolina and nothing happened."[41] As if to buttress his point, the board of education of Topeka, Kansas, voted 5–1 to integrate its schools a full school year before *Brown*'s ruling.[42]

While Marshall forever remained himself, over the year his humor dampened, his marriage suffered.[43] "We still have to complete in a few months what would normally be a two-to-three year job," he told reporters.[44] But months of eighteen-hour workdays peppered with faraway fund-raising speeches taxed his levity. He became short with secretaries and junior counsel—never rude, but newly irascible. "He'd give me hell a lot," William Coleman recalled of the time preparing answers to the Court's five questions.[45] As he labored for yet another year on the most important case of his life, Marshall had taken to wearing ironshoes.

AND SO DECEMBER 7, 1953, dawned on an exhausted Thurgood Marshall. For a week he had been camped in a Washington hotel room, and for months he had been orchestrating a research campaign that eclipsed even the Promethean effort preceding *Brown*'s first oral argument one year ago. Coleman had taken brief leave of his law firm to move into the Wardman Park Hotel with Marshall, and Marshall asked Justice Frankfurter's former law clerk to sit next to him at oral argument. "Weary and haggard from loss of sleep over the cases," reporters Ethel Payne and Arnold de Mille wrote, "Thurgood Marshall still retained his jocular carefree air, but paused soberly to say to members of the press, 'If any of you are in touch with the Man upstairs, you can put in a good word for us on this case please.' "[46]

Spectators had begun lining up on the Court's freezing hard steps at one thirty that morning; the robed justices assumed the bench at the stroke of noon.[47] Spottswood Robinson rose to present a historical argument that the post–Civil War Congress of 1868 "desired and intended" for the Fourteenth Amendment to eradicate segregation in the nation's schools.[48] Robinson spoke for over fifty minutes and was interrupted with questions just twice, the second time being when Justice Stanley Reed, a conservative southerner, asked if Robinson's clients would be in a better position had Congress seen fit to outlaw school segregation. The answer seemed as obvious as Reed's vote seemed unattainable: "If there had been such a statute," Robinson replied, "we wouldn't be in court right now."[49] On behalf of the Department of Justice, Assistant Attorney General J. Lee Rankin next argued powerfully that the Court held both "the power and the duty" to eradicate school segregation.[50]

South Carolina was represented by eighty-one-year-old John W. Davis, the 1924 Democratic nominee for president of the United States and a Supreme Court litigator surpassed in appearances only by the legendary

Daniel Webster. Over his daughter's pleas not to take the case, Davis agreed to represent South Carolina pro bono. The white-haired advocate embodied his client's defiance: "Let me say this for the State of South Carolina. It does not come here in sack cloth and ashes. It believes that its legislation is not offensive to the Constitution of the United States."[51] In his argument Davis referred to Reconstruction as "the tragic era," and closed by reminding the Court of "Aesop's fable of the dog and the meat: The dog, with a fine piece of meat in his mouth, crossed a bridge and saw the shadow in the stream and plunged for it and lost both substance and shadow. Here is equal education, not promised, not prophesied, but present. Shall it be thrown away on some fancied question of racial prestige?"[52] With his impassioned plea Davis brought himself to tears. More than a few in the courtroom, including Marshall, were well aware of Davis's storied reputation before the Court and felt for the old segregationist. Fifteen months later, Davis would die quietly in Charleston, South Carolina.[53]

As Thurgood Marshall rose to speak, the courtroom rustled with anticipation. Marshall was just a few words into his presentation when Chief Justice Earl Warren leaned forward in his leather chair to ask him to expound please on his understanding of the Court's power to declare school segregation unconstitutional.[54] The chief justice nodded as Marshall expanded on Rankin's earlier contention that the Court possessed both the power and the duty to do so.[55]

The associate justices peppered Marshall for the duration of his argument. Justices Jackson and Frankfurter intermittently whispered to each other and fired questions. The fidgety Frankfurter asked, "If you reject the separate but equal doctrine, don't you reject the basis of the *McLaurin* decision?" Marshall had hardly replied, "No," when the justice launched into another question. They cornered him several times and Marshall's performance was, for him, subpar.

When arguments resumed the next day, Marshall quickly regained his footing and pushed hard. "The argument of judicial restraint has no application in this case. There is a relationship between Federal and State, but there is no corollary or relationship as to the Fourteenth Amendment. The . . . duty of following the Fourteenth Amendment is placed upon the states. The duty of enforcing the Fourteenth Amendment is placed upon this

Court."[56] The only way the Court could reason its way to ruling against the plaintiffs was "to find that for some reason Negroes are inferior to all other human beings . . . the only thing can be an inherent determination that the people who were formerly in slavery, regardless of anything else, shall be kept as near that stage as is possible; and now is the time, we submit, that this Court should make it clear that that is not what our Constitution stands for."[57]

WITH DUTIES WRITTEN and oral at last complete, Marshall returned to New York City to face the mammoth debt incurred in preparing the second *Brown* brief and argument. Thirty lawyers had donated their time, and anonymous thousands had mailed in contributions humble and great, but tens of thousands of dollars in unpaid travel, printing, courier and research expenses commanded Marshall back to the road on a seemingly endless itinerary of fund-raising speeches. Venues North and South burst with folks eager to see "Mr. Civil Rights" in person, to hear the easy baritone about which they had read so much in the papers.

One Sunday five months after December's arguments, Marshall had finished addressing an audience in Mobile, Alabama, and was preparing for the next day's speech in Los Angeles when he received a telephone call. Return to Washington, the unidentified caller advised him, come to the Supreme Court tomorrow.[58]

He was sitting in the Court with James Nabrit and George Hayes a few minutes before one the following afternoon when Chief Justice Earl Warren, ensconced between his eight brethren, began reading from the judgment in his hands. After briefly reciting the cases' history and applicable precedent, Warren read the gist: "We come then to the question presented: Does segregation of children in public schools solely on the basis of race, even though the physical facilities and other 'tangible' factors may be equal, deprive the children of the minority group of equal educational opportunities? We believe that it does."[59] Marshall stared at Kentucky-born Justice Stanley Reed, who, to his shock, had filed no dissent; Reed stared back and did not look away once while the chief justice read history into the record: "We conclude—unanimously—that, in the field of public education, the doctrine of 'separate but equal' has no place. Separate educational facilities are inherently unequal."[60]

———————————

NEARLY TWENTY YEARS EARLIER Charles Hamilton Houston had told the nation's black lawyers that, regarding segregated education, "we need to break this up or perish."[61] From his deathbed Houston assigned one of his local cases to two friends who "owed" him, and four years later, the Court decided that case along with *Brown* to declare Washington, D.C.'s segregated schools unconstitutional.[62] Had he lived to see it, the day surely would have been one of the happiest in Houston's life.

Even after *Brown's* unanimous holding, however, segregated education would not break up easily. The day after the Court delivered its opinion, the *Washington Post* reported that "there were numerous indications that it will take considerable time before the Court's unanimous ruling takes effect in all the states where segregation is in force."[63] Georgia, South Carolina and Mississippi took steps to privatize their public schools, with Georgia's governor, Herman Talmadge, promising "to map a program to insure continued and permanent segregation."[64] North Carolina's governor was "terribly disappointed" by the ruling.[65] President Eisenhower's press secretary, like the governor of Mississippi, refused to comment on *Brown v. Board of Education*.[66]

For segregation's opponents, *Brown* was, as the historian John Hope Franklin remembered, "a sweet, momentous, historical decision."[67] He recalled that "there was dancing in the streets in Washington, D.C., and a number of other places."[68] Nobel Peace Prize recipient Ralph Bunche was withdrawing twenty-five dollars in cash from the bank teller on the fourth floor of the United Nations building in New York City when nearby reporters informed him of the Court's decision. Bunche became so excited at what he called "an historic event" that he forgot to take his money and had to be chased down by a bank employee.[69]

Thurgood Marshall waxed optimistic to reporters over the next few days. He predicted that segregation would disappear from America's public schools "within a very few years now."[70] He did not think any southern state would follow through with a threat to privatize its schools, but if one did, "we will have them in court the same morning."[71] A few weeks later, Nashville, Tennessee's mayor, Ben West, presented Marshall with a golden key to the city in front of a crowd gathered from twenty states.[72]

THE COMING YEARS would present struggles unforeseen by those celebrating during the days following *Brown*. Through the years and trials to come,

Thurgood Marshall remained compass-true to the legal notions of justice he learned years ago as a student, then colleague and friend of Charles Hamilton Houston. When Marshall was appointed to the U.S. Court of Appeals for the Second Circuit, the prominent New York City attorney Lawrence Bailey recalled that when Marshall attended Howard Law School, "the public image of the Negro lawyer was a poor one." Charles Houston, Bailey wrote, had "conceived, designed and developed a plan to train and educate the Negro lawyer to be his people's own liberator," and, by 1961, "the exploits and accomplishments of Thurgood Marshall" were admired by lawyers and citizens of all races.[73] President Lyndon Johnson later asked Marshall to serve as solicitor general and later still appointed him to the Supreme Court of the United States. At each promotion, Marshall surely had the same thought expressed by so many who observed *Brown*'s oral argument: "If only Charlie were here."[74]

Charlie's fight was Thurgood's fight. So it had been and forever would be. Time loosened neither man. "The [desegregation] cases started with law schools and graduate schools," Marshall recalled, "solely because it was thought the issues could be made clearer in such cases than cases involving elementary and high schools."[75] Ever since the two men had launched the legal campaign in 1935, the lawyers held as their "single objective the destroying of racial segregation in public education."[76]

Within a few months after *Brown*, however, it became clear to Marshall and the NAACP Legal Defense Fund attorneys that despite their unanimous Supreme Court victory, they had not yet achieved their objective— racial segregation persisted in the nation's public schools. "Do not lose heart if victory does not come at once," Houston had encouraged them years ago. "Persevere to the end."[77] The lawyers returned to the Supreme Court to argue *Brown II*, in which the Court ordered that school desegregation should proceed "with all deliberate speed."[78] Southern officials seized the phrase as license to desegregate at a pace of their own choosing and, accordingly, their integration efforts all but ceased.

Nineteen years later, Justice Thurgood Marshall dissented in a 5–4 decision by which the Court allowed Detroit's public school system to remain segregated as a matter of fact. Detroit had the nation's fifth-largest school district and, like many districts across the country, it remained segregated not by law but by custom and practice. In a dissent joined by three of his brethren, Justice Marshall wrote with an authority borne from pain and triumph at once known and unknowable to his fellow justices. The fight unceasing trundled forth anew each day, and Thurgood Marshall, like Charles Hamilton Houston before him and with him, rose again to meet its unwelcome familiar daybreak, rose again to bring justice to law. It was the Supreme Court's duty, Marshall reminded his fellow justices, "to eliminate root and branch all vestiges of racial discrimination."[79]

NOTES

ABBREVIATIONS

The following abbreviations are used in the notes to designate frequently cited individuals.

CHH   Charles Hamilton Houston
TM   Thurgood Marshall
WW   Walter White

CHAPTER 1: SOUTHERN JUSTICE ON TRIAL

1. Frank Getty, "The Dramatic Leesburg Murder Trial," *Washington Post*, December 31, 1933.
2. "Yankee Common Sense," *Time*, May 8, 1933.
3. Getty, "The Dramatic Leesburg Murder Trial."
4. Walter Francis White, *A Man Called White: The Autobiography of Walter White* (University of Georgia Press, 1995), p. 3.
5. Ibid., pp. 5–6.
6. "Honeymoon," *Washington Post*, February 5, 1933.
7. "Yankee Common Sense."
8. "Virginia Wins Right to Try Killer Suspect," *Washington Post*, October 17, 1933.
9. Ibid.
10. Genna Rae McNeil, *Groundwork: Charles Hamilton Houston and the Struggle for Civil Rights* (University of Pennsylvania Press, 1983), p. 90.
11. Ibid.

12. "Court to Rule on Crawford Defense Today," *Washington Post*, November 7, 1933.

13. Ibid.

14. Ibid.

15. Ibid.

16. Ibid.

17. "Race Refuted as Crawford Jury Factor," *Washington Post*, November 8, 1933.

18. McNeil, *Groundwork*, p. 91.

19. "Make Appeals for Crawford," *New York Amsterdam News*, November 22, 1933.

20. McNeil, *Groundwork*, p. 93.

21. "Court to Rule on Crawford Defense Today."

22. The Library of Virginia, "Working Out Her Destiny—Timeline," available at http://www.lva.virginia.gov.

23. "All White Panel Chosen to Try Crawford Case," *Washington Post*, December 13, 1933.

24. Frank Getty, "Hope of Alibi for Crawford Is Abandoned," *Washington Post*, December 15, 1933.

25. Frank Getty, "Crawford Case Goes to Jury This Morning," *Washington Post*, December 16, 1933.

26. Ibid.

27. Getty, "The Dramatic Leesburg Murder Trial."

28. Ibid.

29. Ibid.

30. Ibid.

31. Helen Boardman and Martha Gruening, "Is the N.A.A.C.P. Retreating?" *Chicago Defender*, June 30, 1934.

32. CHH and Leon Ransom, "The Crawford Case," *Chicago Defender*, July 14, 1934.

CHAPTER 2: AMBITIOUS, SUCCESSFUL, HOPEFUL DREAMS

1. Juan Williams, *Thurgood Marshall: American Revolutionary* (Three Rivers Press, 1998), p. 25.

2. Ibid., p. 27.

3. Ibid., pp. 27–28.

4. "Poolroom Like a Church," *Washington Post*, November 30, 1904.

5. "Pen and Pencil Club Dines," *Washington Post*, February 15, 1903.

6. Walter J. Leonard, "Charles Hamilton Houston and the Search for a Just Society," *North Carolina Central Law Journal* 22, no. 1 (1996): 4.

7. Richard Kluger, *Simple Justice: The History of* Brown v. Board of Education *and Black America's Struggle for Equality* (Vintage, 1977), p. 153.

8. Ibid., p. 125.

9. Genna Rae McNeil, *Groundwork: Charles Hamilton Houston and the Struggle for Civil Rights* (University of Pennsylvania Press, 1983), p. 53.

10. "Woodrow Wilson: A Portrait," *American Experience*, available at http://www.pbs.org.

11. "A Chronology of African American Military Service from WWI through WWII," available at http://www.redstone.army.mil/history/integrate/CHRON3.html.

12. Peter Perl, "The Washington, D.C. Race Riot of 1919," *Washington Post*, March 1, 1999.

13. Ibid.

14. "Detective Sergeant Wilson Victim; Other Officers Hurt; Negro Runs Amuck, Wounding Many in Flight," *Washington Post*, July 22, 1919.

15. Ibid.

16. Perl, "The Washington, D.C. Race Riot of 1919."

17. "Riots Elsewhere Forecast by Negro," *Washington Post*, July 25, 1919.

18. Ibid.

19. "Soviet Influence Behind Race Riots," *Washington Post*, August 27, 1919; "Topics in the Pulpits," *Washington Post*, July 26, 1919.

20. "Asks a Riot Inquiry," *Washington Post*, July 23, 1919.

21. "Denouncing Wave of Crime Here, Officials, Ministers and Others Declare Police Are Too Few," *Washington Post*, July 21, 1919.

CHAPTER 3: NO TEA FOR THE FEEBLE

1. CHH, "The Need for Negro Lawyers," *Journal of Negro Education* 4 (1935), CHH Collection, Moorland-Spingarn Research Center, Howard University.

2. Richard Kluger, *Simple Justice: The History of* Brown v. Board of Education *and Black America's Struggle for Equality* (Vintage, 1977), p. 156.

3. Genna Rae McNeil, *Groundwork: Charles Hamilton Houston and the Struggle for Civil Rights* (University of Pennsylvania Press, 1983), p. 71.

4. Memorandum from CHH to Howard Law faculty, February 5, 1931, CHH Collection.

5. Ibid.

6. McNeil, *Groundwork*, p. 82

7. Ibid., p. 73.

8. "Howard White Law Faculty Resigns," *New York Amsterdam News*, August 13, 1930.

9. Ibid.

10. Memorandum from CHH to Howard Law faculty, October 9, 1931, CHH Collection.

11. McNeil, *Groundwork*, p. 83.

12. Ibid., p. 84.

13. TM, "A Tribute to Charles H. Houston," *Amherst Magazine*, Spring 1978, p. 273.

14. CHH, "Saving the World for 'Democracy,'" *Pittsburgh Courier*, August–October 1940, CHH Collection.

15. Ibid.

16. Ibid.

17. Ibid.

18. Ibid.

19. Ibid.

20. Ibid.
21. Ibid.
22. Ibid.
23. Ibid.
24. Ibid.
25. Ibid.
26. Ibid.
27. McNeil, *Groundwork*, p. 69.
28. Ibid.
29. Ibid.
30. Ibid.
31. Ibid.

CHAPTER 4: THE SOCIAL ENGINEERS

1. Juan Williams, *Thurgood Marshall: American Revolutionary* (Three Rivers Press, 1998), p. 55.
2. Ibid., p. 35.
3. Ibid., pp. 41–42.
4. Ibid., p. 349.
5. Ibid., p. 56.
6. "Washington's Alleys," *Washington Post*, May 12, 1930.
7. "More Police Necessary," *Washington Post*, January 6, 1930.
8. TM, "A Tribute to Charles H. Houston," *Amherst Magazine*, Spring 1978, p. 273.
9. Richard Kluger, *Simple Justice: The History of* Brown v. Board of Education *and Black America's Struggle for Equality* (Vintage, 1977), pp. 128–29.
10. Mark V. Tushnet, *Making Constitutional Law: Thurgood Marshall and the Supreme Court, 1961–1991* (Oxford University Press, 1997), p. 185.
11. Kluger, *Simple Justice*, p. 128.
12. Genna Rae McNeil, *Groundwork: Charles Hamilton Houston and the Struggle for Civil Rights* (University of Pennsylvania Press, 1983), p. 82.
13. Kluger, *Simple Justice*, p. 128

CHAPTER 5: SOUTH JOURNEY CHILDREN

1. Juan Williams, *Thurgood Marshall: American Revolutionary* (Three Rivers Press, 1998), p. 59.
2. Ibid., p. 60.
3. Michael J. Klarman, *From Jim Crow to Civil Rights: The Supreme Court and the Struggle for Racial Equality* (Oxford University Press, 2004), p. 119.
4. Statement of Charles H. Houston before the Sub-Committee of the United States Judiciary Committee in Hearings on the Costigan-Wagner Bill, S. 1978, 73d Cong., 2d Sess., February 20, 1934, CHH Collection, Moorland-Spingarn Research Center, Howard University.

5. Ibid.

6. Ibid.

7. Richard Kluger, *Simple Justice: The History of* Brown v. Board of Education *and Black America's Struggle for Equality* (Vintage, 1977), p. 164.

8. Ibid.

9. Williams, *Thurgood Marshall*, p. 60.

CHAPTER 6: THE LAW OFFICES OF THURGOOD MARSHALL, ESQ.

1. WW to CHH, October 6, 1993, CHH Collection, Moorland-Spingarn Research Center, Howard University.

2. WW to CHH, February 28, 1935, CHH Collection.

3. WW to CHH, November 17, 1933, CHH Collection.

4. Louis Campbell to WW, 1934, CHH Collection.

5. WW to CHH, October 13, 1934, CHH Collection.

6. CHH to WW, August 9, 1934, CHH Collection.

7. Genna Rae McNeil, *Groundwork: Charles Hamilton Houston and the Struggle for Civil Rights* (University of Pennsylvania Press, 1983), pp. 111–12.

8. Ibid., p. 112.

9. Roger Goldman and David Gallen *Thurgood Marshall: Justice for All* (Carroll & Graf, 1992), p. 27.

10. Ibid.

11. Juan Williams, *Thurgood Marshall: American Revolutionary* (Three Rivers Press, 1998), p. 63.

12. Ibid.

13. "Order Trial of Howard U Law Student," *New York Amsterdam News*, November 30, 1935.

14. Ibid.

15. Ibid.

16. Williams, *Thurgood Marshall*, p. 74.

CHAPTER 7: *MURRAY V. MARYLAND*

1. Leland B. Ware, "Setting the Stage for Brown: The Development and Implementation of the NAACP's School Desegregation Campaign, 1930–1950," *Mercer Law Review* 521 (2001): 631.

2. Ibid.

3. Ibid., p. 643.

4. Richard Kluger, *Simple Justice: The History of* Brown v. Board of Education *and Black America's Struggle for Equality* (Vintage, 1977), p. 186.

5. Ibid.

6. Ibid., p. 187.

7. Ibid.

8. Ibid., p. 189.

9. "Smash Ban on Race Students at University of Maryland," *Chicago Defender*, June 6, 1935.

10. CHH to TM, August 24, 1935, NAACP Papers, Manuscript Division, Library of Congress.

11. Kluger, *Simple Justice*, p. 188.

12. "Negro, Rejected by College, Sues," *Washington Post*, April 20, 1935.

13. *Black's Law Dictionary*, revised 4th ed. (West Publishing, 1968).

14. Ware, "Setting the Stage for Brown," p. 649.

15. Ibid., p. 645; see also Kluger, *Simple Justice*, pp. 188–89.

16. Kluger, *Simple Justice*, p. 190.

17. Ibid.

18. Mark V. Tushnet, *The NAACP's Legal Strategy against Segregated Education, 1925–1950* (University of North Carolina Press, 1987).

19. "Court Studies Suit of Negro to Enter School," *Washington Post*, November 6, 1935.

20. Mark V. Tushnet, *Making Civil Rights Law: Thurgood Marshall and the Supreme Court, 1936–1961* (Oxford University Press, 1994), p. 14.

21. CHH to TM, August 23, 1936, NAACP Papers.

22. Ibid.

23. Roger Goldman and David Gallen, *Thurgood Marshall: Justice for All* (Carroll & Graf, 1992), p. 30.

24. Ware, "Setting the Stage for Brown," p. 651.

25. CHH to Charles Harris Wesley, December 7, 1935, NAACP Papers.

26. Ibid.

27. CHH to TM, December 7, 1935, NAACP Papers.

28. TM to CHH, December 21, 1935, NAACP Papers.

29. Ibid.

30. CHH to TM, December 24, 1935, NAACP Papers.

31. Rayford Logan to CHH and TM, January 15, 1936, NAACP Papers.

32. CHH to TM, January 3, 1936, NAACP Papers.

33. Ibid.

34. "Race Barrier Still Down in Baltimore," *New York Amsterdam News*, October 17, 1936.

35. Ibid.

36. "First to Graduate from University of Maryland Law School," *New York Amsterdam News*, June 18, 1938.

37. Murray trial Exhibit 1, CHH Collection, Moorland-Spingarn Research Center, Howard University.

CHAPTER 8: DON'T SHOUT TOO SOON

1. Richard Kluger, *Simple Justice: The History of* Brown v. Board of Education *and Black America's Struggle for Equality* (Vintage, 1977), p. 195.

2. CHH, "Don't Shout Too Soon," *Crisis*, March 1936, p. 79, NAACP Papers, Manuscript Division, Library of Congress.

3. Ibid.

4. Ibid.

5. Ibid.

6. Ibid.

7. Michael J. Klarman, *From Jim Crow to Civil Rights: The Supreme Court and the Struggle for Racial Equality* (Oxford University Press, 2004), p. 168, quoting an unnamed historian.

8. CHH, "Don't Shout Too Soon."

9. Klarman, *From Jim Crow to Civil Rights*, p. 165.

10. CHH, "Don't Shout Too Soon."

11. Ibid.

12. TM to CHH, February 15, 1936, NAACP Papers.

13. Kluger, *Simple Justice*, p. 195.

14. CHH to TM, February 10, 1936, NAACP Papers.

15. Ibid.

16. "Gentleman from Illinois," *Time*, November 19, 1934.

17. Juan Williams, *Thurgood Marshall: American Revolutionary* (Three Rivers Press, 1998), p. 82.

18. "Carl J. Murphy: Publisher, Civil Rights Activist, Educator," *Baltimore Sun Reporter*, February 13, 2007.

19. Sandy M. Shoemaker, "We Shall Overcome, Someday: The Equal Rights Movement in Baltimore, 1935–1942," *Maryland Historical Magazine* 89, no. 3 (Fall 1994).

20. Genna Rae McNeil, *Groundwork: Charles Hamilton Houston and the Struggle for Civil Rights* (University of Pennsylvania Press, 1983), p. 127.

21. Ibid., p. 140.

22. Ibid.

23. "Charles Houston Speaks in Memphis at Metropolitan," *Atlanta Daily World*, April 17, 1936.

24. Ibid.

25. "Charles Houston Thanks N.Y. Daily," *Chicago Defender*, June 6, 1936.

26. McNeil, *Groundwork*, p. 126.

27. "Refused Admittance to Baltimore School," *Chicago Defender*, June 13, 1936.

28. McNeil, *Groundwork*, p.141.

29. Williams, *Thurgood Marshall*, p. 80.

30. "Negroes to Sue to Gain High School Admittance," *Washington Post*, January 17, 1936.

31. Ibid.

32. Ibid.

33. "Refused Admittance to Baltimore School," *Chicago Defender*, June 13, 1936.

34. Mark V. Tushnet, *Making Civil Rights Law: Thurgood Marshall and the Supreme Court, 1936–1961* (Oxford University Press, 1994), p. 17.

35. Williams, *Thurgood Marshall*, p. 83.

36. Prentice-Hall, Inc. to TM, July 17, 1936, NAACP Papers.

37. TM to Prentice-Hall, Inc. July 27, 1936, NAACP Papers.

38. CHH to TM, September 21, 1935, NAACP Papers.

39. TM to CHH, May 25, 1936, NAACP Papers.

40. Ibid.

41. "Negro Attorney Has Great Chance, Says Houston," *Atlanta Daily World*, September 25, 1932.

42. Ibid.

43. Tushnet, *Making Civil Rights Law*, p. 18.

44. TM to CHH, May 25, 1936, NAACP Papers.

45. "Negro Attorney Has Great Chance."

46. McNeil, *Groundwork*, p. 145.

47. Ibid.

48. Ibid.

49. TM to F. O. Reinherd, October 8, 1936, NAACP Papers.

50. Williams, *Thurgood Marshall*, pp. 84–85.

51. "Parents Gain Much Ground; May Win," *Atlanta Daily World*, August 17, 1936.

52. Ibid.

53. Williams, *Thurgood Marshall*, p. 80.

Chapter 9: Special Counsel and Assistant Counsel

1. Juan Williams, *Thurgood Marshall: American Revolutionary* (Three Rivers Press, 1998), p. 95.

2. Howard Ball, *A Defiant Life: Thurgood Marshall and the Persistence of Racism in America* (Crown, 1998), p. 49.

3. Mark V. Tushnet, *Making Civil Rights Law: Thurgood Marshall and the Supreme Court, 1936–1961* (Oxford University Press, 1994), p. 17; "Houston understood that in Marshall he had a student who had the potential to surpass him."

4. CHH, tentative itinerary to New York, September 3, 1936, CHH Collection, Moorland-Spingarn Research Center, Howard University.

5. Ibid.

6. CHH, itinerary, October 1936, CHH Collection.

7. Ibid.

8. "6,000 School Children Are Out in Street," *New York Amsterdam News*, November 21, 1936.

9. "Thurgood Marshall in Speech at Lincoln U," *Chicago Defender*, November 28, 1936.

10. "Legal Counsel to Speak," *New York Amsterdam News*, January 16, 1937.

11. Roger Goldman and David Gallen, *Thurgood Marshall: Justice for All* (Carroll & Graf, 1992), p. 31.

12. Ibid.

13. "Unfair Teachers' Salaries to Be Fought," *New York Amsterdam News*, November 28, 1936.

14. Ibid.

15. Ibid.

16. Ibid.

17. Mark V. Tushnet, *The NAACP's Legal Strategy against Segregated Education, 1925–50* (University of North Carolina Press, 1987), pp. 59–60.

18. Eileen S. McGuckian Franklin, *Rockville: Portrait of a City* (Hillsboro Press, 2001).

19. Ibid.

20. Tushnet, *The NAACP's Legal Strategy*, p. 60.

21. Richard Kluger, *Simple Justice: The History of* Brown v. Board of Education *and Black America's Struggle for Equality* (Vintage, 1977), p. 197, quoting Edward Lovett.

22. Ibid., pp. 197–98.

23. Ibid., p. 198.

24. "Houston Addresses Large Crowd, Closing NAACP Meet," *Atlanta Daily World*, April 26, 1937.

25. Ibid.

26. "Fraternity Helps to Push School Fight," *Chicago Defender*, March 20, 1937.

27. "Washington's Social Whirl," *Chicago Defender*, May 1, 1937.

28. Ibid.

29. CHH, "Making the World Safe for Democracy," *Pittsburgh Courier*, October 1940, CHH Collection.

30. Memorandum from CHH to WW, August 16, 1935, CHH Collection.

31. Ibid.

32. Kluger, *Simple Justice*, p. 200.

33. WW to CHH, March 12, 1935, CHH Collection.

34. Herman E. Irving to WW, March 10, 1935, CHH Collection.

35. Ibid.

36. Ibid.

37. CHH to WW, undated, CHH Collection.

38. Ibid.

39. Ibid.

40. Tushnet, *The NAACP's Legal Strategy*, pp. 59–60.

CHAPTER 10: ON THE CUSP IN MISSOURI

1. Douglas O. Linder, "Before *Brown*: Charles H. Houston and the *Gaines* Case," p. 1, available at http://www.law.umkc.edu.

2. Ibid.

3. Ibid.

4. Mark V. Tushnet, *The NAACP's Legal Strategy against Segregated Education, 1925–1950*, (University of North Carolina Press, 1987), pp. 70–71.

5. Juan Williams, *Thurgood Marshall: American Revolutionary* (Three Rivers Press, 1998), p. 97.

6. CHH, "Tentative Findings Regarding Negro Lawyers," February 1920, CHH Collection, Moorland-Spingarn Research Center, Howard University.

7. Leland B. Ware, "Setting the Stage for Brown: The Development and Implementation of the NAACP's School Desegregation Campaign, 1930–1950," *Mercer Law Review* 52 (Winter 2001): 631, 654.

8. Richard Kluger, *Simple Justice: The History of* Brown v. Board of Education *and Black America's Struggle for Equality* (Vintage, 1977), p. 203.

9. Ibid.

10. Ibid.

11. Ibid.

12. Linder, "Before *Brown*," p. 12.

13. *Missouri ex rel. Gaines v. Canada.*, 342 Mo. 121, 127 (1937) (en banc).

14. Linder, "Before *Brown*," p. 14.

15. Kluger, *Simple Justice*, p. 204.

16. Ibid.

17. Linder, "Before *Brown*," p. 14.

18. Ibid.

19. Ibid.

20. Ibid., p. 15.

21. Ibid.

22. Ibid.

23. Ibid.

24. Ibid.

25. Ibid., p. 16.

26. "White Missouri," *Time*, August 3, 1936.

27. *Missouri ex. rel. Gaines v. Canada*, 342 Mo. 121, 113 S.W. 2d 783 (Mo. 1937).

28. Ibid. at 131.

29. Ibid.

30. Ibid. at 132.

31. Ibid. at 133.

32. "White Missouri."

33. Genna Rae McNeil, *Groundwork: Charles Hamilton Houston and the Struggle for Civil Rights* (University of Pennsylvania Press, 1983), p. 150.

34. A. Leon Higginbotham, Jr., and William C. Smith, "The Hughes Court and the Beginning of the End of the 'Separate But Equal' Doctrine," *Minnesota Law Review* 75 (1992): 1099, 1109.

35. Leonard Baker, *Brandeis and Frankfurter: A Dual Biography* (Harper and Row, 1984), pp. 357, 370.

36. William Orville Douglas, *The Court Years, 1939–1975: The Autobiography of William O. Douglas* (Random House, 1980), pp. 14–15.

37. Robert L. Carter, "The Long Road to Equality," *Nation*, May 3, 2004.

38. "Columbians Ahead of Their Time: Charles Evans Hughes," *Columbia 250*, http://www.c250.columbia.edu.

39. *Missouri ex rel. Gaines v. Canada*, 580 U.S. 337, 347 (1938).

40. Ibid. at 349.

41. Ibid. at 351.

42. Ibid. at 350–51.

43. Higginbotham and Smith, "The Hughes Court," p. 1124.

44. Linder, "Before *Brown*," p. 18.

45. "Editorial Comment on 'The Gaines Decision,' " *New York Times*, December 13, 1938.

46. Linder, "Before *Brown*," p. 18.

47. Ibid.

48. "Sixteen States Are Affected by 'The Gaines Case,'" *New York Times*, December 13, 1938.

49. "Lloyd Gaines Becomes a Civil Rights Leader, but Only Wanted to Go to Law School," http://www.blackmissouri.com, February 5, 2008; see also M. Zapp, "Who Was Lloyd Gaines?" *Vox* magazine, December 2006.

50. Chad Garrison, "The Mystery of Lloyd Gaines," *Riverfront Times*, April 4, 2007.

51. Ibid.

5? Ibid.

53. Ibid.

54. Ibid.

55. "Editorial Comment on 'The Gaines Decision.'"

56. Linder, "Before *Brown*," p. 19.

57. "Family Seeks Lloyd Gaines," *New York Amsterdam News*, October 21, 1939.

58. Ibid.

59. Ibid.

60. "Principal in the Gaines Case Missing," *Chicago Defender*, October 21, 1939.

61. Ibid.

62. "NAACP Still Seeking Missing Lloyd Gaines," *Atlanta Daily World*, March 14, 1940.

CHAPTER 11: AN OUTSIDE MAN

1. WW to TM, November 14, 1934, NAACP Papers, Manuscript Division, Library of Congress.

2. TM to Senator Millard Tydings, January 28, 1935, NAACP Papers.

3. Ibid.

4. Ibid.

5. Senator Millard Tydings to TM, February 16, 1935, NAACP Papers.

6. Ibid.

7. TM to Senator Millard Tydings, March 18, 1935, NAACP Papers.

8. Ibid.

9. Senator Millard Tydings to TM, March 21, 1935, NAACP Papers.

10. WW to TM, April 9, 1935, NAACP Papers.

11. Ibid.

12. TM to Representative Ambrose J. Kennedy, April 1, 1936, NAACP Papers.

13. Ibid.

14. WW to TM, April 20, 1936, NAACP Papers.

15. "NAACP Devises New Way of Protesting Lynching," *Atlanta Daily World*, September 17, 1936; "Anti-Lynch Flag Flying Over 5th Ave," *Chicago Defender*, September 19, 1936.

16. "President Told He Now Has Chance to Hit Lynching, Walter White Wires," *Atlanta Daily World*, November 21, 1936.

17. "13 Lynchings in '36, NAACP Says," *Atlanta Daily World*, January 3, 1937.

18. "New Lynching Record Set with Three in Six Days," *Atlanta Daily World*, May 14, 1936.

19. Juan Williams, *Thurgood Marshall: American Revolutionary* (Three Rivers Press, 1998), p. 100.

20. "Houston Urges Citizens to Oppose Emasculation of 14th Amendment," *Chicago Defender*, March 6, 1937.

21. Genna Rae McNeil, *Groundwork: Charles Hamilton Houston and the Struggle for Civil Rights* (University of Pennsylvania Press, 1983), p. 149.

22. "Houston Rewed After Divorce," *New York Amsterdam News*, October 2, 1937.

23. Ibid.

24. Ibid.

25. Mary McLeod Bethune to CHH, November 8, 1937, NAACP Papers.

26. McNeil, *Groundwork*, p. 148.

27. Richard Kluger, *Simple Justice: The History of* Brown v. Board of Education *and Black America's Struggle for Equality* (Vintage, 1977), p. 160.

28. Ibid.

29. Ibid., p. 205.

30. "Houston Leaves NAACP New York Office," *Atlanta Daily World*, July 19, 1938.

CHAPTER 12: HOPE LOOMS

1. "Round of Festivity," *New York Amsterdam News*, June 25, 1938.

2. "Louis Destroys Schmeling in Rematch," International Boxing Hall of Fame, http://www.ibhof.com, 1997.

3. Roger Goldman and David Gallen, *Thurgood Marshall: Justice for All* (Carroll & Graf, 1992), p. 144.

4. "Round of Festivity."

5. Juan Williams, *Thurgood Marshall: American Revolutionary* (Three Rivers Press, 1998), p. 99.

6. CHH to TM, August 26, 1936, NAACP Papers, Manuscript Division, Library of Congress.

7. "Ask New Trial for Boy, 15, Facing Death Sentence," *Chicago Defender*, June 17, 1939.

8. Ibid.

9. "Kentucky Boy May Get Another Trial," *New York Amsterdam News*, May 27, 1939.

10. "Ask New Trial for Boy, 15, Facing Death Sentence."

11. CHH to WW, February 2, 1939, CHH Collection, Moorland–Spingarn Research Center, Howard University.

12. Ibid.

13. Ibid.

14. Ibid.

15. Genna Rae McNeil, *Groundwork: Charles Hamilton Houston and the Struggle for Civil Rights* (University of Pennsylvania Press, 1983), p. 148.

16. Ibid.

17. "NAACP Carries Murder Case to High Court," *Atlanta Daily World*, February 15, 1938.

18. Ibid.

19. Ibid.

20. Petitioner's Brief on Argument, *Commonwealth of Kentucky*, Leon A. Ransom, Charles H. Houston, Counsel for Petitioner; Thurgood Marshall, Edward P. Lovett, of Counsel, 1938, available at 1938 WL 39312 (U.S.).

21. Ibid., citing *Strauder v. West Virginia*, 100 U.S. 303 (1879); *Commonwealth v. Wright*, 79 Ky. 22 (1880).

22. Ibid. at 6.

23. *Hale v. Commonwealth of Kentucky*, 303 U.S. 613, 614 (1938).

24. Ibid. at 616.

25. " 'Lily-White' Jury Trials Lose Again," *Chicago Defender*, April 23, 1938.

26. Telegram from William Houston to CHH, April 11, 1938.

27. "NAACP Carries Murder Case to High Court," *Atlanta Daily World*, February 15, 1938.

28. CHH, "Don't Shout Too Soon," *Crisis*, March 1936, NAACP Papers.

29. "Invade Court; Eject Juror, School Head Tossed from Court House," *Chicago Defender*, October 8, 1938.

30. "Congratulate Texan on His Firm Stand," *Atlanta Daily World*, October 11, 1938.

31. Ibid.; see also Williams, *Thurgood Marshall*, p. 102.

32. "Invade Court; Eject Juror, School Head Tossed from Court House."

33. "Congratulate Texan on His Firm Stand."

34. Ibid.

35. "Investigate Jury-Eviction Case," *Atlanta Daily World*, October 11, 1938.

36. "Congratulate Texan on His Firm Stand."

37. "What Next in Texas?" *Chicago Defender*, October 15, 1938.

38. "N.A.A.C.P. Probes Attack on Texas Venireman," *Chicago Defender*, October 15, 1938.

39. Ibid.

40. Ibid.

41. "When Racial Friction Almost Rubbed Out a Future Justice," *Dallas Morning News*, January 24, 2006.

42. Williams, *Thurgood Marshall*, p. 103.

43. Ibid.

44. Ibid.

45. "N.A.A.C.P. Probes Attack on Texas Venireman."

46. "Gov. Allred Keeps Word; Makes Arrest in Jury Room Assault Case," *Chicago Defender*, November 12, 1938.

47. Ibid.

48. Williams, *Thurgood Marshall*, p. 104.

49. Ibid.

50. Ibid.

51. "Prosecution of Juror's Attackers Asked of G-Men," *Atlanta Daily World*, October 31, 1938.

CHAPTER 13: MARSHALL AT THE HELM

1. Earl Lewis, *In Their Own Interests: Race, Class and Power in Twentieth-Century Norfolk, Virginia* (University of California Press, 1991).

2. *Alston v. School Board of City of Norfolk*, 112 F.2d 992, 995 (4th Cir. 1940); see also Mark V. Tushnet, *The NAACP's Legal Strategy against Segregated Education, 1925–1950*, (University of North Carolina Press, 1987), p. 79.

3. Mark V. Tushnet, *Making Civil Rights Law: Thurgood Marshall and the Supreme Court, 1936–1961* (Oxford University Press, 1994), p. 25.

4. "Virginia Teachers to Appeal," *Atlanta Daily World*, February 18, 1940.

5. "NAACP to Contest VA. Salary Case Decision," *Atlanta Daily World*, March 4, 1940.

6. "As Equal Salary Suit Was Fought," *Atlanta Daily World*, February 20, 1940.

7. "Virginia Teachers Salary Case Up in U.S. Court June 13," *Atlanta Daily World*, June 6, 1940.

8. "Court Holds Up Va. Teachers' Contracts," *Chicago Defender*, April 20, 1940.

9. "Appellate Court Ponders Teachers' Wage Fight," *Chicago Defender*, June 22, 1940.

10. Richard Kluger, *Simple Justice: The History of* Brown v. Board of Education *and Black America's Struggle for Equality* (Vintage, 1977), p. 216.

11. "Unequal Teachers Pay Is Ruled Out," *Atlanta Daily World*, June 24, 1940.

12. "Court Holds Up Va. Teachers' Contracts."

13. "NAACP Pushes Fight on Jim-Crow Schools," *Chicago Defender*, September 30, 1939.

14. Pam Johnson, "The Unforgettable Miss Bluford," *Poynteronline*, http://www.poynter.org, February 23, 2004.

15. "Famous Missouri Journalists," State Historical Society of Missouri, available at http://www.shs.umsystem.edu.

16. Tushnet, *The NAACP's Legal Strategy*, pp. 83–84.

17. Ibid., p. 85.

18. Johnson, "The Unforgettable Miss Bluford."

19. Ibid.

20. "NAACP Pushes Fight on Jim-Crow Schools."

21. Ibid.

22. "Rush Tennessee U. Campus; Demand Admittance," *Chicago Defender*, October 7, 1939.

23. Ibid.

24. CHH, "Don't Shout Too Soon," *Crisis*, March 1936, NAACP Papers, Manuscript Division, Library of Congress.

25. Tushnet, *Making Civil Rights Law*, p. 26.

26. Genna Rae McNeil, *Groundwork: Charles Hamilton Houston and the Struggle for Civil Rights* (University of Pennsylvania Press, 1983), p. 155.

27. Tushnet, *Making Civil Rights Law*, p. 26.

28. Ibid., p. 27.

29. Roger A. Fairfax, Jr., "Wielding the Double-Edged Sword: Charles Hamilton Houston and Judicial Activism in the Age of Legal Realism," *Harvard Black Letter Law Journal* 14 (1998): 17, 24.

30. "Name Students at Howard U. to Get Fellowship Awards," *Chicago Defender*, October 1, 1938.

31. "Marshall in Talk," *New York Amsterdam News*, May 21, 1938.

32. "Movers Fight for Fat Plum," *New York Amsterdam News*, July 31, 1937.

33. "NAACP Branch Now in Bronx," *New York Amsterdam News*, April 13, 1940.

34. "NAACP's Famed Thurgood Marshall Speaks Here Tonight," *Atlanta Daily World*, May 21, 1940.

35. Ibid.

36. "Predict Passage of Anti-Lynching Bill Today," *Atlanta Daily World*, January 10, 1940.

37. Ibid.

38. Ibid.

39. Ibid.

40. Ibid.

41. Charles P. Howard, "The Observer," *Atlanta Daily World*, August 15, 1940.

42. Tushnet, *The NAACP's Legal Strategy*, p. 55.

43. "Continues Fight for Admittance to Tennessee U," *Atlanta Daily World*, October 11, 1940.

44. Ibid.

45. "Man Appeals Attack Case Conviction," *Chicago Defender*, June 18, 1938.

46. "Execution of Ala. Torture Victim Halted," *Chicago Defender*, March 23, 1940.

47. Ibid.

48. Ibid.

49. "To Die for Killing," *New York Amsterdam News*, June 11, 1938.

50. Ibid.

51. "Alabama Man Is Found Guilty in Death of Nurse," *Atlanta Daily World*, June 9, 1938.

52. "Seek Fourth Reprieve for Doomed Man," *Chicago Defender*, January 20, 1940.

53. Ibid.

54. "Supreme Court Reverses Another Death Sentence," *Atlanta Daily World*, March 17, 1940.

55. "Alabaman Gets Life Term in Second Trial," *New York Amsterdam News*, December 21, 1940.

CHAPTER 14: GREENWICH RAILROAD BONES

1. Daniel J. Sharfstein, "Saving the Race," *Legal Affairs*, March/April 2005.

2. "Rap State for Jailing Spell After Acquittal," *Chicago Defender*, February 8, 1941.

3. Ibid.

4. Juan Williams, *Thurgood Marshall: American Revolutionary* (Three Rivers Press, 1998), p. 119.

5. Sharfstein, "Saving the Race."

6. Ibid.; "Hint 'Something Wrong' in Woman's Rape Charge," *Chicago Defender*, December 21, 1940.

7. "Probe Casts Doubt on Socialite's Rape Story," *Chicago Defender*, December 28, 1940.

8. Sharfstein, "Saving the Race," p. 2.

9. "Hint Socialite Mrs. Strubing May Not Prosecute Butler Accused of Attacking Her," *New York Amsterdam News*, January 4, 1941.

10. Sharfstein, "Saving the Race," p. 2.; "Hint 'Something Wrong' in Woman's Rape Charge."

11. Sharfstein, "Saving the Race," p. 3.

12. Ibid.

13. Ibid., p. 4.

14. Ibid.

15. "Rap State for Holding Spell After Jury Acquits Him of Charges," *Chicago Defender*, February 8, 1941.

16. Ibid.

17. Ibid.

18. Ibid.

19. Genna Rae McNeil, *Groundwork: Charles Hamilton Houston and the Struggle for Civil Rights* (University of Pennsylvania Press, 1983), p. 156.

20. Ibid., pp. 156–57.

21. Richard Kluger, *Simple Justice: The History of* Brown v. Board of Education *and Black America's Struggle for Equality* (Vintage, 1977), pp. 229–30.

22. Ibid., p. 230.

23. Ibid.

24. Ibid., p. 231.

25. McNeil, *Groundwork*, p. 163.

26. Kluger, *Simple Justice*, p. 231.

27. Ibid.

28. McNeil, *Groundwork*, p. 158.

29. Kluger, *Simple Justice*, p. 232.

30. *Steele v. Louisville & N.R. Co. et al.*, 323 U.S. 192 (1944).

31. "First Negro Makes Oral Plea in Ala. High Court," *Chicago Defender*, December 4, 1943.

32. Ibid.

33. "Writer Contends Court Evaded Issue in Fireman's Case," *Atlanta Daily World*, January 18, 1944.

34. WW to CHH, May 27, 1948, NAACP Papers, Manuscript Division, Library of Congress.

35. Ibid.

36. J. Clay Smith, Jr., "A Tribute to Charles Hamilton Houston: Remembered Hero, Forgotten Contribution: Charles Hamilton Houston, Legal Realism and Labor Law," *Harvard Black Letter Law Journal* (Spring 1998): 6.

37. Ibid., p. 9.

38. Ibid.

39. Ibid., p. 10.

40. "Supreme Court Gets Plea of Firemen to Save Jobs on Dixie Railroads," *Chicago Defender*, November 25, 1944.

41. Ibid.

42. Ibid.

43. Ibid.

44. Ibid.

45. *Steele v. Lousville & N.R.Co. et al.,* 323 U.S. 192, 199 (1944).

46. Ibid. at 201.

47. "Supreme Court Decision Gives Job Hope to 4,000," *Chicago Defender,* December 30, 1944.

48. Roy Wilkins to CHH, December 21, 1944, NAACP Papers, Manuscript Division, Library of Congress.

49. "High Court Rail Union Ruling Gives Negro Workers New 'Bill of Rights,'" *Chicago Defender,* January 6, 1945.

50. Ibid.

51. Williams, *Thurgood Marshall,* pp. 113–14.

52. "Lyons Gets Life Term in Slaying," *Atlanta Daily World,* February 7, 1941.

53. Ibid.

54. Ibid.

55. TM to WW, February 2, 1941, NAACP Papers.

56. Ibid.

57. "Lyons Gets Life Term in Slaying."

58. TM to WW, January 28, 1941, NAACP Papers.

59. "File Appeal in Torture Case," *Chicago Defender,* October 30, 1943.

60. Williams, *Thurgood Marshall,* p. 114.

61. TM to WW, January 28, 1941, NAACP Papers.

62. Ibid.

63. TM to WW, February 2, 1941, NAACP Papers.

64. Ibid.

65. Ibid.

66. Ibid.

67. Ibid.

68. Ibid.

69. "Triple Slayer Suspect to Face Trial in January," *Chicago Defender,* November 15, 1941.

70. "Oklahoma Slaying Case Goes to Supreme Court," *Chicago Defender,* May 6, 1944; *Lyons v. State of Oklahoma,* 322 U.S. 596 (1944).

71. "Lyons Conviction Upheld in D.C.," *Atlanta Daily World,* June 6, 1944.

CHAPTER 15: WAR AT HOME AND ABROAD

1. Author's interview with William T. Coleman, Jr., July 18, 2008.

2. Ibid.

3. Ibid.

4. Ibid.

5. Memorandum from CHH to Legal Defense Fund, November 19, 1943, NAACP Papers, Manuscript Division, Library of Congress.

6. Ibid.

7. "Soldier Beaten Because He Would Not Take Off Uniform, Convicted," *Atlanta Daily World*, December 7, 1943.

8. Ibid.

9. Ibid.

10. Juan Williams, *Thurgood Marshall: American Revolutionary* (Three Rivers Press, 1998), p. 125.

11. Alvin E. White, "Negro Is Loyal, But Wants to Share in Benefits of Democracy, O.F.F. Is Told," *Atlanta Daily World*, March 25, 1942.

12. "'Defend Democracy at Home,' NAACP Slogan," *Atlanta Daily World*, June 11, 1941.

13. "Removal of Army, Navy Jim Crow Is Urged," *Atlanta Daily World*, October 19, 1937.

14. Eleanor Roosevelt Papers, "Fair Employment Practices Committee," in *Teaching Eleanor Roosevelt*, ed. Allida Black, June Hopkins et. al. (Eleanor Roosevelt National Historic Site, 2003), http://www.nps.gov/archive/elro/glossary/fepc.htm (accessed August 28, 2008).

15. "To Name Executive Secretary of FEPC," *New York Amsterdam News*, August 9, 1941.

16. "Two Howard U. Educators Get Defense Posts," *Washington Post*, October 26, 1940.

17. "Judge Hastie Named Aide in War Department," *Atlanta Daily World*, October 27, 1940.

18. Ibid.

19. "Army Refused to Let Hastie Resign," *Atlanta Daily World*, January 25, 1942.

20. "Whites, Others Also Call on FEP Committee," *Atlanta Daily World*, November 16, 1941.

21. "FEPC Disappoints on First Hearing," *New York Amsterdam Star-News*, August 16, 1941.

22. "McNutt Stops FEPC Dixie Rail Hearings," *Atlanta Daily World*, January 13, 1943.

23. CHH to Roy Wilkins, March 8, 1944, NAACP Papers.

24. Ibid.

25. "Atty. Houston Succeeds Young as Member of FEPC Committee," *Atlanta Daily World*, March 7, 1944.

26. *Grovey v. Townsend*, 295 U.S. 45 (1935).

27. Mark V. Tushnet, *Making Civil Rights Law: Thurgood Marshall and the Supreme Court, 1936–1961* (Oxford University Press, 1994), p. 105.

28. Prentice Thomas to TM, January 1, 1942, NAACP Papers.

29. Ibid.

30. Ibid.

31. TM to Prentice Thomas, January 5, 1942, NAACP Papers.

32. Ibid.

33. Tushnet, *Making Civil Rights Law*, p. 105.

34. Ibid., p. 104.

35. "White Primary Case Opens in Houston, Texas," *Atlanta Daily World*, April 22, 1941.

36. Ibid.

37. Ibid.

38. Michael J. Klarman, *From Jim Crow to Civil Rights: The Supreme Court and the Struggle for Racial Equality* (Oxford University Press, 2004), pp. 454–55.

39. Williams, *Thurgood Marshall*, p. 112.

40. CHH to President Harry S. Truman, December 3, 1945, NAACP Papers.

41. Telegram from WW to CHH, December 3, 1945, NAACP Papers; letter from President Harry S. Truman to CHH, December 7, 1945, NAACP Papers.

CHAPTER 16: SUPREME BROKEN COVENANT

1. Genna Rae McNeil, *Groundwork: Charles Hamilton Houston and the Struggle for Civil Rights* (University of Pennsylvania Press, 1983), p. 167.

2. Michael J. Klarman, *From Jim Crow to Civil Rights: The Supreme Court and the Struggle for Racial Equality* (Oxford University Press, 2004), p. 176

3. Ibid., p. 175

4. "Houston Says Negro Struggle for Status Faced by Three Forces," *Atlanta Daily World*, December 6, 1945.

5. Sidney P. Brown, "House of Alpha," adapted with fraternal gratitude.

6. Klarman, *From Jim Crow to Civil Rights*, p. 177.

7. Eric Pace, "Spottswood W. Robinson III, Civil Rights Lawyer, Dies," *New York Times*, October 13, 1948.

8. Dillard Stokes, "Covenant Case Arguments End; Decision Unlikely for Months," *Washington Post*, January 17, 1948.

9. Mark V. Tushnet, *Making Civil Rights Law: Thurgood Marshall and the Supreme Court, 1936–1961* (Oxford University Press, 1994), p. 87.

10. Ibid.

11. McNeil, *Groundwork*, p. 178.

12. Stokes, "Covenant Case Arguments End."

13. Juan Williams, *Thurgood Marshall: American Revolutionary* (Three Rivers Press, 1998), p. 150.

14. Tushnet, *Making Civil Rights Law*, pp. 91–92.

15. "Restrictive Covenants," *Chicago Defender*, January 31, 1948.

16. McNeil, *Groundwork*, p. 177.

17. Ibid.

18. Stokes, "Covenant Case Arguments End."

19. Tushnet, *Making Civil Rights Law*, p. 94.

20. Ibid., p. 93.

21. Williams, *Thurgood Marshall*, p. 150.

22. Ibid.

23. Tushnet, *Making Civil Rights Law*, p. 93.

24. Ibid.

25. "D.C. Racial Restrictive Covenant Cases Concluded," *Atlanta Daily World*, January 20, 1948.

26. Stokes, "Covenant Case Arguments End."

27. "Statement of Mr. Charles Houston before the Presidential Committee on Civil Rights," May 15, 1947, CHH Collection, Moorland-Springarn Research Center, Howard University.

28. TM to CHH, September 7, 1948, CHH Collection.

29. TM to CHH, June 11, 1948, CHH Collection.

30. CHH to TM, June 14, 1948, CHH Collection.

31. WW, "Intentional Repetition," *Chicago Defender*, May 22, 1948.

32. *Shelley v. Kraemer*, 334 U.S. 1, 20 (1948).

33. *Hurd v. Hodge*, 334 U.S. 24, 34 (1948).

34. Ibid. at 35–36.

35. "Dixie School Compact Hit by Negroes," *Washington Post*, March 14, 1948.

36. Ibid.

37. Ibid.

CHAPTER 17: PEACE OF MIND

1. Genna Rae McNeil, *Groundwork: Charles Hamilton Houston and the Struggle for Civil Rights* (University of Pennsylvania Press, 1983), p. 200.

2. Memorandum from TM to CHH, September 10, 1946, NAACP Papers, Manuscript Division, Library of Congress.

3. Ibid.

4. Ada Lois Sipuel Fisher with Danney Goble, *A Matter of Black and White: The Autobiography of Ada Lois Sipuel Fisher*, (University of Oklahoma Press, 1996), p. 51.

5. Ibid., p. 50.

6. Ibid., p. 95.

7. Ibid., p. 90.

8. Roscoe Dunjee to TM, January 15, 1946, NAACP Papers.

9. Ibid.

10. Memorandum from TM to CHH, September 10, 1946, NAACP Papers.

11. Ibid.

12. Ibid.

13. Richard Kluger, *Simple Justice: The History of* Brown v. Board of Education *and Black America's Struggle for Equality* (Vintage, 1977), p. 259.

14. Dillard Stokes, "Supreme Court Questions Oklahoma Counsel on Banning Negro Girl from Law College," *Washington Post*, January 9, 1948.

15. Ibid.

16. *Sipuel v. Oklahoma State Board of Regents*, 332 U.S. 631 (1948).

17. "Students at OU Equally Divided on Court Ruling," *Daily Oklahoman*, January 13, 1948.

18. Harriett Bunn, "Oklahoma's Dual School Idea on Trial," *Washington Post*, June 6, 1948.

19. "It's a Wonderful Constitution, Ada Says on Return to State," *Daily Oklahoman*, January 15, 1948.

20. Memorandum from CHH to TM and Marian Wynn Perry, February 23, 1949, CHH Collection, Moorland-Springarn Research Center, Howard University.

21. TM to CHH, February 10, 1949, CHH Collection.

22. CHH to TM, February 22, 1949, CHH Collection.

23. TM to Lillie Jackson, April 4, 1949, CHH Collection.

24. Ibid.

25. TM to Carl Murphy, April 13, 1949, CHH Collection.

26. TM to CHH, April 13, 1949, CHH Collection.

27. CHH to TM, April 6, 1949, and April 15, 1949, CHH Collection.

28. Earl Conrad, "The Battle of the NAACP," *Chicago Defender*, May 24, 1947.

29. "Sweatt Says Negro Law School Unsatisfactory," *Chicago Defender*, September 27, 1947.

30. Conrad, "The Battle of the NAACP."

31. Charles T. McCormick to Grover Sellers, February 26, 1946, Charles T. McCormick Papers, Rare Books and Special Collections, Tarlton Law Library, University of Texas at Austin.

32. Grover Sellers to Charles T. McCormick, March 16, 1946, Charles T. McCormick Papers.

33. Mark V. Tushnet, *The NAACP's Legal Strategy against Segregated Education, 1925–1950* (University of North Carolina Press, 1987), p. 126.

34. "Negro Again Denied Right to Admission to Texas University," *Atlanta Daily World*, May 20, 1947.

35. "Texas Votes Millions for New University," *Chicago Defender*, March 8, 1947.

36. Charles T. McCormick to C. D. Simmons, September 17, 1947, Charles T. McCormick Papers.

37. Ibid.

38. "Sweatt Tests Legality of Jim Crow Schools," *Atlanta Daily World*, May 18, 1947.

39. "Negro Again Denied Right to Admission to Texas University," *Atlanta Daily World*, May 20, 1947.

40. "White Texans Form NAACP Group," *Atlanta Daily World*, April 4, 1947.

41. Ibid.

42. "Sweatt Case Opens in Texas," *Atlanta Daily World*, May 14, 1947.

43. Kluger, *Simple Justice*, pp. 262–63.

44. "Texas Governor Signs Bill for Law School," *Chicago Defender*, March 15, 1947.

45. "Texas Vet Files Appeal in Jim Crow School Suit," *Chicago Defender*, February 22, 1947.

46. CHH to TM, April 20, 1949, CHH Collection.

47. McNeil, *Groundwork*, p. 192.

48. Ibid., p. 191.

49. Ibid., p. 192.

50. Kluger, *Simple Justice*, p. 266.

51. Ibid., p. 268.

52. Memorandum from TM to CHH et. al., October 19, 1948, CHH Collection.

53. Memorandum from TM to CHH et. al., January 3, 1949, CHH Collection.

54. Ibid., p. 202.

55. Ibid., p. 193.

56. *Sweatt v. Painter*, 339 U.S. 629 (1950).

57. *McLaurin v. Oklahoma State Regents for Higher Education*, 339 U.S. 637 (1950).

58. *Sweatt v. Painter*, 339 U.S. 629 (1950).
59. McNeil, *Groundwork*, p. 209.
60. Ibid., p. 210.
61. Ibid., p. 212.
62. Ibid., p. 211.
63. Ibid.

CHAPTER 18: ROOT AND BRANCH

1. Mark V. Tushnet, *Making Civil Rights Law: Thurgood Marshall and the Supreme Court, 1936–1961* (Oxford University Press, 1994), p. 147
2. TM, "Tribute to Charles H. Houston," *Amherst Magazine*, Spring 1978, p. 274.
3. Ibid.
4. "Truman, Noted Jurists Mourn Charles Houston," *Chicago Defender*, May 6, 1950.
5. Genna Rae McNeil, *Groundwork: Charles Hamilton Houston and the Struggle for Civil Rights* (University of Pennsylvania Press, 1983), p. 212.
6. Untitled photographs, CHH Collection, Moorland-Spingarn Research Center, Howard University.
7. CHH to the National Conference of Bar Examiners, February 18, 1942, CHH Collection.
8. "Profile of Marshall in 'Life' Mag," *Atlanta Daily World*, June 10, 1955.
9. Mary McLeod Bethune "Woodson, Drew and Houston: Three Great Negroes Who Gave Their Lives for Progress," *Chicago Defender*, May 20, 1950.
10. "Charles Houston Named 35th Spingarn Medalist," *Atlanta Daily World*, May 24, 1950; "Negro Publishers Name Truman, Nine Others for Russwurm Award," *Chicago Defender*, July 1, 1950.
11. Richard Kluger, *Simple Justice: The History of* Brown v. Board of Education *and Black America's Struggle for Equality* (Vintage, 1977), p. 291.
12. Tushnet, *Making Civil Rights Law*, p. 147.
13. Kluger, *Simple Justice*, p. 294.
14. Ibid., pp. 317–18.
15. Juan Williams, *Thurgood Marshall: American Revolutionary* (Three Rivers Press, 1998), p. 197.
16. Kluger, *Simple Justice*, p. 318.
17. Ibid., p. 316.
18. Jack Greenberg, *Warriors in the Courts* (Basic Books, 1994), p. 123.
19. Williams, *Thurgood Marshall*, p. 201.
20. Greenberg, *Warriors in the Courts*, p. 123.
21. Williams, *Thurgood Marshall*, p. 201.
22. Greenberg, *Warriors in the Courts*, p. 123.
23. Ibid., p. 124.
24. "Separate But Equal Is Unfair," *New York Amsterdam News*, March 15, 1952.
25. Kluger, *Simple Justice*, p. 291
26. Ibid., pp. 291–92.
27. Williams, *Thurgood Marshall*, p. 205.

28. Andrew B. Lewis, "A Brief History of Prince Edward County's School Desegregation Fight," Capitol Square Civil Rights Memorial Foundation, available at http://www.vacivilrightsmemorial.org.

29. Ibid.

30. Kluger, *Simple Justice*, p. 471.

31. "Highlights of 1949: The Local and National Scene," *New York Amsterdam News*, December 31, 1949.

32. "Poppy Tells Secrets of Husband's Choice Foods," *Chicago Defender*, October 13, 1951.

33. "Walter White Dies in New York," *Atlanta Daily World*, March 22, 1955.

34. "Walter White, 61; NAACP Leader," *Washington Post*, March 22, 1955.

35. "Thurgood Marshall Speaks to AME Group," *Atlanta Daily World*, November 25, 1953.

36. James T. Patterson, Brown v. Board of Education: *A Civil Rights Milestone and Its Troubled Legacy* (Oxford University Press, 2001), p. 52.

37. Ibid., p. 57.

38. Ibid., p. 60.

39. "Rehearing School Case Cost Bared," *Chicago Defender*, December 19, 1953.

40. "Miss. Solon Sees 'Tar, Feathers' for Race," *Atlanta Daily World*, December 12, 1953.

41. "Thurgood Marshall Speaks to AME Group," *Atlanta Daily World*, November 25, 1953.

42. "Topeka, Kansas Board Votes to End School Segregation," *Atlanta Daily World*, September 8, 1953.

43. Williams, *Thurgood Marshall*, p. 212.

44. "Thurgood Marshall Says NAACP to Press School Bias Fight," *Atlanta Daily World*, August 9, 1953.

45. Author's interview with William T. Coleman, Jr., July 18, 2008.

46. "Rehearing School Case Cost Bared."

47. Ibid.

48. "School Decision Expected by June," *Chicago Defender*, December 19, 1953.

49. "First Session Is Packed With Drama," *New York Amsterdam News*, December 12, 1953.

50. "School Decision Expected by June."

51. Oral argument transcript, *Briggs v. Elliott*, Supreme Court of the United States, December 8, 1953.

52. Ibid.

53. "John W. Davis Passes at 81," *Atlanta Daily World*, March 25, 1955.

54. "First Session Is Packed With Drama."

55. Ibid.

56. Oral argument transcript, *Briggs v. Elliott*.

57. Ibid.

58. Williams, *Thurgood Marshall*, p. 225.

59. *Brown v. Board of Education*, 347 U.S. 483 (1954).

60. Ibid.

61. McNeil, *Groundwork*, p. 138.

62. Ibid., p. 210; *Bolling v. Sharpe*, 347 U.S. 497 (1954).

63. Chalmers M. Roberts, "South's Leaders Are Shocked at School Integration Ruling," *Washington Post* and *Washington Times Herald*, May 18, 1954.

64. Ibid.

65. Ibid.

66. Ibid.

67. John Hope Franklin, "Behind the Brown Decision: A Conversation with John Hope Franklin," *Stetson Law Review* 34 (Winter 2005): 423, 440.

68. Ibid.

69. Roberts, "South's Leaders Are Shocked at School Integration Ruling."

70. Ibid.

71. Ibid.

72. *Chicago Defender*, July 17, 1954.

73. Lawrence Bailey, "Comment," *New York Amsterdam News*, October 14, 1961.

74. WW, "The Late Charlie Houston Would Have Been Proud of 'His Boys,'" *Chicago Defender*, December 26, 1953.

75. TM, "Thurgood Marshall Tells School Campaign Story in His Own Words," *Atlanta Daily World*, July 4, 1954.

76. Ibid.

77. McNeil, *Groundwork*, p. 142.

78. *Brown v. Board of Education*, 394 U.S. 294 (1955).

79. *Milliken v. Bradley*, 418 U.S. 717 (1974).

INDEX

A Note on the Author

A graduate of Yale University and Duke University School of Law, Rawn James, Jr., has practiced law for nearly ten years in Washington, D.C., where he lives with his wife and their son.